The Diagnosis & Correction of Vocal Faults

James C. McKinney

BROADMAN PRESS

Nashville, Tennessee

4268-11

ISBN: 0-8054-6811-0

Dewey Decimal Classification: 784.9

Subject Headings: VOICE / / SINGING

Library of Congress Catalog Card Number: 82-72226

Printed in the United States of America

Contents

List of Illustrations

Figure

Acknowledgments

First, I would acknowledge my indebtedness to my teacher and friend, the late William Vennard, Professor of Voice at the University of Southern California. The influence of his teaching, his ability to accept opinions and methods differing from his own, and his encyclopedic magnum opus *Singing— the Mechanism and the Technic* are apparent throughout this book. Also, I would express appreciation to Van Christy, whom I have never met, for his books, especially the two-volume set *Expressive Singing*, in which I found corroboration for many of the ideas which I had arrived at empirically in the voice studio before I first encountered his writing in 1961.

Second, I would like to thank Robert Burton, who through a long friendship has helped me to refine my knowledge of and approach to the teaching of singing and who served as consultant on this book, and my other colleagues in the voice department of Southwestern Baptist Theological Seminary, who have shared their ideas, their studios, and even their students freely with me.

Third, a special word of gratitude is due to Noelle Barker, Michael Pilkington, and Alan Tait of the Guildhall School of Music and Drama, London, England, for permitting me to observe pedagogical procedures in that school while I was on sabbatic leave.

Fourth, I am grateful to the administration of Southwestern Seminary for granting me the sabbatic leave which made the writing of this book possible, and to Nancy Brown and Rhonda Turner, who helped in the final preparation of the manuscript.

Finally, I want to give credit to my wife, Elizabeth, without whose constant support and sympathetic understanding my long-standing dream of writing such a book would not have been brought to fruition.

Introduction

The initial impulse toward this book came from our youngest son, Kevin, when he was about five years old. I had been asked to serve as a substitute choir director at a church in a nearby town. My wife was away from home adjudicating in some piano auditions, so I took Kevin with me to the Sunday morning service, carefully instructing him to sit on the front row and to listen attentively. The presiding minister introduced me at some length as Dr. McKinney, and called me by that title several times. After the service, as we were sitting in the car and putting on our seat belts, I became aware that Kevin was studying me rather intently, with a puzzled look on his face. Then came the question, "Daddy, what kind of a doctor are you?" Obviously he was struggling with his memories of trips to a doctor's office and of the assorted needles and other tools to which he had been exposed, and with his new awareness that his own father might be one of *those*. While I was trying to decide how to explain to a five-year-old the difference between a medical doctor and a "teaching" doctor, the second question came, "Do you doctor sick voices?" With the direct approach to truth which children often employ, he had answered his own question. It was apparent that he knew more about my vocation than I had ever imagined. Out of the mouths of babes. . . .

Although I was already teaching courses in how to teach singing and was vitally interested in correcting vocal problems, these two innocent questions started me along a train of thought which has culminated years later in this book. The second impulse came from an invitation to direct two sessions on correcting vocal faults at a summer workshop of the National Association of Teachers of Singing. For the first session I decided to present a comparative study of the way a medical doctor would diagnose the health problems of a person and the way a singing teacher would diagnose the vocal problems of a student. For the conclusion of that session I prepared a tape recording of ten vocal faults to be played for those attending the workshop. Each person was asked to answer three questions about each example of a vocal fault. The questions were:

> What is wrong with the sound that you are hearing?
> What do you think is causing it?
> What would you do about it if you were the teacher?

At the second session the tape was played again, but this time it was stopped after each example, and the particular fault was identified and discussed under the headings Symptoms, Causes, and Cures, to carry out the parallel with medical diagnosis. Even though the workshop attendees represented many years of teaching experience and some of them posessed excellent aural discrimination, hardly any of them had received training in the diagnosis and correction of vocal faults, and most of them found the test difficult.

In subsequent years I have had the opportunity to repeat this presentation, and others growing out of it, on a number of occasions for college and university voice teachers and students and for various groups of choral directors and ministers of music. The results of the test have remained rather constant. In general, those hearing the tape recording have been more proficient at recognizing that something is wrong with the sound than they have been at knowing what causes the fault and what should be done about it. The elimination of this gap in the training of many teachers of singing and choir directors has been a prime motivating factor in the writing of this book.

Testing the ability of students to diagnose and correct vocal faults is a regular part of the final examination in my classes on the teaching of singing. Ten examples of faulty singing usually are included, although sometimes one example of more or less correct singing is included. All of the examples are presented in live performance; in five of them the singer can be heard only; in the other five he is both audible and visible. This trains the student to observe both auditory and visual clues to vocal faults. The hundreds of students who have passed through these classes have served as laboratory guinea pigs and as a proving ground for many of the ideas contained herein. The rapidity with which some student teachers have gained facility in handling vocal problems has encouraged me as to the validity of the approach and has provided a further stimulus to me to put it in written form.

The first chapter is devoted to diagnostic procedures—to suggested methods of identifying and evaluating auditory and visual clues to vocal problems. This is the cornerstone of effective voice teaching and choral work—discriminatory hearing assisted by observation. Until one can hear and see what is wrong with a sound, he is building on the wrong foundation. The second chapter is included for those who may not have an adequate knowledge of the nature of sound. Since sound is the basic material with which teachers of singing are concerned, it is essential that they have a basic awareness of how it functions.

The remaining chapters discuss the faults related to certain specified areas and some possible means of eliminating them. In any discussion of what is wrong in a particular area it is essential that there be a statement of what, in the author's opinion, is right. Where there are recognized authorities, they will be quoted. In problematical areas, where no consensus or authority exists, the author must fall back on his own experience and on what has worked for him. In other areas, such as the mechanism of the larynx, the musculature of the breathing apparatus, or acoustics, only a modest amount of background information will be given and the reader will be referred to more detailed sources.

A major problem with the classification of vocal faults is that they often can be assigned to more than one area. For example, the vowel logically can be discussed under either articulation or resonation; an argument can even be developed for including it under phonation, since it affects vocal cord action. In such cases the author has made an arbitrary decision. If a certain fault is not found where you expect it to be, you should check the Index for its location.

The purpose of this book is revealed in its subtitle, "A Manual for Teachers of Singing and Choir Directors." It is designed to serve as an instructional handbook or a reference manual on the diagnosis and correction of vocal faults. Some sections could prove helpful to a speech teacher, but that has not been a major objective. It definitely has not been intended for use in connection with any pathological conditions of the voice. Treatment of such conditions should be left to medical specialists, who often will refer students to voice teachers or speech therapists when they feel the problems are functional and not organic. The voice teacher should make every effort to learn which vocal problems lie within the domain of the voice studio and may be worked with safely. Some excellent books concerning pathological conditions of the voice are listed below. [1]

---

1. Friedrich S. Brodnitz, *Keep Your Voice Healthy.* (New York: Harper & Bros., 1953).

   Brodnitz, *Vocal Rehabilitation.* (Rochester, Minn.: Whiting Press, 1959).

   Morton Cooper, *Modern Techniques of Vocal Rehabilitation.* (Springfield, Illinois: Charles C. Thomas, 1973).

   Margaret C. L. Greene, *The Voice and its Disorders,* 3rd ed. (Philadelphia: J.B. Lippincott Company, 1972).

Lee E. Travis, ed., *Handbook of Speech Pathology*. (New York: Appleton-Century-Crofts, 1957).

Robert West, Merle Ansberry, and Anna Carr, *The Rehabilitation of Speech*, 3rd ed. (New York: Harper, 1957).

1
Diagnosing Vocal Faults

The Diagnostic Process

Diagnosis: "The process of determining by examination the nature and circumstances of a diseased condition."[1]

When you enter the office of a medical doctor, the diagnostic process often begins before you are aware that it is taking place. Although the process may not be obvious, a well-trained doctor will start at once to collect information and seek clues which will help him evaluate your condition. The handshake with which he greets you may reveal important facts about your muscle tone, your body temperature, the condition of your skin, or the state of your nerves. Even the seemingly casual words with which he opens the conversation may be highly purposeful, as he listens to your voice, notices your posture and overall appearance, observes the color of your skin, looks at the circles under your eyes, and checks the condition of each cornea. An observant doctor can accumulate a surprising amount of information about a patient before starting his formal examination.

At this stage in the process the doctor may ask you to describe how you feel—in other words, to discuss your symptoms. (A symptom is "any sensation or change in bodily function experienced by a patient that is associated with a particular disease."[2]) He does not expect a technical discourse from you in correct medical terminology, but he does expect you to explain in simple terms why you came to see him. He wants to know what, in your opinion, is not functioning properly, or, more directly, what hurts. Much of this information can be determined by tests, but often some of it can only be supplied by the patient. Your self-evaluation of what is wrong with you may be of crucial importance to the doctor in arriving at a correct diagnosis. Only you can describe your own sensations.

After listening to your recital of symptoms, the doctor usually begins his routine checking of temperature, pulse rate, blood pressure, and so forth, and makes any specialized tests which may have been indicated by your symptoms.

He examines the areas where trouble frequently appears—such as the eyes, ears, nose, throat, chest, and heart—even when there is no apparent connection with the symptoms you have listed. This systematic gathering of evidence continues until a recognizable pattern of indicators has emerged, and the doctor is reasonably confident that he knows what is wrong with you. Three basic techniques have been used to accumulate this evidence: (1) informal observation of the patient, (2) self-evaluation by the patient, and (3) systematic testing by the doctor.

If the diagnostic process were to stop at this point, the patient would be no better off than he was when the examination began. One definition of diagnosis is "thorough analysis of facts or problems in order to gain understanding and aid future planning."[3] This definition implies that the end purpose of diagnosis is not identification of a disease through its symptoms; rather, the end result is gaining knowledge about the disease and planning proper corrective procedures. Certainly this is what the patient has in mind when he approaches a doctor's office; he wants to know what is making him feel so bad and what he can do to get rid of it. The doctor, then, must ask three fundamental questions about each patient he examines: (1) What are the symptoms? (2) What are the causes of these symptoms? (3) What are the possible remedies? Reduced to its simplest form, his plan of action is *symptoms, causes, cures.*

By now you may be saying to yourself, "I thought this was a book about correcting vocal problems, not about practicing medicine." Your point may be well taken, but perhaps the next section will reveal some strong parallels between diagnosing medical problems and diagnosing vocal faults.

Identifying Vocal Problems

In large measure, the ability of a person to change for the better the vocal sounds which he hears coming from a singer, a speaker, or a choir will determine how effective he is as a singing teacher, a speech teacher, or a choir director.[4] Vocal sound is the raw material with which he is working; if he cannot make adjustments in it, he is about as effective as a mechanic who does not know how to tune engines. Being able to change sounds implies that you know the nature of sound, that you know how musical instruments function, and that you understand the relation of the vocal instrument to the physical processes that govern it. Being able to change sounds also implies that you have established standards for good sounds which you have arrived at by listening to recognized artists, especially ones who have had lasting success and who continue to demonstrate vocal freedom and tonal beauty. This is one of the most elusive facets of the vocal art, for both student and teacher; and unfortunately, when questioned, many students reveal that they really do not know how they should sound. If you are going to work with voices, it is essential that you have a tonal ideal based on the physical laws of sound and the tone quality of artist performers against which you can measure the sounds you are hearing. This is the starting point in identifying vocal problems.

There are established standards for judging the health of a person—for example, normal body temperature, acceptable limits for pulse rate and blood pressure, the number of red and white corpuscles in the blood, and so forth. The diagnostic procedures previously discussed reveal how an individual differs from those standards when he is ill. Similar procedures may be used for the identification of vocal problems once you have established some standards for acceptable vocal sound. When a student walks into your studio, he is entrusting you with one of his most precious possessions—his voice. It is imperative that you develop some of the same types of diagnostic skills acquired by a doctor. Doctors usually treat people who have health problems, not people who exhibit glowing good health. In similar fashion, voice teachers seldom work with people who have no vocal problems; they spend their time with persons who have not yet achieved the status of artist singers. (Even artist singers may need a checkup periodically to be certain that all is going well, just as an apparently healthy person may take a routine physical examination.) It is the task of the teacher to spot the imperfections which may be present and to plan a course of action which, in due time, should remove them.

It has been stated earlier that the teacher must have a clear-cut conception of good vocal sound to serve as a standard of judgment when hearing sounds which are lacking in some desirable attribute. Some of the features of a good sound will be mentioned later. For the present it will be assumed that you have that skill and that you have just recognized certain vocal imperfections in one of your students. Your next task is to communicate this information to the student in such a way that he will accept your analysis and want to make the desired change. To perform this task well you will need at least three things: (1) comprehensive knowledge of the vocal mechanism and how it works, (2) ability to express yourself in terms the student can understand, and (3) some of the skills of a master psychologist. Sometimes it is difficult to tell a student that his tone is less than perfect without hurting his feelings to such an extent that inhibitory patterns are set up. The teacher must always be careful to couch his criticism in positive terms which offer a remedy to the problem.[5] The teacher-student relationship must be based on mutual respect and an awareness of the complex personal feelings that each person brings into the studio.

Diagnosis in the Teaching Studio

Every teacher should establish a systematic approach to the diagnosis of vocal faults as a prescribed part of his teaching technique. This approach should not, and probably cannot, be the same for any two teachers. If two teachers use exactly the same approach, one of them is a mere copy of the other, and is essentially noncreative. There are too many variables in the teaching process for this to ever happen. It is equally inconceivable that one teacher will teach two students in exactly the same way. Each student brings his own personality, his own problems, his own physical makeup, and his own learning capabilities to the studio. Attempting to pour every student in the same mold is like returning to the Procrustean bed, and the results may be just as violent.[6] Any system of teaching voice which does not permit individuals to vary should be considered suspect. Even two students who have the same vocal problems may need to be approached differently. Please avoid the misconception that there are secret methods and magical formulas that will solve all problems if they are followed religiously. It cannot be repeated too often: each student is an individual and must be allowed to seek vocal truth for himself under your guidance. Resist the temptation to turn your students into vocal clones of yourself.

That having been said, it must be stated again that each teacher should have a systematic approach to diagnosing vocal faults. If not, it is likely that some faults will go unnoticed and uncorrected. If you do not set up some system of checks and counterbalances, you will tend to ignore some problems and to forget others for extended periods of time. Many studio teachers will testify to the difficulty of maintaining a balanced approach to all phases of vocal technique. It is a good habit to keep a card file or notebook on each student as a record of problems encountered, corrective techniques attempted, and results achieved, in addition to literature assigned, memorization, and so forth. It is also a good idea to design a checklist, perhaps in printed form, for use in auditioning students, and for comparative purposes in later lessons to see what progress has been made and to remind you of the goals toward which you are working.

Your systematic approach to diagnosing vocal faults could be patterned on that mentioned earlier as a possible approach to medical diagnosis. The three basic techniques transferred to teaching would become (1) informal observation of the student, (2) self-evaluation by the student, and (3) systematic analysis by the teacher.

As soon as the student walks into your studio, you can begin accumulating information that may help you do a better job in the identification of his vocal faults—his stance, his posture, the presence or absence of tension or nervous mannerisms, the quality of his speaking voice and fluency of delivery, his command of language and freedom of expression, his apparent attitude toward you, his mental alertness, and so forth. These first impressions and observations may prove to be quite significant later on.

After the customary introductory pleasantries, ask the student some questions which will encourage him to indulge in self-evaluation—such questions as, "What are your goals as a singer? What do you hope to gain from studying with me? What previous vocal training have you had? Are you aware of any specific vocal problems that you have? What kind of songs do you most enjoy singing?" Develop questions which are compatible with your own teaching situation, but do give the student a chance to reveal whatever he can about his own goals and problems. Some of your most important clues to his vocal production may come from his response.

The third and most structured phase of the diagnostic procedure would be to have the student sing for you while you make a systematic analysis of his voice production and other pertinent factors. This is where a predesigned checklist will save time, ensure complete coverage of all areas, and provide a permanent file on the audition.[7] Just as a doctor would make certain standard tests—temperature, pulse rate, blood pressure, and so forth—so could a teacher evaluate certain areas of vocal technique and tone quality. For example, is the vibrato normal, too fast, too slow, exaggerated, irregular, or lacking? Is the basic phonation breathy, tight (tense), or relatively balanced? Is the intonation sharp, flat, inconsistent, or relatively true? A checklist constructed with your own favorite vocal terms could be used to evaluate quickly such areas as posture, breathing, support, articulation, tone quality, volume, and so on. It is very important that this first hearing, and the immediately following ones, should be carefully conducted. There is an unwritten law in voice teaching and choral work which states that bad sounds and incorrect pitches which are not heard on the first hearing become increasingly less likely to be heard with each subsequent hearing. It is also true that the longer you teach a student without correcting a particular vocal fault, the more inclined you are to accept it as an inborn characteristic of that person and leave it uncorrected.

In this first hearing it is the better part of wisdom to let the student sing the entire song without stopping him for suggestions or corrections. Let him present his musical offering uninterrupted, and then find something positive to say about his presentation. It may be difficult, but there must be some good aspect you can ferret out to comment on! Above all, do not give him a catalog of all his vocal problems. It is essential that you build a good working relationship with him; nothing can get the process started quicker than a few well-chosen words of praise. This is much more important than amazing (or crushing) him with your ability to identify his vocal problems.

Sometimes you will encounter a student who wants to stop after almost every phrase to apologize for his singing or to explain what was wrong with it. There are several possible causes for this type of behavior; regardless of the cause, insist from the first that he sing the song or a designated section of it from beginning to end without stopping. Encourage him to think in larger musical units and to get on with it. Until he quits his stop-and-go tactics, you will have little success in correcting other problems.

In summary, try to make your first hearing of any student a positive experience. Let him know that you enjoy teaching and that you want your experience with him to be an enjoyable one. Avoid negative criticism, but do lay down some firm guidelines and clear expectations for him.

The Classification of Vocal Faults

There are several possible ways to classify vocal faults. One would be to classify them according to their relation to the essential properties or elements of a musical sound: for example, (1) faults related to pitch, (2) faults related to intensity, (3) faults related to duration, (4) faults related to timbre, and (5) faults related to sonance. Another method of classification would be according to their relation to the physical processes involved in the singing act: that is, (1) faults related to respiration, (2) faults related to phonation, (3) faults related to resonation, and (4) faults related to articulation. A third way might be classification by the part of the vocal mechanism involved, such as: (1) faults of the tongue, (2) faults of the jaw, (3) faults of the lips, (4) faults of the soft palate, and so forth. Still another way could be by the area of vocal technique involved: faults related to range extension, registers, vibrato, flexibility, legato, dynamics, and so on. The listing of classification systems could be carried still further, but it is already obvious that it is quite difficult to come up with one all-inclusive system.

For the purposes of this book the system related to the physical processes in the singing act has proved to be the most convenient and to allow the most logical sequence of presentation. The next chapter should clarify some of the reasons behind this choice. As subcategories within the various classifications, the faults are grouped as faults of *hypofunction* or *hyperfunction*.[8] Faults of hypofunction are those in which there is not enough activity of the mechanism involved. Faults of hyperfunction are those in which there is too much activity or too much tension—overuse.

A Plan of Action

Just as a doctor may ask himself three basic questions about a patient, a teacher may ask himself three related ones about each student who enters his studio. These questions are:

(1) What is wrong with the sound I am hearing?

(2) What is causing it to sound that way?

(3) What am I going to do about it?

The teacher's plan of action is to *recognize symptoms, determine causes,* and *devise cures.*

In order to *recognize symptoms,* the teacher will need to evaluate two types of clues—audible ones and visible ones. Test your own powers of perception by listening to one of your students with your eyes closed and then with your eyes open. You may be surprised to learn that some people sound better when you do not watch them and that others sound better when you do. When a person presents a pleasing or captivating appearance, your eye may deceive your ear into accepting vocal sounds which are less than good; the converse also is true. As a general rule, however, when vocal faults are clearly audible, visible clues are readily apparent, also. These visible clues will be discussed in later chapters; for the present the following will serve as examples: postural rigidity, collapsed chest, tight jaw, furrowed brow, raised shoulders, tilted head, white knuckles, knees locked back, shaking legs, heaving chest, and so on. Among the audible clues would be included such factors as (1) breathiness, nasality, vibrato, intonation, hoarseness, and volume level, (2) elements of vocal technique, such as flexibility, diction, legato, range, and evenness of scale, and (3) the more imprecise terms used to describe tone quality and resonance, which will be discussed in due time. The important thing is to form the habit of critical listening and looking as a standard part of your studio technique, so that valuable symptoms will not pass unnoticed.

In order to *determine causes,* the teacher will need to be intimately acquainted with the vocal mechanism and with the physics of sound. It is possible to be an excellent singer or speaker and at the same time remain almost completely ignorant of how your voice works and what acoustics are. Such people are called natural singers or speakers; they seldom develop into outstanding teachers because they have little factual information to pass on to a student. Some of them are highly intuitive and manage to inspire others, but it is also a matter of record that some of the strangest books on voice gracing the shelves of our libraries have been written by former singers who may have sung beautifully but never bothered to learn the basic facts about sound and the vocal mechanism. This explains the amusing and sometimes scientifically impossible ideas promulgated therein. Knowing the function of the vocal mechanism and the nature of sound will help you to avoid making ambiguous, inaccurate, or misleading statements about the voice. It will also lead you more directly to the cause of vocal faults.

One of the most effective techniques used in analyzing the cause of a particular fault is to empathize with the student—to try to feel in your own vocal mechanism the actions that are taking place in his—to enter so completely into what he is doing that your own mechanism subconsciously attempts to reproduce his vocal production. This form of imitation or motor mimicry can be developed to the point where it is one of the quickest and most valuable methods of identifying the cause of a fault. It is a skill that you should cultivate and bring to the highest level possible. Coupled with your knowledge of how the voice works and of sound, this empathetic skill will help you communicate directly and effectively to the student what is wrong with the sound he is making and what you think is causing it.

The ability to *devise cures* for vocal faults comes mainly from applied knowledge and gained experience. For example, in the case of a breathy sound, knowledge will reveal that the vocal cords are not closing completely enough (and likely are not staying closed long enough in any given cycle), thus permitting too much air to escape. The cure is obvious: the vocal cords must be trained to make a more efficient closure. But how? Experience will reveal which methods have been most successful in the past; the logical answer is to use those methods first. However, experience will also reveal that the same approach will not work on all students. It is important to accumulate as many cures as possible for each vocal fault. Some students will respond to the first one tried; others will exhaust everything you come up with. The essential element is that you keep trying. Do not begin to tolerate or accept the incorrect sound just because you have not been able to change it. Be resourceful; be creative; adapt your techniques; consult other teachers; keep searching until you find an answer. If you know what is causing a bad sound, you nearly always can correct it, provided that the student is giving you his full cooperation and really wants to make the change.

This first chapter has been devoted to a discussion of diagnostic procedures and to some suggested methods of identifying, classifying, and evaluating auditory and visual clues to vocal problems. The primary purpose has been to stimulate you to think about your own studio approach and to analyze the process by which you listen to and observe students. The next chapter will explore some basic facts about the nature of sound, especially in relation to the vocal instrument.

Remember the plan of action:
(1) Recognize symptoms,
(2) determine causes,
(3) devise cures.

Notes

1. *The American College Dictionary* (New York: Random House, 1961).

2. *Collins Dictionary of the English Language* (London: William Collins Sons, 1979).

3. *Collins English Dictionary.*

4. From this point forward, in the interest of brevity, the singing teacher, speech teacher, or choir director will be called the teacher, and the person with whom he is working, the student. The basic facts are the same in each area, and specialized application can be made as needed.

5. There is an interesting discussion about changing a natural sound into a normal sound in William E. Ross, *Secrets of Singing* (Bloomington, Ind.: By the Author, 1959), p. 2.

6. Procrustes was a legendary robber in ancient Greece who cut off or stretched his victims to make them fit the length of his bed!

7. A sample audition checklist is provided in Appendix 1.

8. This terminology was used by Emil Froeschels to classify dysphonias. William Vennard, in his voice pedagogy classes at the University of Southern California, expanded the use of the terms to include underactivity and overactivity in certain phases of the singing act for the classification of vocal faults.

2
A Basic Approach to Vocal Sound

The Nature of Sound[1]

What is sound? One dictionary states that sound is "the sensation produced in the organs of hearing when certain vibrations (sound waves) are caused in the surrounding air or other elastic medium, as by a vibrating body."[2] This is the classic definition which insists that for a sound to exist it must be heard. Actually, four elements are essential to the existence of sound: (1) a vibrating object, (2) a power source to make the object vibrate, (3) a medium through which the vibrations are transmitted, and (4) an apparatus to receive the vibrations. Stated another way, there must be a vibrator, an actuator (or stimulus), a transmitter, and a receiver.

Air is the usual medium through which sound waves are transmitted, although liquids and solids also may serve in this capacity. The velocity at which sound travels is approximately 1,000 feet per second or 750 miles per hour; it varies with the density of the air. How does sound pass through the air? Does the air itself move at the speed of sound? What property of air enables it to serve so effectively as a conductor of sound waves (vibrations)?

> The air about us is made up of submicroscopic units of matter, called molecules. They move about independently, but tend to stay a certain distance apart, other conditions remaining the same. If they are forced closer together they fly apart again, and if they are forced apart, they fly back together again. This property of matter is called *elasticity*.[3]

Due to this property of elasticity, when the molecules of air adjacent to a vibrating object are compressed, they tend to fly apart, thus compressing the molecules adjacent to them on all sides; these molecules, in turn, fly apart, and the chain reaction continues until all the energy in the sound wave has been used up. The strength of the sound drops off more and more rapidly as the distance from the source increases. (Intensity is in inverse proportion to the square of the distance.) The alternate action of molecules moving closer together and springing apart is referred to as a compression wave and a rarefaction wave. These waves move out from the power source in a series of concentric spheres, ever-increasing in size until they run out of energy. Elasticity keeps the molecules from flying off in space after they have been disturbed. It is this molecular action that passes the sound waves along—not the actual passage of air. Air moving at 750 miles per hour would vastly exceed hurricane force!

The vibrator and the actuator may be best discussed in their functions as essential parts of musical instruments further on in this chapter; therefore, they will be omitted here. The function of the ear is to receive the alternate waves of compression and rarefaction and transmit them to the brain, where they are interpreted. Research has revealed much about how the ear encodes messages for the brain, but all the secrets of the process are still not known. The important fact for this discussion is that the ear does function as the receiving mechanism for the sound waves.

Sounds often are divided into two basic categories—noises and musical tones. With the incorporation of noise elements in so much contemporary music, this is not as convenient a division as it once was; however, it is still appropriate for the purposes of this study. How can you distinguish between noises and musical tones? The usual distinction which is made is that between regularity and irregularity, between symmetry and asymmetry. A musical tone is one in which the sound wave pattern repeats itself regularly; a noise is a sound which does not have a recognizable pattern because of its irregularity and lack of order. The contrast is between recurrent form and chaos. In singing and speaking the vowel is most nearly related to musical tone; the consonant, to noise; but the distinction is not absolute. More about this later.

Characteristics of a Musical Tone. How would you go about describing a sound? First of all, you could identify it as either a musical tone or noise. Assuming that it is a musical tone, how could you describe it? Musical tone has five characteristic properties or essential elements: duration, intensity, pitch, sonance, and timbre. Each of these properties has a specific meaning which can be expressed in concrete, objective terms; in other words, each is capable of accurate measurement by scientific methods. Each property, however, may be interpreted subjectively by the listener, and therefore may be given an imprecise evaluation.

Duration is self-explanatory. Simply stated, it is how long a musical tone lasts. This property can be measured accurately by a metronome or by a chronometer. In actual practice the measurement is made subjectively by the performer, without recourse to any mechanical devices. Teaching people how to observe duration values should be a standard part of basic musicianship courses; it should be reinforced in the voice studio, especially for music requiring an orchestral accompaniment.

Intensity is not so readily defined. The term tends to be used interchangeably with loudness and volume, even in scientific areas where more precise meanings might be observed. Intensity deals with the amount of energy in the sound—the strength of the sound—and can be measured objectively by its decibel level. The intensity of a sound is represented by the amplitude of its wave. The amplitude is determined by the extent to which the molecules have been displaced—the greater the displacement, the greater the intensity. In this sense intensity and amplitude are synonyms: both indicate the amount of energy in a sound; both indicate the extent to which the equilibrium of molecular structure has been disturbed by the vibrating object.

The term *loudness* is also used to describe the strength of a sound, but often with more subjective connotations than intensity. Loudness tends to be measured by the human ear, not by scientific equipment. What is loud to one person may be soft to another. A trained listener can accept a greater quantity of sound with comfort than an untrained one. Some eardrums are more affected by the pressure variations of sound waves (which actually indent the eardrum) than others, and so forth. William Vennard states:

> Increase the intensity and you will increase the loudness, but the ear adjusts itself so that doubling intensity will not double loudness. Having twice as many people in your chorus will make it louder, and perhaps better, but not twice as loud, and probably not twice as good. It is also interesting to note that a high tone sounds louder than a low one of the same intensity; the ear is more sensitive to high pitches.[4]

The most ambiguous term used to describe this property of sound is probably *volume*. Its various meanings include loudness and softness of sound, amount of sound, fullness of sound, intensity of sound, and a control on electronic equipment for adjusting the intensity of sound. Perhaps it is best to limit this term to one of its more basic meanings related to three-dimensional measurement or library usage. Then intensity can be used to mean the objective measurement of the strength of a sound, and loudness to mean the listener's subjective evaluation of that strength.

Some teachers speak of intensity when discussing resonance, vocal efficiency, tone quality, or interpretation. It has valid shades of meaning in all these areas, but other words could serve just as effectively and avoid possible confusion by the student.

Pitch is the frequency of vibration of a musical tone as expressed in the number of vibrations per second. One complete vibration consists of a compression wave and a rarefaction wave, and is called a cycle. Frequency may be indicated in cycles per second, or in hertz (Hz). 440 Hz means that a vibrating object is sending out vibrations at the rate of 440 times each second; this is the standard concert pitch for the A above middle C.

Pitch usually is referred to as being high or low. These terms are not really descriptive, and actually can be damaging psychologically to a singer. (One wit has pointed out that the right end of a piano keyboard is no higher than the left end!) Reaching up for "high" notes and pushing down for "low" notes are bad mental images for a singer to have and frequently lead to vocal problems. Unfortunately, no one has come up with any substitute terms for high and low pitches that have gained wide acceptance. It would be more accurate to speak of fast pitches and slow pitches because of the frequency rates involved, but these terms have proved to be practically meaningless to persons who are performing music. For this reason the use of high and low will be continued here, but only in the sense that high refers to a higher (greater) number of vibrations per second and low refers to a lower (smaller) number.

It should be pointed out that the frequency rates of the tones which make up an interval have a fixed mathematical ratio. For example, in an octave the higher tone has a frequency exactly twice that of the lower tone; the octave above A440 would be A880. In a perfect fifth the ratio of the higher tone to the lower is 3:2; the tone a fifth above A440 would be E660. The frequency rate of a vibrating object is determined by several factors: size, shape, elasticity, and mass. If these factors remain constant, the pitch will not vary, regardless of how strongly the vibrator is set in motion.[5]

The relationship between pitch and intensity is often illustrated by the act of throwing a stone into a still pond of water. The waves created by the stone will move out from the point of impact at the rate of so many waves per unit of time; this is symbolic of pitch. The vertical height of the waves, which becomes less and less as the waves move further away from the point of impact, represents the intensity or amplitude of the wave form. The rate of speed of a sound wave remains stable, but the amplitude changes as the energy in the wave is dissipated.

Sonance and timbre, the two remaining properties of a musical tone, present some problems of definition. Although sonance is an essential characteristic of tone, it has not gained general acceptance as a term and is not even mentioned in some authoritative sources. Timbre, on the other hand, is in widespread use and has various shades of meaning. Synonyms for timbre include tone quality, tone color, and *klangfarbe* (German for tone color). It has both objective and subjective aspects. Objectively, *timbre* is the characteristic tone quality of a sound as determined by the presence and relative strength of its component partials. Timbre is the primary factor which enables you to distinguish between two instruments or voices performing the same pitch with the same intensity. One dictionary defines timbre as:

> that characteristic quality of a sound, independent of pitch and loudness, from which its source or manner of production can be inferred: the saxophone and clarinet have different timbres, and so do the vowels of *bait* and *boat*. Timbre depends on the relative strengths of the components of different frequencies, which are determined by resonance.[6]

The musical tones which you hear are complex sounds. Simple sounds exist in theory and in the laboratory, but seldom in the actual performance of music. The vibrator which supplies the basic pitch also provides other frequencies at the same time; resonators may add still other frequencies. The basic pitch is called the fundamental or the first partial. The other frequencies are called overtones or higher-numbered partials.[7] All of these generated frequencies combine to form a complex structure which your ear accepts and interprets as one musical tone.

Subjectively, *timbre* has many subtle, and often imprecise, shades of meaning. Teachers use it to describe a certain kind of vocal sound; they may speak of a "reedy" timbre, a "tinny" or a "metallic" timbre, a "velvet" timbre, and so forth; or they may say that a voice is lacking in timbre. Such descriptive terms are in common use in many teaching studios, and, no doubt, have some validity if they are applied consistently by the teacher and understood by the student. The problem lies in getting groups of teachers to agree on the exact meanings of the terms and on the desirability or undesirability of any particular sound. If agreement could be reached on the correct labels for certain sounds, it is quite possible that objective scientific analysis could confirm the accuracy of the teacher's subjective evaluation. Until that day arrives, timbre will continue to have a variety of subjective meanings.

Like timbre, *sonance* also is concerned with the identifying characteristic elements of sound; however, instead of being limited to the frequency structure of the sound, it is related to patterns of change in the sound, including changes of timbre. According to Carl Seashore, *sonance* is the pattern of change in timbre, pitch, intensity, or admixture of noise in a given tone. This definition implies that in order for sonance to exist, a sound must last long enough for patterns of change to be established. A prime factor in sonance, then, is vibrato, which is made up of changes in pitch, intensity, and timbre. In speech, inflectional patterns and changing rates of delivery are important elements of sonance, and are of great assistance in identifying a particular speaker.

All musical instruments, including the human voice, have some character-istic noise elements present in the tone which contribute to the identity of each instrument, even though the listener may be unaware of their presence. The scraping of a bow on a string, the thudding of piano hammers, the clicking of valves or keys, the chiff of an organ pipe, the plucking of a string, the formation of consonants—all of these noise elements affect the listener's concept of musical tone and help him to distinguish the various instruments.

The Nature of Musical Instruments

A musical instrument is a device engineered to produce musical tones, even though those tones may contain noise elements, as has just been mentioned. Each instrument has three essential parts: an actuator, a vibrator (or vibrators), and a resonator (or resonators). The function of the actuator (also referred to as the exciter or the stimulus) is to furnish the energy or power needed to set the vibrator in motion. The function of the vibrator is to generate a series of sound waves—alternate waves of compression and rarefaction. The function of the resonator is to influence the intensity and/or timbre of the sound waves. How the resonator does this will be discussed in a later chapter. For now it may be helpful to think of the resonator as a secondary vibrator which is set into motion by the main vibrator and which adds its own characteristics to the generated sound waves.

The classification of musical instruments may be approached at several different levels.[8] For this study a basic division into three groups will be used—wind instruments, stringed instruments, and percussion instru-ments—and the approach will be general. In the wind instruments, the actuator is the breath of the player as controlled by the breathing mechanism; the sound waves are set up in the enclosed column of air by the vibratory action of the lips in contact with the mouthpiece or reed of the instrument; the tubing of the instrument functions as the resonator. (Some interesting sidelights concern the vibrator of a flute, the influence of the vibrating column of air on the pitch of a reed instrument, and the effect of different materials on the quality of resonators.)

In the stringed instruments, the actuator is the bow in conjunction with the arm of the player, the vibrator is the string or strings, and the resonator is the body of the instrument. (Interesting sidelights concern the resonance function of the bridge, sound holes and sound post, and the cause of wolf tones.) In the percussion instruments, the actuator is the mallet in conjunction with the arm of the player, the vibrator is the object struck, and the resonator is the body of the instrument.

To see if you understand the nature of musical instruments, make a list of common orchestral instruments and see if you can identify the actuator, vibrator, and resonator of each. Be certain that you include instruments of each basic type.

The human voice does not fit neatly into any of these three types, although it exhibits some relationship to two of them. It most nearly resembles the brass instruments of the wind family, especially in regard to the actuator. The actuator is the breath of the person, the vibrators are the vocal cords, and the resonators primarily are the cavities located above them. (The vocal resonators will be discussed in detail in chapter 8.) Breath pressure is applied to the vocal cords, causing them to initiate vibration; this vibratory action of the vocal cords resembles that of the lips of a brass player, but there the similarity ends, since there is no parallel for the mouthpiece. The pitch-producing mechanism of the singer is much more complicated than that of a brass player, and the resonator system is infinitely more flexible and versatile.

Comparisons sometimes are drawn with stringed instruments and their determination of pitch by the changing of tension. It is risky to carry this analogy too far; there probably are more differences than there are similarities. However, one of the most effective devices for getting a singer to produce a better legato and more efficient breath control is to suggest that he imitate the smooth bowing technique of an experienced string player. Suggestions borrowed from the technique of various instruments frequently are helpful in solving vocal problems, just as orchestral conductors may ask instrumentalists to make the music "sing." However, vocal music has properties that are exclusively its own.

The Nature of Vocal Sound

The act of producing vocal sound is made up of four physical processes: respiration, phonation, resonation, and articulation. These processes occur in the sequence given: (1) breath is taken, (2) sound is initiated in the larynx, (3) the resonators receive the sound and influence it, and (4) the articulators shape the sound into recognizable units. These processes will be considered individually in successive chapters as they relate to the diagnosis and correction of vocal faults. For the present they will be discussed briefly.

Respiration is the process of moving air in and out of the body—inhalation and exhalation. Breathing for singing and speaking is a more controlled process than is the ordinary breathing used for sustaining life. The controls applied to exhalation are particularly important.

Phonation is the process of producing vocal sound by the vibration of the vocal cords. It takes place in the larynx (voice box) when the vocal cords are brought together (approximated) and breath pressure is applied to them in such a way that vibration ensues.

Resonation is the process by which the basic product of phonation is enhanced in timbre and/or intensity by the air-filled cavities through which it passes on its way to the outside air. Various definitions of resonator, resonance, and resonation include such terms as amplification, enrichment, enlargement, improvement, intensification, and prolongation; all of these terms seem to indicate that the end result of resonation is, or should be, a better sound.

Articulation is the process by which the joint product of the vibrator and the resonators is shaped into recognizable speech sounds through the muscular adjustments and movements of the speech organs. These adjustments and movements of the articulators result in verbal communication and thus form the essential difference between the human voice and other musical instruments. Singing without understandable words limits the voice to nonverbal communication.

The following illustration may help you differentiate between respiration, phonation, resonation, and articulation. Count out loud from one to five; you are employing all four processes. Now whisper the numbers from one to five; try to analyze which processes have been either eliminated or changed. You may be using more breath while whispering, but the basic breathing method remains the same as before. Your articulators are working as vigorously as they were previously, so the articulation process also is unchanged. Whisper the word *who*, and keep holding it until you can hear a rustling sound somewhere inside your head. Is this phonation or resonation? By definition phonation is the production of vocal sound by the vibration of the vocal cords. When you whisper, the vocal cords do not vibrate; this eliminates phonation. In a soft whisper the vocal cords approach each other, but do not touch. In a forced whisper the cords close firmly for two-thirds of their length, but the back one-third remains open. In either type of whisper the sound which you are hearing is created by the friction of air passing through the partially closed vocal cords (this is known as glottal friction); this frictional sound passes into the resonance cavities and is amplified by them. The resonation process is still there, but it is not as obvious as it was when phonation also was present. Now continue your experiment by counting from one to five without making any sound whatsoever; pretend that you are trying to communicate with someone through a thick glass door without anyone else hearing you. If you do this correctly, only one process should remain—articulation. Now repeat the entire exercise—counting out loud, whispering, counting silently—observing carefully the differentiating factors.[9]

Although these four processes are to be considered separately, in actual practice they merge into one coordinated function. With an effective singer or speaker you seldom are aware of the individual processes involved; the mind and the body of the performer are so coordinated that you perceive only the resulting unified function. It is difficult during the learning stages for a student to achieve this level of coordination. Inevitably he will be more concerned with one area of technique than another; the various processes will progress at different rates and therefore will be out of balance with each other. Many vocal faults result from a lack of coordination. Some of these will be considered as they relate to one particular process; others will be treated in a separate chapter on problems of coordination.

Interpretation sometimes is listed as a fifth physical process involved in the production of vocal sound. Without doubt it will influence the kind of sound you are making and is an essential element in artistic performance; but, strictly speaking, it is not a physical process (just as musicianship is not). The student must acquaint himself with musical style and performance practices, and the teacher may suggest certain interpretative effects, but in the final analysis interpretation can not be taught. If the student does not have enough creative imagination to react aesthetically to the text and the music, and enough freedom of personality to express what he feels, no amount of instruction can redeem the situation. Failure to interpret well is not a vocal fault which can be corrected by attention to the four physical processes; neither is the failure to sight-read music well. Problems related to interpretation and musicianship are not primarily vocal problems, even though they may affect vocal sound significantly; therefore, they will receive little discussion here.

The Classification of Vocal Sounds.[10] It has been stated earlier that sounds are divided into two basic categories, musical tones and noises; the determining factor is the presence or absence of a regularly recurring sound wave pattern. Vocal sounds also are divided into two basic categories—vowels and consonants—with a wide variety of subclassifications possible. As a group, the vowels are identified as musical tones, and the consonants as noises, but the distinction is not absolute. Some consonants (the so-called semivowels: [l], [m], [n], [ŋ], and [r] can function as vowels, and some vowels (the so-called glides) can function as consonants—for example, the first sound in the word "you" is really [i] rapidly formed, and the first sound in "will" is [u].[11] Wise has pointed out the difficulties involved in producing an accurate, all-inclusive definition of terms such as vowel, consonant, and phoneme.[12] For the purposes of this study it will be sufficient to establish some working definitions, with explanatory comments.

"A *vowel* is a speech sound which may constitute a syllable or the nucleus of a syllable."[13] "A voiced speech sound whose articulation is characterized by the absence of friction-causing obstruction in the vocal tract, allowing the breath stream free passage."[14] Several characteristics of the vowel can be drawn from these two definitions: (1) it is an unrestricted speech sound; (2) it is capable of being sustained (that is, it is a continuant); (3) it normally is a voiced (phonated) sound, although it can be whispered; (4) it is the basic building material of vocal tone—the vowel carries the tone; (5) it has a definite shape or form—it is molded by the articulators.

Some speech sounds contain two or more vowels in succession. A *diphthong* is a complex of vowel sounds beginning with one easily identifiable sound and ending with another; it functions as a single vowel does within a syllable. In the English language the first vowel is stressed (long) and the second is unstressed (short). There are five common English diphthongs, as found in the following words: bay, by, now, know, boy. Although some authorities do not recognize its existence, a *triphthong* is "a composite vowel sound during the articulation of which the vocal organs move from one position through a second, ending in a third."[15] Words fitting this description would include "fire," "oil," "mail," and slang expressions such as "yeah" and "wow." The three elements of a triphthong may not meet all the requirements of vowel forms, but they do exhibit some of the characteristics.

"A *consonant* is a speech sound which is used marginally with a vowel or diphthong to constitute a syllable."[16] A consonant is "(as a member of a syllable) a sound subordinated to another sound that has greater sonority; . . . (as a member of an articulation class) a sound made with more or less obstruction of the breath stream in its passage outward. . . . "[17] Vennard states that a consonant is a speech sound, chiefly noise, used with vowels to form sound patterns having symbolical meaning.[18] Several characteristics of consonants can be drawn from these three definitions: (1) they are more or less restricted speech sounds; (2) they contain more or less conspicuous noise elements due to the degree of restriction present; (3) they are subordinate to vowels in sonority; (4) they do not form the center (nucleus) of syllables, but define the borders of them; (5) they function as sound interrupters or sound stoppers and thus separate the vocal tone into recognizable units which can communicate meaning. More will be said about the subclassification of consonants in a subsequent chapter.

Semantic Problems in Describing Vocal Sound. At its best, the act of describing vocal sound is an inexact science; at its worst, it is a mishmash of flowery phrases, illogical terminology, and apocryphal statements that contain scattered elements of truth—a veritable semantic maze. Why is vocal sound so difficult to describe? Why does the act of singing result in so many differing explanations of what is taking place? At the center of the problem is the fact that the human voice is a self-contained instrument. Since the vocal instrument is internal, there are no keys to press, no valves to open, no tactile or visual clues to the determination of pitch; and even the ability to monitor the sound produced is complicated by the vibrations carried to the ear through the Eustachean tube and the bony structures of the head and neck. The main guides of the singer are sensations—vibratory sensations resulting from the closely related processes of phonation and resonation, and kinesthetic ones arising from muscle tension and movement, body position, and distribution of weight (kinesthetic responses also are referred-to as *muscle sense*). Describing these subjective sensations to another person in such a way that the person can duplicate them and achieve the same kind of sound is a most difficult task—there are too many intangible elements present and too many variables.

Another major problem in describing vocal sound lies in the vocal vocabulary itself. Most of the descriptive terminology is *drawn from other disciplines*, as a result of the intangible nature of tone quality. The following terms borrowed from other arts, sciences, and nature are sometimes used by teachers to describe various tone qualities: warm, white, dark, light, round, reedy, spread, focused, covered, swallowed, forward, ringing, hooty, bleaty, plummy, mellow, pear-shaped, and on and on. The real problem lies in knowing what the terms mean and in getting teachers to agree on what they mean. Where teacher and student both understand what they mean, such terms can be an effective means of communication; however, care does need to be exercised concerning their standardization.[19]

A third semantic problem may arise from the mechanistic and psychological controls employed in the act of singing. Extreme advocates of the mechanistic approach believe that singing is largely a matter of getting the right parts in the right place at the right time, and that correcting vocal faults is accomplished by calling direct attention to the parts which are not working well. At the other extreme are those who believe that attention should never be directed to any part of the vocal mechanism—that singing is a matter of producing the right mental images of the desired tone, and that correcting vocal faults is achieved by learning to think the right thoughts and by releasing the emotions through interpretation of the music. As is often the case, the truth lies between these two extremes and is a composite of both approaches.[20] There are certain times and certain students with whom a mechanistic approach seems to be the only solution; there are other times and other students with whom only the psychological approach seems to bring results. With most students and most teachers a combination of approaches probably will be most effective; the more ways you can surround a problem, the better chance there is that you will find a solution.

At some time in the future it may be possible to furnish your teaching studio at reasonable cost with electronic equipment which can give you instantaneous feedback on the particular tone a student is producing; this information might include such items as vowel accuracy, harmonic spectrum, vibrato rate and extent, vocal faults present, probable causes, and suggested techniques for correction. If and when this day arrives, much of the creativity and a lot of the joy of teaching likely will have been lost. Until that day comes, teachers will do what they have done for centuries: they will listen to students and will make a subjective evaluation of what they hear and see, and will set out to change that which they do not like. They will have legitimate differences of opinion, especially about tone quality. Who is to say that a person who likes a "brighter" sound is more right than a person who prefers a "darker" sound? It is to be hoped, however, that standards can be agreed upon whereby a sound may be classified as too "bright" or too "dark" for normal singing, or that a point may be reached at which nasality becomes excessive.

The tape recording which is supplied with this book includes examples of the major faults associated with tone quality. The purpose of the recording is not to attempt to establish standards for tone quality; rather, it is designed to let the listener know what the author means when he says that a certain sound is too nasal, or too dark, or too straight, or too whatever. It lets the reader have firsthand knowledge of the sound the author is describing. This is the moment of truth when you experience in actual vocal sound what has been communicated verbally on the printed page. You may agree or disagree with the diagnosis—that is your privilege—the important thing is that you know what is meant by the terms used. This is the starting point in any true communication.

The remaining chapters deal with specific vocal faults as they relate to the physical processes involved in singing and their coordination. The first ones to be considered are those related to posture, breathing, and support.

respiration vibrate
phonation—vibrate—enhance
resonate
articulate

psychological vs. mechanistic

Notes

1. It is beyond the scope of this book to engage in an extended discussion of acoustics or to defend the facts presented. Readers seeking more detailed or technical information will find the following sources helpful:

John Backus, *The Acoustical Foundations of Music* (New York: Norton, © 1977).

Wilmer T. Bartholomew, *Acoustics of Music* (New York: Prentice-Hall Inc., 1942).

Charles A. Culver, *Musical Acoustics* (Philadelphia: Blakiston, 1951).

Robert M. Taylor, *Acoustics for the Singer* (Emporia: Kansas State Teachers College, 1958).

2. *American College Dictionary.*

3. William Vennard, *Singing—the Mechanism and the Technic* (New York: Carl Fischer, Inc., 1967), p. 1.

4. Vennard, *Singing*, p. 3.

5. Greene, *The Voice*, p. 9.

6. *American College Dictionary.*

7. For an extended discussion of timbre and the harmonic series, see Vennard, *Singing*, pp. 4-12.

8. See *Harvard Dictionary of Music*, 2nd ed., s.v. "Instruments," "Wind Instruments," "Brass Instruments," and "Reed."

9. I have used this illustration for years but no longer remember its origin.

10. For a comprehensive discussion of the production and classification of sounds see Claude Merton Wise, *Applied Phonetics* (Englewood Cliffs, N.J.: Prentice-Hall, 1957), pp. 33-80.

11. The symbols here are drawn from the International Phonetic Alphabet (known as the IPA). See Appendix 2 for a list of the IPA symbols used in this book.

12. Wise, *Applied Phonetics*, pp. 65-78.

13. Ibid., p. 73.

14. *Collins English Dictionary.*

15. Ibid., s.v.

16. Wise, *Applied Phonetics*, p. 74.

17. *American College Dictionary.*

18. Vennard, *Singing*, p. 258.

19. The voice teaching profession owes a debt of gratitude to Victor Alexander Fields and William Vennard for their efforts to establish a standard terminology.

20. Kenneth Pike tells an amusing story about his conversion from a mechanistic position to one where the psychological approach also played a part as the result of a voice class experience in his *Phonetics* (Ann Arbor: University of Michigan Press, 1943), pp. 17-20.

3
Posture

A Rationale for Good Posture

Why defend good posture? Doesn't everyone believe in it, even if they don't practice it? Strange to say, there are those who feel that posture has little relation to the singing act and that the less said about it, the better. There are some well-known singers who exhibit poor posture, and there are some teachers who never mention posture in a lesson. Granted that too much emphasis on posture may result in rigidity and tension, it is true, nonetheless, that good posture and good singing are strongly interrelated. There are several basic reasons why this is so.

First of all (and apart from singing), the body functions best when certain conditions exist. The main purpose of the hard framework called the skeleton is to support, protect, and give shape to the body; the main purpose of the muscles is to produce movement and to assist in positioning the body. It is very important not to confuse these purposes; for example, standing with the body out of line or with the head hanging forward of the shoulders causes muscles to take over some of the function of the skeleton, resulting in unnecessary tension and eventual fatigue. When the skeletal structure is in proper alignment, the muscles are left free to produce movement and to assist in positioning the body; unnecessary tension can be kept at a minimal level. Good posture allows the skeletal framework and the muscular components of the body to fulfill their basic functions efficiently without any undue expenditure of energy.

Second, the actuator of the vocal instrument functions best when certain conditions exist. It is obvious that the ability to move air in and out of the body freely and to obtain the needed quantity of air can be seriously affected by the posture of the various parts of the breathing mechanism. A sunken chest position will limit the capacity of the lungs, and a tense abdominal wall will inhibit the downward travel of the diaphragm. Good posture allows the breathing mechanism—the actuator—to fulfill its basic function efficiently without any undue expenditure of energy.

Third, the vibrator and resonators of the vocal instrument function best when certain conditions exist. It is much easier to initiate phonation and to tune the resonators when the vocal mechanism is in proper alignment and unnecessary tension has been eliminated. No other instrument has such a complex system of resonators with so many variables present. It is essential that the singer avoid superfluous movement of the parts of the vocal mechanism and harmful tensions. Good posture facilitates the functioning of the vibrator and resonators.

Fourth, the singer himself functions best when certain conditions exist. When good singing posture is an established habit, the mere act of assuming it is like putting on a comfortable pair of shoes or dressing up in your favorite outfit. The fact that you are doing something familiar—something that has worked for you before—can create confidence and a feeling of well-being. Even in a stressful situation, such as singing in public, habitual good posture can lend a sense of assurance and poise. There is a psychological boost or lift that comes from knowing that you look well and that you are performing a familiar act. Good posture can be a psychological asset to a singer.

Fifth, the audience functions best when certain conditions exist. The appearance of a performer is one of the major determinants of audience reaction. An obviously nervous singer creates an uncomfortable group of listeners; one who appears confident and poised puts an audience at ease. Some very interesting studies have been made which compare audience reaction to two performers on the same instrument when the performers are seen and when they are not seen. Suffice it to say, the studies proved that performer appearance is a crucial factor in audience reaction. Good posture can help a singer secure a positive reaction from an audience.

Finally, the general health of an individual can be benefited by good posture. Vital body processes, such as blood circulation and breathing, take place more easily with proper posture. The various organs can function more efficiently if they are not cramped, mashed, or pushed out of place because of poor posture. Habitual good posture can relieve much of the tension and fatigue caused by sitting or standing improperly.

Taken as a whole, the case in favor of good posture is rather conclusive. The person who seeks to establish habitual good posture has everything to gain and virtually nothing to lose, aside from time and energy expended. As a prelude to discussing postural faults, the next section is devoted to a description of good posture.

Arriving at Good Posture

In order to arrive at good posture you should set up positive thought patterns about it. Try to visualize the following descriptive adjectives in relation to your own posture: buoyant, expansive, erect, alert, free-to-move, vibrant, flexible, poised, tall, loose, free, happy, balanced. A few of these words may have more meaning to you than the rest; if so, concentrate on them. Avoid any sensation of rigidity or of being locked in one position. Form the habit of practicing in front of a mirror (preferably full-length); this is an excellent way to avoid those distracting mannerisms which singers are prone to adopt. Check to see if the mirror accurately reflects what you are thinking; if it does not, experiment until you get the desired result. Many students are reluctant to use a practice mirror; this is unfortunate, for it is one of the quickest and most effective means of correcting postural faults and mannerisms. If you can satisfy yourself about your appearance, you can satisfy most audiences about it.

Tension probably is the greatest enemy of the public performer. Proper thought patterns and postural habits can do much to keep it under control. It is foolish to speak of eliminating tension; the body cannot operate without tension; excessive tension is what must be recognized and avoided. One way to do this is to learn where excess tension is likely to occur and to be alert for it. Another way is to loosen the body up and make certain it is functioning properly before you attempt to practice or perform. No competent athlete would attempt to perform his particular skill without first engaging in a series of bending, stretching, and shaking-out exercises designed to tune his muscles to an ideal state of tonus. Tonus is "a normal state of slight continuous tension in muscle tissue which facilitates its response to stimulation."[1] Many singers and speakers start using their voices at full strength without making any effort to warm them up or to see that their bodies are adequately prepared for the work of producing sound. Many of the problems encountered in singing and speaking can be avoided by proper preparation of the body as a whole. It is a good idea to establish a regular warm-up procedure to be used *before* you practice or perform. Until you have decided on your own warm-up system, the following suggested routine may be helpful:

(1) General bending and stretching exercises, such as reaching as high as you can; touching the left foot with the right hand and the right foot with the left hand alternately; rolling the body around in circles from your waist; deep knee bends; touching both toes simultaneously; and so forth;

(2) roll your head around in circles clockwise several times and then

reverse the direction, letting your head flop freely;

(3) move your shoulders around in circles, first to the back and down several times, and then reverse the direction;

(4) with your arms hanging loosely at your sides, shake your hands back and forth as fast as you can while keeping your upper arms as loose as possible;

(5) stand with your feet close together and, without lifting your toes from the floor, raise each heel alternately as if you are walking in place, gradually increasing the tempo until your legs seem to be shaking all over;

(6) nod your head back and forth in such a large arc that your chin touches your chest and the back of your head touches your back;

(7) flop your jaw up and down freely while saying "yah";

(8) bubble air between your lips until you are making a sound resembling that of a motorboat or motorbike;

(9) pretend you are chewing a very large bite of food.

These exercises are designed to improve your muscle tone in general and to remove interfering tensions from those areas surrounding the vocal mechanism in particular.

A Description of Good Posture

The previous section stated that good posture may be described by words such as these: alert, balanced, buoyant, erect, expansive, flexible, free-to-move, happy, loose, poised, vibrant; more words of this genre, no doubt, will come to your mind. These are general concepts which apply to the mental attitude of the performer. The specifics of posture will be considered in relation to the area of the body which is involved.

The Feet. The weight should be evenly distributed between the feet, with the toe of one foot slightly in front of the other. It does not matter which foot is in front; in fact, in a long performance it is a good idea to change the front foot now and then to avoid tension and fatigue. The balance of the weight should be forward toward the balls of the feet, but not to the point that you resemble the Leaning Tower of Pisa. The feet should be fairly close together; the space between them will vary with the size of the individual. Some teachers feel that a girl or woman who is wearing high heels looks better on stage if she stands with the heel of one shoe touching the side of the instep of the other. Otherwise, it is better for the feet to be slightly separated.

Good posture, like good construction work, starts with a firm foundation.

Check your foot position in a mirror; the proper foot position should look natural and feel good.

The Legs. Since your legs are helping to support your body, it is impossible for them to feel completely relaxed when you are standing properly. The ideal feeling is that your legs are freely flexible and ready to move at all times. Avoid any sensation of rigidity or of being locked in one position. The legs, trunk, and head should conform as nearly as possible to a vertical line drawn from a point midway between your heels up to the top of your head. This is true regardless of whether a person is looking at you from the front or the side.

The Knees. The knees, also, should feel loose and ready to be moved at all times. Pulling the knees back and locking them there should be avoided. Some teachers suggest that the knees should be kept slightly forward to ensure looseness and to lessen tension.

The Hips and Buttocks. The hips and buttocks should conform as closely as possible to the vertical line drawn from your feet to your head. Neither hip should stick out further to one side than the other, and the buttocks should be gently tucked under and forward as if you are trying to straighten the small of your back. If the previous suggestions about the feet, legs, and knees have been followed, and if your carriage is truly erect, it should be an easy task to bring your body into vertical alignment.

The Abdomen. In discussing posture and breathing it is helpful to divide the abdominal area into two parts—the lower abdomen and the upper abdomen. The abdomen is that part of the body between the thorax (chest) and the pelvis; it is the visceral cavity, which contains most of the digestive organs, and is separated from the chest cavity by the diaphragm. The lower abdomen is the area extending from the waistline down to the pelvis; the upper abdomen is the area extending from the waistline up to the rib cage.

The *lower abdomen* is important to good posture. You should feel that it is held in *comfortably*, or that it is being pulled in *gently*. If the lower abdomen is allowed to sag forward, the curvature in the small of the back tends to become more pronounced and the buttocks tend to stick out unduly. Pulling in too strongly on the lower abdomen can create unnecessary tension; this is wasted effort and should be avoided.

The *upper abdomen* is especially important to good breathing. You should feel that it is free to move at all times. Pulling in or pushing out the upper abdomen too strongly can cause tension and interfere with the ability to breathe easily and to phonate properly. Avoid the temptation to pull in too hard on this area in an attempt to establish good posture.

The Back. Imagine that you are standing as tall as you can; you will notice a lifting or stretching sensation extending upward along the spinal column. This spinal lift or stretch is a vital part of good posture. Imagine at the same time that your back is as broad or as wide as you can make it. A third valuable thought pattern is that you are straightening the small of your back; notice that when you do this, the lower abdomen is pulled in gently and the buttocks are tucked under and forward without any conscious thought on your part. Thinking of straightening the small of your back also aids in achieving spinal stretch and the proper chest position; this one simple act can have several beneficial results.

The Chest. The chest should be comfortably high at all times; good posture should place it in this position *before* you breathe or sing. The chest does not need to move up or down when you breathe in or out, but should remain comparatively still and quiet; there will be some movement of the ribs, especially the lower ones, but the chest as a whole should remain stable. By thinking of standing tall and stretching the spine you can attain a comfortably high chest position without any conscious effort; the sensation of spinal stretch will help keep the chest in its proper place. If you feel that your chest must be held up in this position, you are doing something wrong. If you feel that it is expanded, spacious, and buoyant, you are on the right track. Avoid any sensation of having to muscle the chest up by pulling in on the upper abdomen; let thoughts, not muscles, hold it up.

The Shoulders. The shoulders should be rolled or pulled back gently and then allowed to drop down until they feel as if they have settled into a socket. They should not move up or forward during the act of breathing or singing, but should remain in this back-and-down position. When the shoulders remain stationary, it is much easier to maintain the comfortably high chest and the feeling of spinal stretch. There should not be any feeling that the shoulders are being forced down or tightened; instead, there should be a feeling of released tension, as if you have just let go of a heavy weight. Avoid any sensation of rigidity or locking.

The Arms and Hands. When the shoulders are pulled back gently and then allowed to drop, your arms will hang freely and naturally at your sides. This is the preferred position for most singers. The hands are extensions of the arms; like the arms, they should hang naturally at the sides, and should be as free from tension as possible. Avoid nervous mannerisms such as rubbing your thumbs and fingers on each other, clenching your fists, feeling your clothes, twitching your hands or fingers, and tensing your arms. These movements add nothing to your singing and often prove distracting to an audience.

Some singers like to hold their hands in front of the body. This is acceptable as long as it looks natural and the hands and arms are not too tense. Clenching the hands or tensing the arm muscles can cause the entire upper body, including the vocal mechanism itself, to be tense. Placing the hands on a piano, music stand, or lectern is acceptable also, if the result looks good and avoids tension. When singing from a book, support it in the palm of one hand and use the other hand to turn pages. Avoid having more tension in your arms than you need to support the book. Changing hands now and then may reduce tension and fatigue.

The Head. The head should be directly in line with the body and centered on the shoulders, whether viewed from the front or from the side. The twin ideas of standing tall and stretching the spine will help to put your head in the correct position. The head should not be allowed to hang forward of the shoulders (like that of a buzzard) or to tilt backward toward them. Your eyes should appear level, and you should look and feel as if your chin has been tucked in slightly. Many people hold the chin too high when singing; thinking of stretching the back part of your neck upward will help you find the best position for your chin.

When you are singing, your head and eyes should remain level. Avoid the bad habit of raising the chin to "reach" for high notes. If any movement is necessary, the chin can be lowered slightly for high notes. If you must look up, raise the eyes only—not the whole head. When the back of the neck is stretched and the chin is not raised, you can move the head freely from side to side without affecting your sound adversely. Some motion of this type is good; it keeps you from locking into one set position and gives you freedom to communicate better.

Seated Posture. When you are seated, the main support for your weight comes from the seat of the chair, so your feet and legs are not as important as they were in standing posture. From the hips up, however, you should feel almost the same way that you did when you were standing. The trunk and head should be in a straight line, with the feeling that you are sitting tall and stretching your spine. Sit with your hips well back into the chair and think of straightening the small of your back. You can lean forward or backward from the hips without affecting your ability to sing well as long as you maintain the correct alignment of your body above the chair seat.

Your foot position should be the same for sitting that it is for standing. This makes it possible to stand up without shifting your position, and also looks good. If you are not holding music, your hands should lie comfortably in your lap. It is best to avoid armchairs; if you must sing in one, be careful not to raise your shoulders.

Summary. Ultimately these separate components of good posture must be brought together as a unified configuration. Good posture must become so habitual that it does not require continual analysis, but will respond readily to the appropriate thought patterns. A major league pitcher no longer has to ask himself how to throw a curveball; if he engages in the right thought patterns, the ball will do what he wants it to. The singer needs to discipline his posture to respond in the same way, with his body functioning as a unit in response to his thought patterns. Remember that the main justification for good posture is its ability to place the parts of the vocal instrument in their most efficient working position.

Faults Related to Posture

Unlike some of the other areas to be discussed, the faults related to posture are almost entirely visible ones. They may be divided into two interrelated types: alignment faults and tensional faults.

Alignment Faults. Alignment faults should be readily apparent to an alert observer. The previous discussion of good posture has prescribed some definite guidelines for both vertical and horizontal alignment of the parts of the body. It should be easy to establish a routine for determining if any parts are out of line. The following checklist is not exhaustive but does call attention to various alignment problems:

(1) Head tilted to right or left, front or back;
(2) chin too high or too low;
(3) raised shoulders or one higher than the other;
(4) slumping posture with collapsed chest;
(5) protruding abdomen and/or buttocks;
(6) too much curvature in small of back;
(7) one hip more prominent than the other;
(8) knees pulled too far back;
(9) feet too far apart or too close together.

Most of these alignment faults can be corrected by calling them to the student's attention and insisting that he or she practice in front of a mirror, both in the teaching studio and in the practice room. If this approach does not work, a more mechanistic one may be effective. For example, if the student seems to be unable to bring the offending member into the proper alignment, try to adjust it for him by manipulation. If his head tilts back every time he starts to sing, gently try to hold it in alignment until he acquires the necessary awareness to control it himself. If he has trouble in maintaining overall body alignment, ask him to try this exercise:

Stand with your heels six to eight inches from a wall. Let your body drop back until your shoulder blades and buttocks are touching the wall. (Normally your head and the small of your back will not be touching the wall.) If both shoulder blades are against the wall, you will discover that your chest is comfortably high, as it should be, and that it is easy to keep it there. Try to place one of your hands between the small of your back and the wall; if you can do so easily, you probably need to straighten that area more. Let your body slide a short distance down the wall by bending your knees and tucking your buttocks under slightly; as you do this, notice that the space between the wall and the small of your back is decreasing, and may even disappear. Maintain this position for a short time to experience this new vertical alignment. Then slide back up the wall by straightening your knees while trying to keep your back as straight as possible. Now, without moving your feet, bounce out from the wall by bumping your lower back against it. You should discover that your general body alignment is much improved and, at least for the moment, is not hard to maintain.

One common feature of the alignment faults is that they contribute to additional faults. Standing with the body out of line not only tends to interfere directly with the function of the vocal instrument, but also to interfere indirectly by placing muscles under unnecessary tension. This is because the supporting function normally carried out by the skeletal structure of the body is being forced upon various muscles in the vicinity of the alignment problem. As an illustration of this fact, perform the following experiment:

Stand before a mirror and place almost all of your weight on your left foot (many people stand this way habitually). Having your weight out of balance calls for several postural adjustments, such as: the left hip sticks out more than the right one, the left shoulder is lower than the right one, the vertical alignment of the body resembles an elongated "s," the head may tilt to the right, and the left knee may be locked back. Careful analysis of stress points may reveal a feeling of strain in the calf muscles of the left leg, in the thigh muscles of the same leg, in the small of the back, beneath the right shoulder blade, and in the left hip joint. If this type of posture is habitual, the strain may not be very apparent because you are accustomed to it, but it is there, nonetheless. Proper alignment will preclude such problems.

Tensional Faults. A muscle is "a tissue composed of bundles of elongated cells capable of contraction and relaxation to produce movement in an organ or part."[2] It performs its work by contracting its fibers, thus shortening its length and exerting a pull on the part to which they are attached; when the muscle relaxes, it returns to its former position and the pull is released. Most muscles pull in only one direction, that direction being determined by the comparative mobility of the parts to which it is attached. The technical names of muscles often reveal the names of the parts to which they are attached and the direction of the pull. The less movable part is named first and is called the *origin* of the muscle; the more movable part is named last and is called the *insertion;* the direction of pull is toward the point of origin. For example, the sternothyroid muscle runs from the sternum (the breastbone) to the thyroid cartilage (the Adam's apple); contracting this muscle tends to pull the thyroid cartilage toward the sternum, thus lowering the larynx—an action associated with yawning.

Since muscles usually pull in only one direction, other muscles are required to reverse the direction of pull. One group of muscles will close the hand into a fist; another group will open it. One set will raise the hand to the shoulder; another will lower it. Opposing groups of muscles often are brought into use simultaneously to stabilize some part of the body so that it may function more effectively. This is particularly true in the process of maintaining body equilibrium and in the act of singing. More about this later.

Muscles perform their work by contracting; however, they perform that work most efficiently when given frequent opportunities to relax. The alternate periods of work and rest of the human heart are a prime example of this principle. If a muscle is held in tension for any length of time, it will begin to protest in various ways. First of all it will tend to quiver or tremble; if the tension is not released, it may begin to shake more violently in what is known as a tetanic flutter—a type of uncontrolled muscle spasm. Rather intense pains may develop, partially from the spasm and partially because contracting a muscle restricts the flow of blood through it. (Soreness and stiffness in the muscle may be a subsequent form of protest.) If the tension still is not released, the muscle eventually will lose its ability to function. Asking a muscle to do more than it has been trained to do can result in the same forms of protest. Almost everyone has had the experience of carrying a heavy suitcase for some distance and then discovering that his hands are quivering so much that he can hardly sign his name. Continuous carrying of a heavy object gives the involved muscles no chance to relax, so they are protesting.

There are two primary visual clues to tensional faults of posture: (1) some form of trembling, quivering, or shaking; and (2) rigidity. If rigidity is prolonged long enough, it, too, may result in some kind of shaking. Remember that shaking is evidence that a muscle is being held in tension too long or is being asked to do more than it has been trained to do. This shaking can occur almost anywhere in the body; it is quite often found in the legs. Many an inexperienced singer has been embarrassed in a public performance by clearly visible shaking of the legs. Shifting the offending member around may temporarily alleviate the distress, but usually it returns and may be more pronounced. Excessive tension in one part of the body tends to be transmitted to adjacent areas.

Trembling of the legs is caused by holding the leg muscles, particularly the ones in the calf, in tension too long. A concomitant fault is pulling back on the knees. Experiment with pulling your knees back as hard as you can and analyzing the resulting places where strain is felt. You will feel tight muscles in both upper and lower parts of the leg, in the feet, and likely in the buttocks. Notice how rigid the calf muscles become. In addition to the tension created, pulling back on the knees poses another hazard; it tends to restrict the flow of blood back to the heart and consequently to the brain. This is a major cause of fainting when choir members are standing on risers and when soldiers are standing at attention. There are three things which can be done to eliminate this problem: (1) loosen the body up and establish proper muscle tonus by doing a warm-up routine before you perform; (2) be aware that the legs are a tension trouble spot and try to avoid tension by thinking of keeping them free-to-move and flexible; (3) bring your knees slightly forward until they are loose feeling and then move them slightly at intervals to prevent locking.

Other places subject to visible shaking would include the head, the chest, the abdomen, the hands and arms, the lips, the jaw, the tongue, and the front of the throat. All of these are not posture-related faults, but they are all tension-related, and the approach to them is similar. Locate the tension, try to determine the cause, and try to eliminate tension by encouraging relaxation techniques or by making smaller demands on the muscles involved.

Some students attempt to solve all problems by sheer muscle power—by local effort; they become so rigid that they resemble statues, with everything locked into place securely and about as much warmth as a block of marble. The best remedy for this problem is movement. Have them walk, march, or dance around the studio; have them do mild calisthenics; have them draw beautiful arches in the air with one or both hands; insist that they sing while they are moving. Motion is the theme; don't let them stop moving long enough to start thinking about local muscles and to lock into one position.

Rigidity may show in many different places in many different guises. It is characterized by lack of movement, by lack of freedom in movement, or by lack of freedom in the vocal sound. At times it may indicate personality problems. A warm, loving relationship in the studio may bring quicker results than any technical answers the teacher can supply.

Because of the influence of posture on the various parts of the vocal mechanism, it is important that postural faults should be corrected early in the student's course of study, before attention is turned to other problem areas. Firm insistence on postural changes should continue until the desired posture has become habitual. As long as good posture is still lacking, avoid the temptation to move on to more interesting areas of vocal instruction, leaving alignment and tensional faults to fend for themselves. Since posture and breathing are so strongly interrelated, it is essential that good posture precede the establishment of good breathing techniques.

In recent years a system for establishing proper posture and freeing the body, mind, and emotions to function as a unified whole has gained wide acceptance. It is known as the Alexander Principle or the Alexander Technique. Classes in the application of various aspects of the Alexander system to musical performance have become a standard part of the curriculum at several notable institutions in Great Britain and in the United States. The author has had the privilege of visiting the Alexander Institute in London and watching skilled technicians apply the Alexander Principle on a private lesson basis. A practitioner who is trained in this system can solve many of the problems of alignment and tension discussed earlier in this chapter. Persons desiring more information on this approach are referred to the sources listed below.[3]

Notes

1. *American College Dictionary.*
2. *Collins English Dictionary.*
3. Wilfred Barlow, *The Alexander Principle* (London: Arrow Books Limited, 1973).
Fernando Duarte, "The Principles of the Alexander Technique," *Journal of Research in Singing* 5 (December 1981): 3-21.

4
Breathing and Support

The Breathing Mechanism

Breathing is a natural process which begins with birth and ends with death. No one instructs a baby in the art of breathing, although he may get a manual assist from the doctor or nurse if he has trouble getting started. The rate of breathing is governed by the body's need of oxygen. If a person is sitting down and not exerting himself, the rate will be about 12-16 times per minute; if he goes to sleep, the rate will decrease; if he starts exercising, it will increase. This type of breathing to sustain life is automatic and needs no conscious controls.

Breathing for life has three stages: (1) a slow intake of air; (2) a somewhat quicker release of air; and (3) a waiting or recovery period before the next intake. If you start analyzing this natural process, it will lose some of its spontaneity because you are bringing it under conscious control. The essential difference between breathing to live and breathing to sing lies in the amount of conscious control exerted.

Air enters the body because of a difference in atmospheric pressure inside and outside the body. This difference in pressure exists because of the action of the diaphragm muscle, which creates a partial vacuum in the lungs. Since the external pressure is greater than the internal, air enters the body through the nose and/or mouth, passes through the throat, the trachea (windpipe), and bronchi, and then enters the lungs—two spongy, elastic, saclike organs located, along with the heart, in the chest cavity. The diaphragm is a dome-shaped partition that separates the chest cavity from the abdominal cavity. It may be described as a floor to the chest and a ceiling to the abdomen. The bottom surface of the lungs is attached to the top surface of the diaphragm by connective tissue. The lungs are nonmuscular and, therefore, must depend on the diaphragm and the muscular movements of the chest, back, and abdomen for expansion or contraction during the act of respiration.

The muscle fibers of the diaphragm are attached to the breastbone, the lowest ribs, and the backbone, with the dome (which may be more accurately described as a double dome) extending upward into the chest cavity from these points of origin. Since the ribs in the front of the rib cage are higher than the ones in the back, the diaphragm extends lower in the back than it does in the front. When these muscle fibers are contracted, the dome of the diaphragm is lowered, compressing the viscera below it and causing the upper abdomen to protrude. At the same time the lungs are stretched downward by this descending movement of the diaphragm, thus increasing the effective capacity of the lungs and creating the partial vacuum referred to earlier which causes outside air to enter the body. It should be mentioned that the descent of the diaphragm does not go as low as the places to which it is attached. The movement visible in the upper abdomen is the result of displaced viscera and relaxed abdominal muscles; some people confuse this movement with that of the diaphragm. The diaphragm cannot descend that low.

The primary muscle for bringing air into the body is the diaphragm. It is assisted by the external rib (intercostal) muscles and by the relaxation of the upper abdomen. When breathing becomes more labored due to strenuous exertion, various other muscles of the shoulders, back, and chest are brought into action; since singing does not demand this level of physical activity, these muscles will not be considered here.[1]

Getting air back out of the body is a somewhat more complicated process than bringing it in. There are several factors involved: (1) the diaphragm relaxes; (2) the lungs are elastic and tend to return to their original shape when the diaphragm quits stretching them; (3) the abdominal organs and abdominal wall return to their original shape and location when the diaphragm quits pushing against and compressing them; (4) the internal rib muscles[2] and the abdominal muscles[3] assist in the expulsion of air. The role of the internal rib and abdominal muscles becomes more prominent as the level of exertion increases.

Breathing normally takes place through the nose until the level of exertion demands so much oxygen that the mouth must assist in taking larger quantities of air more rapidly than is possible through the nose alone. The nose is designed to filter, warm, and add moisture to the incoming air; in order to perform these functions, it is constructed so that it also slows the air down. This factor limits the amount of air that can be inhaled in a hurry through the nose, and therefore becomes quite important in certain singing conditions.

Breathing for Singing

Natural breathing has three stages: a breathing-in period, a breathing-out period, and a resting or recovery period; these stages are not usually consciously controlled. Breathing for singing has four stages:[4] (1) a breathing-in period (inhalation), (2) a setting-up-controls period (suspension), (3) a controlled-exhalation period (phonation), and (4) a recovery period; these stages must be under conscious control until they become conditioned reflexes. Many singers abandon conscious controls before their reflexes are fully conditioned and inherit chronic problems thereby.

Inhalation. The inhalation stage of breathing for singing is quicker, the quantity of air inhaled is greater, and the breath goes deeper into the lungs than in natural breathing. When time permits, the singer should breathe through the nose, so that it may fulfill its cleaning, warming, and moisturizing function. Frequently the music will not allow enough time for breathing through the nose; when this happens, the singer should breathe through mouth and nose simultaneously; this will provide the most breath in the least time.[5]

It is important for a singer to condition his inhalation reflexes by the proper mental preparation. Experiment with the following ideas to see if they have meaning for you:

(1) Pretend you are smelling a flower, even to the point of raising your hand to your nose; notice how the breath enters your body slowly and easily without any conscious effort on your part and how deep the breath goes;

(2) Pretend you are beginning a yawn, but do not actually go into a full yawn; notice how your lower jaw drops free in its socket; notice the gentle lifting feeling in the area of your soft palate; notice that your throat feels deeper; notice the cool air moving easily through your throat; notice how deep in the body your breath goes without any effort;

(3) Pretend that you are drinking a glass of water, raising your hand to your mouth; observe how easily the jaw drops open, how deep and spacious the throat seems, the lifting of the soft palate; if you breathe in this position, the breath will enter the body easily and noiselessly, and will go deep without any effort.

There are three postural conditions which should exist *before* you take a breath—the chest should be comfortably high, the lower abdomen should be comfortably in, and the upper abdomen should be free to move. Check yourself before you breathe by thinking these key words: comfortably up, comfortably in, free-to-move.

When you inhale, the breath seems to move *into* the body, *down* to the lungs, and *out* around the middle of the body. This expansion around the middle of the body is both natural and desirable; it has already been identified as the displacement of the abdominal organs by the descent of the diaphragm. To the singer it feels as if the breath itself is causing the expansion; this is one of those situations for the singer in which what you experience may not coincide with the physical facts. If thinking that your breath moves in, down, and out around the middle has meaning for you, use that thought pattern! The important thing is to establish this feeling of expansion around the middle of your body just below the rib cage. Try this experiment:

Place your hands on your back in such a way that they touch the lowest ribs and the area just below them. Breathe in as if you are smelling a rose; you should feel some expansion beneath your hands. Now place your hands on your sides in such a way that they rest on the lowest ribs and the part of the abdomen just below them. Smell another rose; you should feel some expansion under your hands. Now place your hands on your upper abdomen with your thumbs touching the lowest ribs, your little fingers near your waistline, and your middle fingers touching each other. You should feel more expansion here than in the back and sides.

When the diaphragm moves down, it displaces the abdominal viscera and causes an expansion all the way around the body just below the ribs. The back expands, the sides expand, but the greatest expansion should be in the front of the body. There are two reasons for this: (1) the attachment of the diaphragm to the skeleton is higher in the front of the body than it is on the sides or back; (2) the upper abdomen is capable of more expansion for less expenditure of effort than the sides or back. The singer should strive for expansion in all three of these areas but should focus on frontal expansion. Some teachers have made such a fetish of back expansion or rib expansion that the more normal frontal expansion is limited or even eliminated. This is a case of a partial truth being established as the whole truth, which is an ever-present danger in all facets of teaching singing.

If the upper abdomen is free to move, it is easy to expand around the middle of the body when breathing in, and the main expansion will be in the front of the body. If the upper abdomen is pulled in before you breathe or if it is too tense, it is difficult for that area to expand at all.

A well-performed inhalation should be noiseless and should look effortless.

Audible breathing is a sign that the singer has not fully developed his technique; the path of the incoming air is partially blocked and a gasping or wheezing sound results. The remedy will be discussed in the next major section. The same is true of visible breathing effort.

Suspension. The suspension stage of breathing for singing has no parallel in natural breathing. In natural breathing the end of the inhalation process seems to merge with the beginning of the exhalation process; there are no distinct boundaries between them. In breathing for singing, however, it is very important that the breath should be suspended momentarily just as the act of inhalation is completed. The purpose of this moment of suspension is to prepare the breath support mechanism for the phonation which follows. When properly done, suspension ensures an almost effortless inception of vocal tone without any major readjustment of the mechanism involved. Since it is not part of natural breathing, suspension must be acquired by the singer through the imposition of conscious controls. It should be practiced until its use has become second nature for the singer. Try this experiment:

Breathe in easily and deeply, expanding around the middle of your body as you do so. Just as you are comfortably full of air, stop the downward movement of your diaphragm. Hold this position while you slowly count to five mentally. Do not attempt to hold your breath by closing your vocal cords, lips, etc., but only by keeping the diaphragm contracted. It helps to imagine that you are still breathing in, even after you have stopped doing so. This allows you to set up an equilibrium between the breathing in and breathing out mechanisms which is an essential element of breath support. After holding your breath for a count of five, release it quickly and fully. Repeat this routine of breathing in, suspending, and breathing out several times, holding for at least five counts while suspending. As suspension becomes more habitual, you should shorten the time involved until it is quite brief. Remember that in the suspension stage, however brief it may be, your breath is not moving either in or out. When you suspend your breath, your body should feel comfortably expanded all around, but especially in the front. As long as the diaphragm remains down, it is easy to hold this expanded position.

Controlled Exhalation. The third stage of breathing for singing is a period of controlled exhalation; in coordination with the vocal cords it produces phonation. The length of the period of exhalation is determined by the demands of the musical phrase. In natural breathing the breath leaves the body rather fast due to the relaxation of the diaphragm and the concerted action of various muscles and organs described previously. In singing, however, the breath should be conserved and released quite slowly, as the diaphragm gradually releases its tension and returns toward its original position. Perhaps the best way to gain control of the exhalation process is to try to maintain the expansion around the middle of the body—in the upper abdomen, the lower ribs, and the back—while the diaphragm slowly begins to release its tension. This expansion will decrease in size as breath is expended, but this should happen so gradually that the singer still feels expanded throughout the phrase. Try this experiment:

Place your hands on your upper abdomen with your thumbs touching the lowest ribs, your little fingers near your waistline, and your middle fingers just touching each other. Breathe in deeply and easily until the expansion under your hands has caused your middle fingers to separate slightly. Hold this expanded position for a moment (suspension) before exhaling. Now start making a hissing sound by gently blowing your breath between closed teeth: keep the hiss as steady and even as you can, with a minimum of breath pressure; try to maintain your expansion and to keep your middle fingers from coming back together as long as you can without straining. Now repeat the experiment, but this time blow your breath out forcibly between protruded lips; notice how much more rapidly your expansion collapses. Return to the hissing exercise and repeat it several times always maintaining expansion as long as you can comfortably, and trying to analyze the associated feelings in your abdomen, ribs, and back.

The relationship between the breathing-in muscles and the breathing-out muscles which has been brought into play here will be discussed more fully in the section on breath support.

In a discussion of exhalation Christy states:

The feeling of holding back the breath is essential to establish "Suspension," and continues through the attack and the entire phrase following. It prevents collapse of the resistant breath muscles and establishes a steadiness of control, necessary for all good legato singing. When posture is correct, and all the muscles function properly in singing, there is a feeling of flexible, expansive openness in the body.[6]

Recovery. The fourth stage of breathing for singing is a recovery period. At the end of each breath there should be a brief moment when all the muscles associated with breathing relax; this also applies to the muscles associated with phonation, resonation, and articulation. Muscles perform their task of contracting most efficiently when allowed ample opportunity to rest and recover. If the recovery stage is insufficient, the muscles may become more and more tense with each succeeding breath, particularly under the added pressure of public performance. In natural breathing the recovery period is fairly long; in singing it often is instantaneous because the music insists on an immediate return to action. This pressure to get a quick breath and start singing again causes many inexperienced singers to slight the recovery phase and to accumulate tension. The four stages of breathing for singing should be practiced slowly and deliberately until the technique is secure; then the suspension and recovery phases can be speeded up. Try this experiment:

Practice the four stages while counting silently. Breathe in for three counts, suspend for three, breathe out for three while hissing softly, relax for three before breathing in again. Repeat the whole procedure several times. Then shorten the suspension and recovery phases to two counts for a while. Finally shorten suspension and recovery to only one count.

Sometimes it is necessary to breathe so rapidly that you do not have time to take a normally deep breath. This occurs when you must breathe between two notes of short duration or when you must break a phrase because of its extreme length, as in the extended melismatic passages of the baroque era. A quick breath of this type is called a *catch breath* and requires some adjustment of the basic breathing technique. Both the recovery and inhalation stages need to be accelerated without introducing unnecessary tension. The best approach is to drop the lower jaw quickly open while breathing as if you have been startled or surprised. If the dropping of the jaw and the taking of the breath are properly synchronized, there will be no noise involved and a large quantity of air can be inhaled in a very short time. Direct the breath deep into the body, and avoid any jerking of the upper chest or shoulders. The secret of the catch breath lies in getting the air passages completely open, so that there is nothing to restrict the flow of air or to create frictional noises.

Breath Support

The breath of the singer is the actuator of the vocal instrument. The pressure of the breath against the vocal cords sets them in vibration and phonation ensues. Increasing the breath pressure can affect phonation in two ways; it can increase the frequency of vibration (the pitch) and/or the amplitude of vibration (the intensity). In other words, breath pressure contributes to both the pitch and the intensity of the vocal tone.

Breath support is a dynamic relationship between the breathing-in muscles and the breathing-out muscles whose purpose is to supply adequate breath pressure to the vocal cords for the sustaining of any desired pitch or dynamic level. When a person establishes the correct posture, breathes in properly, and then suspends the breath, a balanced tension is set up between the muscles of inhalation and the muscles of exhalation. By a process of trial and error—empirically—the singer learns to adjust this balanced tension just enough to supply the needed breath pressure for a given pitch and dynamic level. With an inexperienced singer the breath energy seems to come in uneven spurts—too much for one desired sound, too little for the next— somewhat like a small child learning to make large (gross) movements before he can make more delicate coordinations. Only time and disciplined practice will bring the support mechanism to its full potential for supplying fine adjustments of breath pressure to the vocal cords.

Although the terms "breath support" and "breath control" often are used interchangeably, they really are not the same thing. *Breath support*, as previously defined, is a function of the breathing muscles. Breath control mainly is a function of the vocal cords themselves. It may be defined as a dynamic relationship between the breath and the vocal cords which determines how long you can sing on one breath. If that relationship is not an efficient one, if the vocal cords are not closing properly, it is possible to run out of air very quickly, regardless of how well your support mechanism is functioning. The following exercises will help you distinguish between breath control and support:

> Take a deep breath through your mouth; leave your mouth hanging open and blow your breath out; notice how quickly all your breath is exhausted from your body, because you are doing nothing to control the passage of the air. Now take another deep breath, but this time as you blow your breath out, shape your lips into a pucker as if you are about to whistle; notice how much longer it takes to blow the breath out of your body this way. This is because you have begun to control your breath through the use of your lips. Take another deep breath and this time exhale with a hissing noise as you have done earlier, sustaining the sound as long as you can; you are now controlling the breath through the use of your tongue and teeth. Take another deep breath, but this time say "one, one, one . . . " smoothly and continuously while you exhale, sustaining the sound as long as you can. You are now controlling the breath through the use of your vocal cords, which is the way it is normally done in speaking and singing. This is the meaning of the term *breath control*. Now make a soft hissing noise and then a loud one; observe very carefully what you feel in your abdomen when you make the soft sound and then the loud one. This

sensation is *breath support*; observe that it takes more support to make the loud sound than the soft one. Repeat the soft, then loud sequence, but this time say "one, one . . . " softly, then loudly, once again observing the support sensations.

Breath support is a dynamic, ever-changing relationship between the forces which bring air into the body and the forces which cause air to leave the body. In the suspension phase of breathing, these forces are brought into equilibrium; the breath does not move in or out. When phonation is initiated, the balance is tipped in favor of the breathing-out mechanism so that breath pressure may be supplied to the vocal cords; however, the breathing-in muscles—the diaphragm and the external rib muscles—must remain active as a counterbalancing force which resists the breathing-out muscles, but not enough to win the tug-of-war. To the singer it feels much as if he is staying in a breathing-in posture, even though air gradually is moving out of his body.

The area of the upper abdomen just below the tip of the breastbone and bounded on both sides by the ribs is called the epigastrium. The importance of this area can be overemphasized, and its action can be exaggerated; nevertheless, singers need to be aware of how it functions. Try this experiment:

Press the fingers of each hand into the epigastrium—the softer area just below the breastbone. While you are doing so, cough. Notice the reflex action of the epigastrium pushing out against your fingers; this is sometimes called the "bouncing" epigastrium.[7] Continue pressing in and say "hey" loudly; you should feel the same outward reflex action. Now say "hey" softly; you should feel a gentle firming of the abdominal wall, still going outward.

Summary of Breathing Concepts

Like good posture, the separate components of good breathing technique ultimately must be brought together as a unified configuration. The breathing technique needs to be kept under conscious control until it becomes so habitual that it does not require continual analysis, but instead will respond readily to appropriate thought patterns. Some breathing concepts which may prove to be helpful in establishing good habits include:

(1) Good posture precedes good breathing;
(2) breathe in as if smelling a rose;
(3) breathe in as if beginning a yawn;
(4) in—down—out around the middle;
(5) comfortably up—comfortably in—free to move;

    (6) inhalation, suspension, controlled exhalation, recovery;
    (7) breathe in as if drinking a glass of water;
    (8) breathing is effortless and noiseless;
    (9) for a catch breath drop the jaw and breathe as if surprised;
  (10) the chest is comfortably high before, during, and after breathing.

Faults Related to Breathing and Support

There are four methods of breathing which are to some degree inefficient or tension-producing and therefore may be considered as breathing faults. These methods are identified by the portions of the anatomy involved: (1) upper-chest breathing, (2) rib breathing, (3) back breathing, and (4) belly breathing. The semantic problems mentioned in an earlier chapter become evident here; there is little agreement among teachers concerning the names of different breathing methods. For example, there is no widely accepted name for the method of breathing previously advocated in the section on breathing for singing, even though it is in common use; it has been referred to as diaphragmatic, costal, pancostal, intercostal, rib, belly, and diaphragmatic-intercostal breathing by various authors, and this is not an exhaustive list! Neither is it easy to come up with a name that is both accurate and descriptive. All breathing methods involve the diaphragm to some extent; there is some rib action in all of them. Perhaps the most descriptive name for the advocated method is this somewhat unwieldy one: diaphragmatic-intercostal-upper abdominal breathing; at least it indicates where the action is taking place. The reasoning behind the names of the four incorrect methods listed above will become apparent as each is discussed separately.

Upper-chest breathing, which is also known as clavicular breathing, draws its name from the highly visible rising and falling movements of the chest. This method is not taught, but is naturally present in the majority of beginning students. It is interesting to observe that babies and many preschool children breathe correctly; by the time the child has attended school for two or three years, it is likely that upper-chest breathing will have been adopted. The chief cause of this is the postural faults which arise from sitting at a desk or table several hours a day and leaning over it to write, draw, and read. In the general populace upper-chest breathing is the predominant method, especially among women. Its characteristic feature is that the chest rises during inhalation and falls during exhalation.

Upper-chest breathing is undesirable for the following reasons:
    (1) It limits (inhibits) the downward travel of the diaphragm;

(2) It is visually distracting to the audience;

(3) It wastes energy and is physically tiring because of the effort expended in raising the chest;

(4) It often is associated with poor posture;

(5) Tension in the muscles of the chest and shoulders may be transmitted to the neck area and the vocal mechanism itself;

(6) It is inefficient, tending to be shallow.

Place your hand on your upper abdomen and breathe in while raising your chest; observe what is taking place under your hand. The upper abdomen is pulled in to assist in the action of raising the chest. Pulling in on the upper abdomen prevents the diaphragm from making its full descent; it thereby limits the capacity of the lower lung area and interferes with the free functioning of the support mechanism. This is the primary weakness of the upper-chest method.

The corrective procedures are largely a matter of establishing the correct postural and breathing techniques previously discussed. The student must be made aware of the appropriate goals and must constantly be reminded of them until they have become habitual. Do not yield to the temptation to move on to more interesting tonal and musical goals before posture and breathing are secure technically.

Some students have a difficult time breaking down the upper-chest syndrome; for them it may be necessary to impose mechanical controls. Those who are addicted to pulling in strongly on the upper abdomen may have to counter the tendency for a while by actually pushing out on the epigastrium area in order to achieve any expansion around the front of the body; this is a means to an end and should not be continued any longer than necessary. Those who seem unable to stabilize the chest may need to practice while leaning back against a wall in the exercise described under postural faults. Some students can discover the correct action of the diaphragm and the abdominal wall only by lying flat on their backs; some find it beneficial to place a large book on the upper abdomen while in this position so that they can more readily observe and feel the action of the diaphragm. It is important for the student to know how correct breathing looks and feels.

Rib breathing, unlike upper-chest, seldom occurs naturally; it is a method passed on by teachers to their students, and contains certain elements of truth. The rib cage *should* expand during inhalation. In rib breathing, the rib cage *does* expand; the problem is that it is made the sole object of the act of expansion, thus limiting or eliminating expansion in other places. One possible asset of rib breathing is that it often is associated with good posture.

Unfortunately, the good posture may be of the military variety exemplified by the two commands, "Suck in your gut!" and "Squeeze your shoulder blades together until they touch!"—both of which create tensional faults. Another asset is that rib breathing may be almost invisible if the singer is wearing loose-fitting clothing, since the primary expansion is lateral—to the sides. However, one possible visual clue to rib breathing is an outward movement of the elbows when breath is inhaled.

Rib breathing is undesirable, for the following reasons:

(1) It limits (inhibits) the downward travel of the diaphragm;
(2) It wastes energy and is physically tiring because of the effort expended in forcing the ribs outward;
(3) Tension in the muscles of the chest, ribs, and shoulders may be transmitted to the neck area and the vocal mechanism.

Place your hand on your upper abdomen and breathe in while pushing your lower ribs as far out to each side as you can; observe what is taking place under your hand. The upper abdomen is pulled in to assist in the action of pushing the ribs out to each side. As in upper-chest breathing, pulling in on the upper abdomen prevents the diaphragm from making its full descent, limiting the capacity of the lower lung area and interfering with the functioning of the support mechanism. This is the main weakness of the rib-breathing method.

Corrective procedures deal chiefly with the release of postural tension and with the encouragement of upper abdominal expansion while inhaling. Rib breathing is more prevalent among slender people than it is among plump ones; these same slender people tend to have more trouble experiencing expansion around the middle of their bodies, for the reason that they have very little excess tissue to expand. Some of them can experience expansion on inhalation only when sitting down, or, in extreme cases, when sitting down and leaning well forward from their hips. It is important that rib breathers stop pulling in on the upper abdomen, so that it may join the rib cage in expanding; pushing out on the epigastrium area may be necessary for a while to counteract the tendency to pull in.

Back breathing has much in common with rib breathing and could be considered another manifestation of it; however, there is one essential difference. In rib breathing the primary objective is to expand the rib cage to each side; in back breathing, the expansion is in the back itself. There is nothing wrong with expanding the back, unless the act is done in such a way that needed expansion in other areas is limited or eliminated. Unfortunately, too much concentration on expanding the back often has that effect. The back and the ribs should expand during inhalation, but so should the upper abdomen. Paradoxically, concentrating attention on expansion of the back or ribs will virtually eliminate frontal expansion, but concentrating on frontal expansion will result in full and free expansion of the back and the ribs.

When viewed from the front, back breathing may be well hidden. When it is viewed from the back, it is readily visible and may reveal considerable muscle effort. Some teachers advocate pulling the shoulders forward to facilitate expanding the back. It does have that effect, but is not a recommended procedure, for two reasons: it is not good posturally and it tends to further restrict frontal expansion.

Back breathing is undesirable for the following reasons:

(1) It limits (restricts) the downward travel of the diaphragm;
(2) It wastes energy and is physically tiring because of the effort expended in spreading the back;
(3) Tension in the muscles of the back and shoulders may be transmitted to the vocal mechanism;
(4) If the shoulders are pulled forward, it is posturally weak.

If you place your hand on your upper abdomen and breathe in while spreading your back as much as possible, you will discover once again that the upper abdomen is pulled in and the work of the diaphragm is hampered. Upper-chest, rib, and back breathing share this common fault—they limit the downward travel of the diaphragm.

Encouraging frontal expansion during inhalation is the first corrective procedure. There is so much less effort involved in the proper kind of frontal expansion that some back, rib, and upper-chest breathers feel that nothing is happening when they first achieve it; they should avoid the temptation to substitute some other form of muscle effort for the old tense feeling. If a back breather has been taught to roll his shoulders forward, he must learn the proper down-and-back position and the comfortably high chest.

Belly breathing is in a class by itself, having little in common with back, rib, and upper-chest breathing. They all limit the downward travel of the diaphragm during inhalation; belly breathing does not. Instead, it limits the ability of the diaphragm to move upward during exhalation. Students of this method are instructed to "take a deep breath and then push out against your belt while you sing." This has the effect of locking the diaphragm in the lowest position to which it has descended and not allowing it to make its return as air is expended. This is another example of an element of truth being made the basis of a faulty system. Earlier discussion has indicated that the breathing-in muscles stay active during the controlled exhalation stage;

they help retain breath in the body by offering resistance to the breathing-out muscles, and assist in the process of breath support thereby. However, it was pointed out that they remain secondary to the expulsive power of the breathing-out muscles, and the diaphragm readjusts upward as breath is used up. In the belly-breathing method, the breathing-in muscles are so prominent during exhalation that they overpower the breathing-out muscles, and other means must be found to expel the breath. This is accomplished by squeezing the chest down on the lungs or by bending backward from the waist; either approach decreases the size of the chest cavity and forces air from the lungs. Needless to say, this is not the most efficient way to get air out of the body. One visual clue to belly breathing is that the singer may seem to become shorter as a phrase progresses!

There is one unexpected benefit of belly breathing—it seems to help some singers with their lowest notes. Many singers cut off their lowest notes by maintaining too much breath pressure against the vocal cords; since it is difficult to create much breath pressure while belly breathing, the lower voice may benefit in such cases. However, the highest notes can become a disaster area with belly breathing. The disadvantages of belly breathing are:

(1) It restricts the upward travel of the diaphragm during phonation;
(2) It results in poor posture—sunken chest and protruding abdomen;
(3) It severely limits breath support for the upper voice;
(4) It can result in tone quality and vibrato problems.

The most important corrective procedure for belly breathing is postural. It is almost impossible to belly breathe if three postural elements are maintained: comfortably high chest, spinal stretch, and straight back. The belly breather already knows how to get a full descent of the diaphragm on inhalation and expansion around the middle of the body; now he must be convinced that he does not need to push out against his belt.

Hypofunctional breathing, failing to demand enough physical activity of the breathing mechanism, is common only among beginning singers. It consists mainly of the failure to take enough breath as deep in the lungs as it should go; it is caused by a lack of awareness of the actual demands of singing and usually responds readily to treatment. Some students who have never taken a sustained series of deep breaths may become dizzy on first exposure and may ask to sit down; this is no cause for alarm. The quickest cure for hypofunctional breathing is explaining, demonstrating, and asking the student to experience the four stages in breathing for singing. In arriving at enough physical activity of the mechanism, care must be taken not to overemphasize the physical side; hyperfunction can easily result.

Hyperfunctional breathing, demanding too much physical activity of the breathing mechanism, is the province of the experienced singer and is much more prevalent than is generally recognized. Aside from the breath support problems to be considered in a moment, it consists of taking too much air into the body. There are at least two causes for this: (1) the misconception that the ability to sing long phrases is in direct relationship to the quantity of air you can inhale; and (2) the fear of running out of breath in a public performance. The ability to sing long phrases comes primarily from the efficiency of your vocal cord action; it is the result of good laryngeal adjustment, not of lung capacity. If a bicycle tire has a bad valve, the tire will keep going flat, no matter how much air is put in it; if the vocal cords allow too much air to escape, the singer will soon run out of breath, no matter how much air has been inhaled. Taking in too much air not only wastes energy but also creates unnecessary tension in both the breathing mechanism and the larynx. Continued practice in taking bigger and bigger breaths results in too much air being packed into the chest and too much breath pressure pushing back against the vocal cords, with a consequent loss of freedom and flexibility. Try this experiment:

Take a normal breath and suspend it; without exhaling, take in more air; continue this process until you have inhaled four or five times without exhaling, or until you are completely full of air. As you do this, analyze where problems are developing. You will discover that the diaphragm becomes more and more tense; the abdominal wall, rib cage, and back become more and more rigid and inflexible; and pressure builds up under the upper chest to the point of discomfort. If you try to sing or speak, you will find so much pressure against the vocal cords that you can do so only with difficulty.

Limit yourself to taking a *comfortably* deep breath. It is much better to take a moderate breath and learn how to use it efficiently than it is to concentrate on taking vast quantities of air. How much air your body can hold is not nearly as important as how well you use what you have. If you have good breath control and are producing a good vocal sound, it is surprising how long you can sing on a rather small breath. Even though your lungs may feel completely empty after a long phrase, they still contain quite a bit of residual air. In normal breathing over half of the air in the lungs does not move out, but helps to keep the lungs partially inflated until the next inhalation. This residual air can be called upon in emergencies, and can provide some psychological support for the singer who knows it is there. It is possible to blow out most of the air you normally would use for singing and still sing a phrase of average length—if you believe that you can.[8] Many of the problems which singers encounter about running out of breath are psychological ones. If you think you are going to run out, you probably will; the negative thought dictates the result. Underwater swimmers face the same psychological hazards; they must learn to control the almost overpowering urge to breathe. If they can get over this psychological hurdle, the length of time they can remain under water increases greatly. Singers need to develop positive thought patterns about breathing; if you think you can, you often can—faith begets faith.

Hypofunctional breath support, the failure to demand enough activity of the support mechanism, is common only among beginning singers. It consists of the failure to activate the support mechanism enough to provide adequate breath pressure for the proper functioning of the vocal cords. There are several possible causes: (1) no suspension phase in the breathing process; (2) the misconception that the singer is singing much louder than he actually is; (3) an anemic concept of vocal tone; (4) devitalized posture; and (5) a lack of awareness of the nature and function of the support mechanism. In each instance the corrective procedure is the same—make the student aware of the problem and its causes, and ask him to make the necessary adjustments in what he is doing. In the early stages the student may need to exaggerate his responses in order to secure enough physical exertion. Such exercises as panting like a dog or laughing like Santa Claus (Ho! Ho! Ho!) may be helpful in setting up sensations of support.

With more experienced singers breath support presents an interesting paradox. If anything goes wrong with a singer's technique, the first thing to be blamed is the support mechanism, which is accused of failing to supply enough support, and greater effort is invoked. In actual practice, experienced singers seldom are lacking in support; they are much more often guilty of too much support (of hyperfunction). Another facet of the paradox is that support may not have been the problem in the first place. For some unknown reason many singers assume that more support is the universal answer to all vocal faults; this rarely ever is true, and when it is, it applies to a beginner, not to the experienced singer.

Hyperfunctional breath support, demanding too much from the support mechanism, is one of the most frequent vocal faults. It results in malfunction of the phonation, resonation, and articulation systems and, because of their camouflaging effect, often escapes detection. The larynx itself usually receives the blame, due to the kind of sound it is producing; the real culprit is the oversupport which is delivering so much breath pressure to the larynx that it cannot function freely. One cause of too much support has already been mentioned: the misconception that more support is the answer to all vocal evils. Other possible causes are: (1) trying to make a voice bigger than it really is; (2) pulling in on the upper abdomen; (3) eliminating the suspension phase of breathing; (4) excess postural tension; (5) misconception of dynamic level (constantly singing too loudly); (6) a too-muscular approach to singing, etc. Regardless of the initial cause, the usual result is that the abdominal wall is pulled in too strongly, with consequent excess tension and breath pressure. According to Proctor, normal people can produce subglottic breath pressures nearly ten times those ever required in singing.[9]

The best corrective procedure is getting the student to stop exerting so much local effort in the upper abdomen; this is easier said than done. Convincing a student that he does not need to pull in that hard is like persuading a drug addict that he does not need another fix. Reducing tension to the level at which a muscle functions best is one of the most difficult tasks facing a student. There are two reasons for this: (1) removing the familiar sensations of tension leaves the student with little feedback and the feeling that he is doing too little; (2) it is more difficult to judge exactly how much tension has been reduced than it is how much it has been increased. Try this experiment:

> Curl your hand slowly into a fist and gradually keep tightening it until it begins to hurt. It is possible to control the addition of tension rather constantly. Now try to release the tension just as gradually; within a short time it becomes quite difficult to know just how much tension is remaining.

Despite the difficulties involved, the student must learn to relax the upper abdomen enough that it retains its flexibility and freedom of movement. Encourage him to practice the four stages of breathing quite deliberately, making certain that he achieves expansion around the center of the body and that suspension is taking place before he attempts to support a sound. If suspension is effective, it will not be necessary for him to pull in hard on the upper abdomen to start the sound. Ask him to describe what he feels while the suspension stage is in effect; these sensations form the foundation for the support mechanism, and might be described like this:

> There is an expansive, stretching feeling all around the middle of my body, almost as if it is made of gentle elastic.

> There is an expansion downward deep within my body which is hard to localize but also seems to stretch like elastic.

There is a gentle lifting sensation under my upper chest, not forced, but buoyant.

If I start to make a hissing sound, I can feel muscles deep in my lower abdomen start contracting.

Another idea which might encourage less support is to ask the student to sing as if he is singing to a baby.

Since the function of the actuator (the breath) is to bring the vibrator (the vocal cords) into action, respiration and phonation are closely interrelated, and it is difficult to discuss one without referring to the other. Most of the faults related to the breathing mechanism have been considered in this chapter; others will appear in the following chapter on faults related to phonation. Breath control problems fall in this category because they originate from the vibratory action of the vocal cords.

Notes

1. Readers are referred to excellent discussions of the breathing mechanism in Greene, *The Voice*, pp. 19-31, and Vennard, *Singing*, pp. 20-35.

2. The function of the external rib muscles is to lift and separate the ribs; this action increases the vital capacity of the chest cavity. The function of the internal rib muscles is to lower the ribs and bring them closer together; this action decreases the vital capacity.

3. There are several abdominal muscles which can be separately identified. Since they function as a group in the breathing act, they will be referred to here as the abdominal muscles.

4. Van A. Christy, *Expressive Singing*, 2 vols., 3rd ed. (Dubuque, Iowa: Wm. C. Brown Company, 1975), 2:33-35.

5. I cannot agree with those teachers who insist that all breathing must be done through the nose. This approach has at least three weaknesses: (1) the singer often comes in late after a quick breath; (2) the singer often does not get enough breath when breathing quickly; (3) the singer may look funny when attempting to breathe fast.

6. Christy, *Expressive Singing*, 2:35.

7. Vennard, *Singing*, pp. 28-30.

8. Some students refuse to accept this statement without seeing a demonstration of it. Since I have demonstrated it many times in public, I have no hesitation about making such a claim.

9. Quoted in John Large, "Towards an Integrated Physiologic-Acoustic Theory of Vocal Registers," *The NATS Bulletin* 28 (February/March 1972): 33.

5
Phonation

The Mechanism of the Larynx

The larynx forms the uppermost unit of the trachea or windpipe. Its primary purpose is to serve as a valve which keeps food, drink, and other foreign matter out of the lungs and which holds breath in the lungs to assist in the action of lifting and other types of bodily exertion. Its use in speaking or singing—in the act of phonation—is a secondary or superimposed function. When it is used for phonation, the larynx may be more aptly described by its nontechnical name, the voice box, for it is here that vocal sound originates.

This duality of function whereby the larynx serves both as a valve and as a sound-producer is a significant source of problems when these functions are allowed to mix. A typical example occurs when someone attempts to talk and eat at the same time. Using the larynx to produce speech may interfere with its valving action enough that food or drink enters the windpipe and more or less serious choking results. Conversely, speakers and singers often unconsciously introduce unnecessary strain and tension into the larynx by using too much of its valving action while phonating. More about this later. It would be of doubtful value to attempt to duplicate here the extended materials on the mechanism of the larynx which may be found in numerous other sources.[1] The present discussion will be limited to the main structural elements of the larynx and the muscles which are attached to them. It is important for the teacher to be conversant with the basic design and function of the larynx before approaching phonatory faults.

Skeletal Framework of the Larynx. The framework of the larynx consists of five important cartilages and, according to some authorities, one bone. The cartilages are the thyroid cartilage, the cricoid cartilage, two arytenoid cartilages, and the epiglottis; the bone in question is the hyoid bone, from which the larynx is suspended.

The thyroid cartilage serves as a protective housing for the vocal cords and forms the visible projection in the front of the throat known as the Adam's

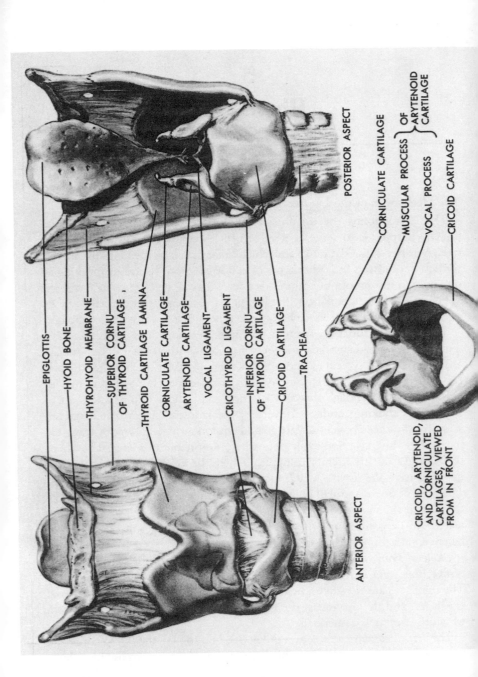

EPIGLOTTIS

HYOID BONE

THYROHYOID MEMBRANE

SUPERIOR CORNU
OF THYROID CARTILAGE

THYROID CARTILAGE LAMINA

CORNICULATE CARTILAGE

ARYTENOID CARTILAGE

VOCAL LIGAMENT

CRICOTHYROID LIGAMENT

INFERIOR CORNU
OF THYROID CARTILAGE

CRICOID CARTILAGE

TRACHEA

ANTERIOR ASPECT

POSTERIOR ASPECT

CORNICULATE CARTILAGE

MUSCULAR PROCESS } OF
ARYTENOID
CARTILAGE

VOCAL PROCESS

CRICOID CARTILAGE

CRICOID, ARYTENOID,
AND CORNICULATE
CARTILAGES, VIEWED
FROM IN FRONT

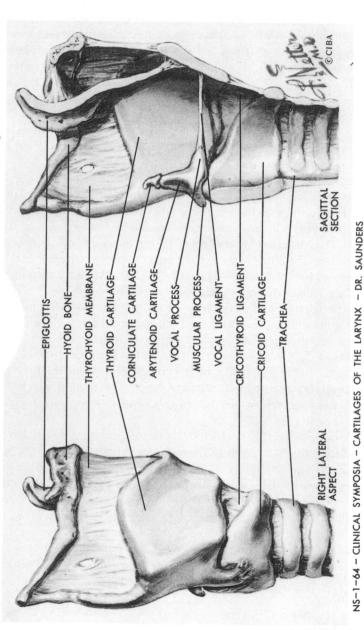

EPIGLOTTIS

HYOID BONE

THYROHYOID MEMBRANE

THYROID CARTILAGE

CORNICULATE CARTILAGE

ARYTENOID CARTILAGE

VOCAL PROCESS

MUSCULAR PROCESS

VOCAL LIGAMENT

CRICOTHYROID LIGAMENT

CRICOID CARTILAGE

TRACHEA

RIGHT LATERAL
ASPECT

SAGITAL
SECTION

NS-1-64 – CLINICAL SYMPOSIA – CARTILAGES OF THE LARYNX – DR. SAUNDERS

Figure 1: The Framework of the Larynx

apple. As a general rule, the more prominent the Adam's apple, the lower the range of the person who possesses it; sometimes there is no visible evidence of the thyroid cartilage. If you feel the front of your Adam's apple with your index finger, you probably will find a notch in the upper portion; this thyroid notch varies in size and may be hard to locate in some higher voices. Projecting upward from the thyroid cartilage are two horns (the superior cornua) which are connected to the hyoid bone by ligaments. Two more horns (the inferior cornua) project downward from the cartilage and form points of articulation with the cricoid cartilage. This articulation permits a rocking motion between the two cartilages.

The cricoid cartilage serves as a base or foundation for the laryngeal framework. The windpipe is made up of a series of circular cartilages which give definite shape to the breathing tube; each cartilage has a section at the back, however, which is made up of muscle and other forms of tissue; this allows the diameter of the tube to be increased or decreased during respiration. The cricoid cartilage sits atop the highest cartilage of the trachea proper and is joined to it by ligament. The cricoid forms a complete circle of cartilage around its bottom edge and resembles the shape of a signet ring, with the narrow band in the front of the throat, and the larger, somewhat rectangular section comprising the back wall of the larynx. The upper surface of this rectangular plate provides points of articulation with the bottom surfaces of the two arytenoid cartilages. In the front, the thyroid and cricoid cartilages are joined together by the cricothyroid ligament. If you feel down the front of your thyroid cartilage below the thyroid notch, you may encounter a second, smaller notch; this is the one between the cricoid and thyroid cartilages.

The arytenoid cartilages, which sit on the top surface of the cricoid plate, are attached to the vocal cords and therefore are vitally related to the position of the cords. The arytenoids are irregular in shape, with the lower part being somewhat pyramidal. Each arytenoid has three prongs: one projects forward into each vocal cord and is called the vocal process; one projects sideways and is called the muscle process; the third projects upward and is called the apex. The apex articulates or is fused with an upward extension called the corniculate cartilage or the cartilage of Santorini, which resembles the handle of a dipper or ladle. The movements of these upward extensions are visible in the collar of the larynx when you are viewing films of vocal cord action.

The epiglottis is a leaf-shaped cartilage which assists in the valving function of the larynx and is also active in the production of certain speech sounds. It is attached by a ligament to the inside surface of the thyroid cartilage just below the thyroid notch, and extends upward to the hyoid bone and the base of the tongue. In the act of swallowing, the epiglottis is pulled toward the back of the throat and down over the opening of the larynx; together with the laryngeal collar it keeps food or drink from entering the trachea.

The hyoid bone is a U-shaped bone which is attached to the base of the tongue and opens toward the back of the throat. The thyroid cartilage is suspended from it; therefore, movements of the tongue will affect both the hyoid bone and the thyroid cartilage. This is an important factor in establishing laryngeal posture for singing or speaking. If you place a thumb on each side of your throat between the lower jaw and the Adam's apple and press in, you can feel the wings of the hyoid bone and can move them about by gentle manipulation.

Musculature of the Larynx.[2] There are two basic categories of muscles involved in laryngeal function: intrinsic and extrinsic. Intrinsic muscles are those which have both ends—the origin and insertion—in the larynx. Extrinsic muscles have one end attached to some point outside it, such as the sternum, the shoulder, or various parts of the head.

The intrinsic muscles of the larynx which are of primary interest are those related to movements of the vocal cords. The most important of these are the thyroarytenoids, the cricothyroids, the cricoarytenoids, and the arytenoids. Intrinsic muscles of secondary interest are those related to the valving function of the larynx, such as the aryepiglottic folds and the thyrohyoid muscle.

The thyroarytenoid muscle, as the name suggests, connects the thyroid and arytenoid cartilages, arising inside the front angle of the thyroid and along its wings and extending back to the two arytenoids, where it is inserted on the vocal and muscle processes. The functions of this muscle are complicated by the fact that there are two distinct folds of it on each side of the thyroid which protrude out into the larynx. The lower set form the vocal cords, which are called the vocalis muscle or the internal thyroarytenoids. The upper set are called the false cords or ventricular bands. The space between the vocal cords and the false cords is called the ventricle; it houses the lubricating glands for the cords. When the larynx functions as a valve, as when swallowing, coughing, or lifting something heavy, both sets of cords assist in closing the air passage. In normal phonation, only the vocal cords are brought into action.

The front end of the vocal cords is attached to the thyroid wall about midway down from the notch and is fixed in this position. The back end of

Figure 2: Intrinsic Muscles of the Larynx

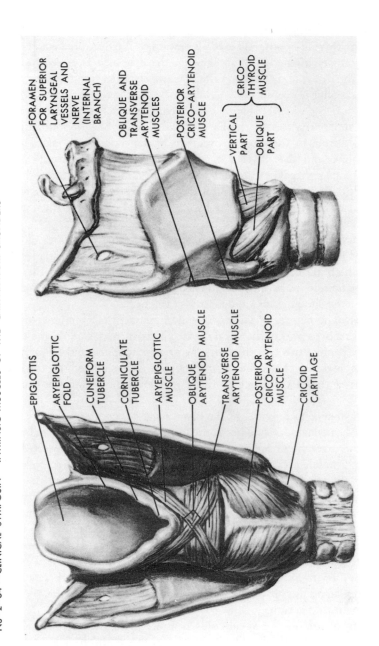

NS–2–64 – CLINICAL SYMPOSIA – INTRINSIC MUSCLES OF THE LARYNX H DR. SAUNDERS

FORAMEN
FOR SUPERIOR
LARYNGEAL
VESSELS AND
NERVE
(INTERNAL
BRANCH)

OBLIQUE
AND
TRANSVERSE
ARYTENOID
MUSCLES

POSTERIOR
CRICO–ARYTENOID
MUSCLE

CRICO–
THYROID
MUSCLE

VERTICAL
PART

OBLIQUE
PART

EPIGLOTTIS

ARYEPIGLOTTIC
FOLD

CUNEIFORM
TUBERCLE

CORNICULATE
TUBERCLE

ARYEPIGLOTTIC
MUSCLE

OBLIQUE
ARYTENOID MUSCLE

TRANSVERSE
ARYTENOID MUSCLE

POSTERIOR
CRICO–ARYTENOID
MUSCLE

CRICOID
CARTILAGE

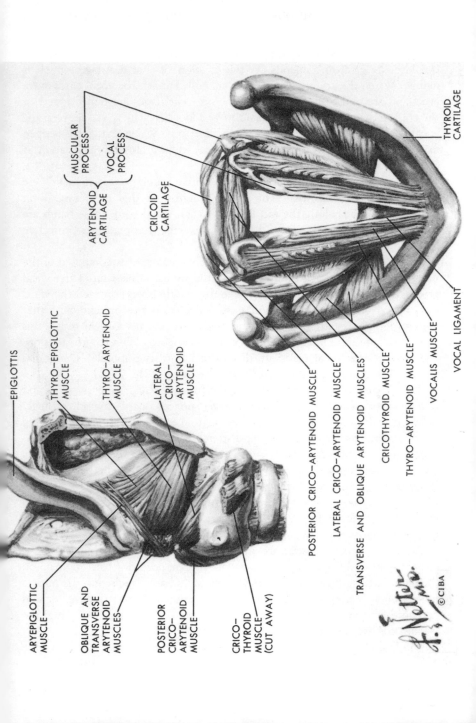

EPIGLOTTIS

THYRO-EPIGLOTTIC MUSCLE

THYRO-ARYTENOID MUSCLE

LATERAL CRICO-ARYTENOID MUSCLE

ARYEPIGLOTTIC MUSCLE

OBLIQUE AND TRANSVERSE ARYTENOID MUSCLES

POSTERIOR CRICO-ARYTENOID MUSCLE

CRICO-THYROID MUSCLE (CUT AWAY)

MUSCULAR PROCESS
VOCAL PROCESS
} ARYTENOID CARTILAGE

CRICOID CARTILAGE

THYROID CARTILAGE

POSTERIOR CRICO-ARYTENOID MUSCLE

LATERAL CRICO-ARYTENOID MUSCLE

TRANSVERSE AND OBLIQUE ARYTENOID MUSCLES

CRICOTHYROID MUSCLE

THYRO-ARYTENOID MUSCLE

VOCALIS MUSCLE

VOCAL LIGAMENT

© CIBA

each cord is attached to the vocal process (the forward prong) of an arytenoid cartilage; its position depends on the location of that cartilage, which is mobile. When the arytenoid cartilages are pulled apart, the vocal cords move apart and are said to be abducted. When the cartilages are pulled together, the cords move together and are said to be adducted. The space between the vocal cords is called the glottis or glottic aperture. When the glottis is open for normal breathing, it is triangular in shape; when it closes for phonation, it becomes a slit.

The underside of the vocal folds is lined with a tough protective membrane called the conus elasticus. The upper margins of this membrane form ligamentous bands along the full length of each vocal cord; these bands are called the vocal ligaments. Like the conus elasticus, they perform a protective function.

The front two-thirds of the length of each vocal cord is composed of the vocalis muscle; the back one-third is cartilaginous, consisting of the vocal process of the arytenoid cartilage. When the muscle fibers contract, the vocal cord is brought into tension and pulls forward on the arytenoids. Other muscles lengthen (stretch) the vocal cords; the vocalis muscle resists this pull. It is called the internal tensor of the vocal cords. The length, tension, and mass of the vocal cords are determined by this principle of muscular antagonism, and this in turn determines the pitch of the sound.

The cricothyroid muscle originates at the front of the cricoid cartilage and fans out upward and backward to the lower surfaces of the thyroid cartilage. When it contracts, it tends to pull the thyroid forward and down, bringing the two cartilages closer together and stretching the thyroarytenoid muscles. (Some sources state that the cricoid is pulled up toward the thyroid. In any case, the net result is the same—the vocal cords are lengthened.) The lengthening of the vocal fold which takes place does not necessarily mean an increase in tension;[3] this is conditioned on the amount of resistance offered by the vocalis muscle to this stretching action. The action of the cricothyroid muscle is important in the singing of low notes.

The cricoarytenoid muscles are divided into two pairs: the posterior cricoarytenoids and the lateral cricoarytenoids. The posterior pair originate on the outer back surface of the cricoid cartilage and are attached to the muscle process of each arytenoid. They have two functions: (1) resisting the forward pull on the arytenoid by the vocalis muscle, and (2) opening (abducting) the vocal cords by pulling the arytenoids out to each side.

The lateral cricoarytenoid muscles originate on the upper surface of the cricoid cartilage and extend up and back at an angle, attaching to the forward face of the muscle process of each arytenoid. Most authorities state that their function is to help adduct (bring together) the vocal cords by pulling forward on the muscular process, thus rotating the vocal processes toward each other and closing the glottis. Vennard assigns this lateral pair an important role in maintaining proper closure of the glottis as longitudinal tension on the vocal folds increases and the glottis tends to gap open. "This pull of the laterals on the muscular processes, causing the vocal processes to press together, is called *medial compression.*"[4]

The arytenoid muscles connect the arytenoid cartilages and are the primary factor in bringing the back end of the vocal cords together. There are three muscles in the interarytenoid group: the transverse arytenoid and a pair of oblique arytenoids. The transverse arytenoid forms a horizontal band across the back surface of the arytenoid cartilages and is the most important means of adducting the vocal cords. The oblique arytenoids form an X across the back of the arytenoid cartilages, running from the apex of each to the muscular process of the other; they assist the transverse arytenoid in pulling the cartilages together, but also function in the act of swallowing and in other valving actions of the larynx.

Intrinsic muscles of the larynx which are more closely related to valving than they are to phonating include the aryepiglottic folds and the thyrohyoid muscle. The aryepiglottic folds run from the arytenoid cartilages to the epiglottis, forming a muscular ring which is called the collar of the larynx. When these muscle fibers contract, the epiglottis is pulled down, the collar moves inward, and the entrance to the larynx is effectively sealed. When the aryepiglottic folds are relaxed, the epiglottis projects upward toward the base of the tongue and the entrance to the larynx is open.

The thyrohyoid muscle may pull in either direction depending upon which end is fixed and which is movable. If the thyroid is stabilized, the hyoid can be pulled downward; if the hyoid is the stable member, the thyroid can be pulled upward. If enough muscular antagonism is present, both actions may be prevented.

The extrinsic muscles of the larynx may be divided into two groups: (1) those that originate above the larynx—the supralaryngeal muscles; and (2) those that originate below the larynx—the infralaryngeal muscles. These extrinsic muscles perform the important task of positioning the larynx by raising, lowering, or stabilizing it. As a general rule, those that originate above the larynx pull up on it, and those that originate below pull down on it. Both sets of muscles can play a part in stabilizing the larynx through the principle of muscular antagonism; however, the infralaryngeal muscles assume a more prominent role during phonation because of the natural tendency of the larynx to rise.

The supralaryngeal muscles are active in such functions as swallowing, chewing, and the tongue movements associated with articulation. They frequently are identified as the "swallowing" muscles or as the "chewing and swallowing" muscles. As an illustration of their effect upon the larynx, perform this experiment:

> Place an index finger gently on the notch of your larynx. Observe what happens when you swallow. You will feel your tongue press up against the roof of your mouth and your larynx pulled up past your finger. Notice how much tension is present just before the swallow actually occurs. Now try to speak or sing while in this position. You will discover that the swallowing muscles are antagonistic to phonation.

There is a sizable number of supralaryngeal muscles; typical examples would include such muscles as the geniohyoid, the hyoglossus, and the mylohyoid. Having a general knowledge of their function is of more importance here than knowing their individual names and specific location.

The infralaryngeal muscles are active in such functions as yawning and inhaling. They are known as the "yawning" muscles and include the sternothyroid, the omohyoid, and the sternohyoid. When they contract, they pull downward on the thyroid cartilage and the hyoid bone, thus lowering the larynx. Try this experiment:

> Place an index finger gently on the notch of your larynx. Observe what happens when you begin to yawn. You will feel the lower jaw drop freely open, the larynx descend slightly, and a gentle lifting in the area of your soft palate as cool air goes deep within your throat and lungs. Now continue the action until it becomes a full yawn, noticing the tension which develops in the throat and lower jaw. Experiment with trying to speak or sing (1) in the beginning-of-a-yawn position and (2) in the full-yawn position. You will discover that the first position is conducive to easy phonation, while the second is somewhat antagonistic.

One other group of muscles deserves some mention because of its proximity to the larynx—*the constrictor muscles*. These are the muscles which line the throat and assist in the act of swallowing by squeezing food down toward the mouth of the esophagus. There are three of them: the upper constrictor, the middle constrictor, and the lower constrictor. They are of particular interest because of their ability to reduce the size of the throat and to create tension in the vicinity of the voice box. The lower constrictor also bears an extrinsic relationship with the larynx because some muscle fibers which arise on the thyroid and cricoid cartilages—the thyropharyngeus and cricopharyngeus muscles—merge with those of the lower constrictor. Because of this connection with the lower constrictor and with the mouth of the esophagus, the cricopharyngeus has an important anchoring effect on the larynx during phonation.

There are additional connections between the esophagus and the larynx. The upward extensions—the corniculate cartilages—of the arytenoids are attached to the front edge of the mouth of the esophagus and assist in opening the esophagus when the larynx moves up during the act of swallowing. Also some muscle fibers from the esophagus are attached to the upper back surface of the cricoid cartilage. Both of these connections can exert a downward drag on parts of the larynx and thereby affect its function.

The Phonatory Process

Phonation is the process of producing vocal sound by the vibration of the vocal cords. It takes place in the larynx when the vocal cords are brought together and breath pressure is applied to them in such a way that vibration ensues. The vocal cords are brought together primarily by the action of the interarytenoid muscles, which pull the arytenoid cartilages together. There are two major theories as to how vibration is initiated: the myoelastic theory and the aerodynamic theory; fortunately, there is no basic conflict between them.

The myoelastic theory states that when the vocal cords are closed and breath pressure is applied to them, the cords remain closed until the pressure beneath them—the subglottic pressure—is sufficient to push them apart, allowing air to escape and reducing the pressure enough for the muscle tension to pull the cords back together again. Pressure builds up once again until the cords are pushed apart, and the whole cycle keeps repeating itself. The rate at which the cords open and close—the number of cycles per second—determines the pitch of the phonation.

The aerodynamic theory is based on the Bernouilli Effect.[5] The theory states that breath is flowing through the glottis while the arytenoid cartilages are being pulled together by the action of the interarytenoid muscles. Due to the

Bernouilli Effect, the breath flowing past the vocal cords causes them to be sucked into vibration before the arytenoids are fully together. When the arytenoids have been pulled together, this same air flow sucks the glottis closed, thus cutting off the air flow until breath pressure pushes the cords apart and the flow starts up again, causing the cycle to repeat.

There is only one minor difference between the two theories, the factor which brings the cords back together in each cycle. The myoelastic theory gives the credit to muscle tension (elasticity); the aerodynamic theory gives the credit to the Bernouilli Effect. It is quite possible that both theories are true and operating simultaneously to initiate and maintain vibration.

A third theory, *the neurochronaxic theory* of Raoul Husson, was in considerable vogue in the 1950s, but has since largely been discredited. It stated that "the frequency of vocal fold vibration is determined by the chronaxy of the recurrent nerve, and not by breath pressure or muscular tension."[6] Advocates of this theory thought that every single vibration of the vocal folds was due to an impulse from the recurrent laryngeal nerves and that the acoustic center in the brain regulated the speed of vocal fold vibration.[7] If it were true, the theory would have obvious psychological advantages for the singer; unfortunately, it has not been validated.

Characteristics of Good Vocal Sound

A necessary prerequisite of establishing good phonatory habits is for the singer or speaker to possess a valid concept of good vocal sound. Mention has already been made of the semantic difficulties inherent in trying to describe the human voice. Nevertheless, the following descriptive expressions represent some of the important characteristics of good vocal sound:

1. Freely produced;
2. pleasant to listen to;
3. loud enough to be heard easily;
4. rich, ringing, and resonant;
5. energy flows smoothly from note to note;
6. consistently produced;
7. vibrant, dynamic, and alive;
8. flexibly expressive.

The following list is made up of negative characteristics which tend to preclude good vocal sound:

1. Constricted, forced, or strained;
2. strident or rasping;

3. too loud, resembling shouting or yelling;
4. hoarse;
5. breathy;
6. weak, colorless, or devitalized;
7. inconsistently produced;
8. shaky or wobbly.

Beautiful sounds start in the mind of the singer. If you cannot think a beautiful sound, it is an accident if you make one. You must learn to "picture" the sound in your mind's eye and "hear" it in your mind's ear before it can become a consistent reality. The best way to achieve the proper mental image of beautiful vocal sound is by listening intelligently to a sizable number of artist singers. You should listen to live performances and recordings until certain recurrent features begin to emerge from most of the singers you are hearing. Likely these features will coincide with some of the characteristics of good vocal sound listed above. The important thing is to arrive at a vocal model which can serve as a guide and goal in your own pursuit of vocal excellence.

It can be dangerous to pattern yourself on one particular singer, no matter how well he or she may sing. In the first place, your physical attributes (length and thickness of vocal cords, size and shape of resonators, etc.) may be so different that you cannot achieve the same kind of sound without forcing or sounding artificial. In the second place, a mature singer with much professional experience can demand more of his voice without hurting it than a novice can. Last, but not least, if you pattern yourself too closely on one singer, you tend to become a pale imitation, with no individuality. It is better to select at least ten singers of your own voice category, decide what strengths they share in common, and work toward those strengths as your vocal ideal.

Three Phases of a Musical Tone. Any musical tone may be divided into three phases or segments: the attack phase, the sustention phase, and the release phase. Stated more simply, these phases consist of starting the sound, holding the sound, and ending the sound. Each phase is important, and each has its own unique problems.

The attack phase is especially important because it tends to affect the entire phonatory process. Starting a tone well prepares the way for the subsequent sustension and release phases to be done well, also. Starting poorly often results in a poor continuation. A good attack originates in the mind of the singer before the physical act takes place; it includes preparation for the correct pitch, the correct tone quality, and the correct dynamic level.

The pitch must be attacked cleanly, without scooping up to it or sliding down to it. In order to do this, the singer must form the habit of hearing the pitch mentally *before* the attack, not during it.

A good attack must be prepared physically as well as mentally. A perfect attack occurs when the breath support mechanism and the vocal cords are brought into action simultaneously and efficiently, without unnecessary tension or wasted breath. This kind of effortless coordination can take place only if the proper preparatory steps are taken. Practice starting good sounds by using this routine:

(1) Breathe in as if beginning a yawn;
(2) feel your body expand around the middle;
(3) suspend your breath just as you are comfortably full of air;
(4) start the sound by merely thinking to do so, without conscious physical effort.

It is not necessary to use any local effort, such as pulling in or pushing out the upper abdomen, to start a sound well. If the breath has been taken properly and good posture has been maintained, you have already established enough support to sing most of your vocal range without any conscious readjustment. All that is needed is the correct mental image of the pitch, tone quality, and dynamic level desired, and reflex action will take place. If the result is not good, something was wrong with the mental or physical preparation. Do not resort to more muscle effort as a corrective measure. Think first!

In a balanced, coordinated attack, the jaw should drop freely open just as the sound starts or very shortly before. The correct motion of the jaw is down and then back; it should never be forced down, pushed forward, or locked in any position, but should always be free to move.

Since you have no direct control over your vocal cords, do not think about them while you are singing. It is much better to think about the kind of sound you want to produce, and about what the sensations of a good sound are. Although phonation actually takes place in the larynx, it feels as if it starts somewhere in the head rather than at the vocal cords. Some singers say that the sound seems to start in the roof of the mouth. This is a good sensation to try to experience because it directs your attention away from the vocal cords; it will be discussed further in the chapter on resonance. There is an old saying which states, "A good singer is a head and a chest with nothing in between." This is an apt description of what the singer should experience.

The sustention phase of a tone lasts from the instant of attack to the instant of release. Its duration is determined by the note or notes to be sung. To sustain something is to hold it up, to support it physically from below, to keep it going, to maintain or prolong it, to keep up its vitality. This is exactly what should take place during the sustention phase: the energy used to start a sound must be kept going; the breathing mechanism must support the sound from below; the sound must be kept vital and headed somewhere. A sustained sound should be steady and consistent; it should not waver and should not change quality or dynamic level except in response to the expressive demands of the music. It is especially important that the breath energy should not come in spurts or surges. There are two factors that will help to ensure a steady supply of energy:

(1) Maintain the expansion around the middle of your body for as long as the sound lasts;

(2) maintain good posture by standing tall and stretching your spine.

With good posture and proper breathing, a balanced tension is set up between the breathing-in and breathing-out muscles. This dynamic relationship—already identified as breath support—is essential to the proper sustaining of a sound.

When sustaining a sound, imagine that the sound is flowing freely out of your body, but that your breath is staying inside your body. Obviously breath is escaping, but it should be released as slowly as possible. Thinking that you are in a breathing-in position while phonating will help to slow the escape of air down and to maintain the expansion around the middle of the body. Your throat should feel relaxed and open from the top to the bottom; maintaining the beginning-of-a-yawn position will ensure this feeling. The roof of your mouth should vibrate much as it does when you hum; this "hummy" feeling will affect both the quality of the sound and the efficiency of the vocal cord action.

It is not necessary to make any movements of the tongue, lips, or jaw while sustaining a single sound. The articulators are active in the attack and release phases of a sound, but not during the sustention phase. Once a sound has been started, the tongue, lips, and jaw have done their main work and can take it easy until the release of the sound. One of the marks of an inexperienced singer is the changing of articulatory posture while sustaining a sound. This can create unnecessary tension and can adversely affect the vowel being sustained.

The release phase of a tone is instantaneous and should be executed with firmness and precision. It should not be ignored, slighted, or exaggerated, but should take place at an exact time and in a definite manner. There should be no doubt that the sound has ended; it should not just fade away or die from lack of energy. The breath support which is necessary to sustain a sound should be continued until the release is finished. Do not let your support sag before the sound is completed; if you do, both the pitch and the quality of the sound may be affected.

Be careful not to anticipate a release. Thinking about the release too soon can cause you to let your support relax too soon or to tighten your throat in preparation for a consonant. A good release is made at the last possible instant, cleanly and precisely. Insecure musicianship is a major cause of poor releases, not to mention its effect on the attack and sustention phases. One of the most important skills a singer can have is the ability to count time accurately. Only in this way can he know when to attack a tone, how long to sustain it, and when to release it.

Most of the words in the English language end with consonants. Because of this fact, consonants are of vital importance in many releases. If a final consonant can be put on quickly, firmly, and exactly at the right time, it usually will result in a good release. Unfortunately, many singers are careless about final consonants and seldom use enough energy or agility when making them. A final consonant should be delayed until the last possible instant and then put on quickly and firmly. Think of the consonant as the actual release of the sound. Do not anticipate the release while you are still on the preceding vowel; wait and let go of the sound by means of the consonant.

Never try to end a sound by stopping (pinching) it in your throat or by cutting off your breath. Such a release creates tension and often sounds strained. Let the organs that shaped the sound—the lips, tongue, and jaw—release it, and the strain will disappear. When a sound ends with a vowel, you should still release the sound as if it has a consonant on it—firmly and quickly—by releasing the articulators. It is not necessary to have different techniques for releasing vowels and consonants.

Actually, at the same instant that the lips, tongue, and jaw release the sound, the vocal cords and the support mechanism release also in a synchronized movement. However, it is best for the singer to feel that the articulators bear the primary responsibility for the release and that they have done the letting go.

Summary. The phonatory process is vitally linked with respiration. It is possible to breathe without phonating, but it is not possible to phonate without the assistance of the breath. In an ideal, balanced phonation, the two processes coordinate in such a way that the desired pitch and dynamic level are achieved with a minimum of effort from the support mechanism. Stated another way, the breath pressure and the vocal cord tension are so perfectly balanced that the desired vibration can take place without unnecessary tension or leakage of breath.

In a discussion of phonation Christy makes these comments:

> Students are advised in phonation (singing):
> 1. *That the chest never collapses, nor do the shoulders move up or down when singing even the longest phrase.* . . .
> 2. *That they not attempt to sing too long phrases on one breath,* but always maintain good quality of tone and sufficient breath reserve first, with the long ideal phrase second in importance. . . .
> 3. *That efficient tone is basic for efficient breath control.* . . .
> 4. *That under no circumstance should the singer try to "pull in" the diaphragm or control its action consciously.* . . .[8]

These statements underline the fact that good phonation is strongly dependent on good posture and good breathing techniques, and that local effort is to be avoided in singing. The singer's body must be trained to function as a whole, under the control of the mind, not as a group of separate parts that are locally controlled. Coordinated action is the basis for good phonation.

Faults Related to Phonation

The phonatory faults to be considered here are those which arise from the basic malfunctioning of the laryngeal mechanism when the singer is using his so-called normal or modal voice. (Phonatory faults related to registers will be discussed in a separate chapter.) As with other areas, these faults are of two types: hypofunctional and hyperfunctional.

Hypofunctional phonation,[9] the failure to demand enough appropriate activity of the laryngeal mechanism, is common among young singers, but can persist throughout the adult life. It is one of the most prevalent vocal faults. The primary cause of hypofunctional phonation is an inadequate or incomplete closure of the glottis—the vocal cords do not approximate properly. The primary evidence of hypofunctional phonation is a breathy sound; air is being allowed to escape by the inadequate glottal closure. Any time the vocal cords do not close adequately enough, breath support will push unused air past them. *Wasted air is wasted tone and should be avoided.* Wasted air also leads to lack of breath control. Just as a tire with a bad valve can go flat quickly, so can a singer run out of breath if his vocal cord closure is too loose or too weak to prevent it. As Christy has said, "Efficient tone is basic for efficient breath control." In this context, efficient tone and efficient vocal cord action are synonymous.

The best corrective procedure for a breathy sound is to train the vocal cords to close properly, thereby eliminating or minimizing the excess breath. If the vocal cords were under direct control, this might be easy; however, such is not the case. It is not possible to command the interarytenoid and lateral cricoarytenoid muscles to close the glottis more firmly and be assured that it will come to pass. This action must be brought about by indirect means—by certain thought patterns and conditioned reflex actions. For example, thinking of the beginning of a yawn or actually beginning a yawn will cause the vocal cords to move out of the way of the anticipated incoming breath; the glottis has been opened. Conversely, the thought of beginning a humming sound will bring the vocal cords together and close the glottis. Try the following procedure:

Take a comfortably deep breath and think of starting to hum. You will find your mouth and your vocal cords closing in preparation for the hum. (If you pull in hard on your abdominal muscles, you can feel the vocal cords holding back the breath.) As you begin the hum, bring your teeth together firmly and try to feel a lot of "buzzy" vibration in the roof of your mouth. This type of hum is somewhat penetrating in quality but is seldom breathy. Now, with your mouth still closed, continue humming while separating your teeth by dropping the lower jaw freely down. Try to maintain as much vibration in the roof of the mouth as possible. This type of hum is more relaxed and has better quality than the first one; it will not be breathy if it is properly produced.

Another way to encourage proper closure of the vocal cords is by asking the student to employ more energy when singing. With many inexperienced singers, the glottal closure is inadequate simply because the body is not working hard enough to produce a vital sound. There are several possible causes for this: (1) poor posture, (2) shallow breathing, (3) lack of the suspension state of breathing, (4) singing too softly (misconception about how loud they actually sound), (5) wrong vocal models, such as certain highly popular entertainers, (6) failure to recognize good vocal quality, (7) lack of involvement in the music.

The breathiness which results from not using enough energy can be approached in several ways. One approach which works well, but is often overlooked, is merely asking the student to sing louder.

In conjunction with this the student may be asked to perform gentle lifting motions, such as pretending to lift something of modest weight by raising the hands from waist level, or actually raising a desk dictionary, or two or three medium-size books, from that level. The vocal cords tend to close to support arm movements of this type; care must be taken, however, not to lift heavy objects, for then the epiglottis and laryngeal collar will tend to close, making phonation difficult, if not impossible.

Another approach is to ask him to imitate an opera singer, or to sing in an affected manner. It is unfortunate that many young persons have this distorted image of an opera singer, but this distortion explains why many of them fail to achieve a vital sound. Nevertheless, asking them to sing like an opera singer can produce surprisingly good results.

A third approach is the obvious one of making certain that good posture and breathing habits have been established, as described in previous chapters. Another is to make the student aware of the function of the breath support mechanism by having him laugh like Santa Claus (with a hearty "Ho, Ho, Ho!") or by asking him to call out several loud "Hey!" sounds as if he is trying to attract the attention of someone who is some distance away. A similar idea is asking students to sing as if they are trying to be heard on the last row of a large auditorium, or actually having them sing in such a place.

The matter of lack of involvement with the music can be approached by selecting songs to which the student can respond readily, by requiring the student to memorize the text and recite it expressively, by suggesting an interpretation of the song which will call for an emotional response, and by exposing the student to artist performances of the same or similar songs. All students need to have firmly established tonal ideals or models; listening to outstanding singers is the most effective way to achieve this goal.

Vowels and consonants may be used to combat a breathy sound, also. The more forward or frontal vowels—such as, [i], [ɪ], and [eɪ]—inherently are more tense in their production than the other vowels are.[10] Because of this fact they are conducive to nonbreathy sounds, with [i] (as in "beet") being especially effective in this regard. As a first step, vocalize the student on one of the forward vowels; if the breathy sound persists, ask him to pull his teeth firmly together while singing the vowel. This clenched jaw position is not recommended for normal singing (!), but as a temporary expedient it does firm up the laryngeal action enough for the student to experience a nonbreathy sound. Its use should be discontinued as soon as the student can go from this position to a relaxed jaw without the sound becoming breathy.

The nasal consonants—[m], [n], and [ŋ]—coupled with other consonants that require firm lip and/or tongue action may be effective in eliminating breathiness. Experiment with the following combinations, sung to descending five-note scale patterns or other simple melodic patterns: ding, ding, ding, ding, ding; boom, boom, boom, boom, boom; no, no, no, no, no; wing, wing, wing, wing, wing; voom, voom, voom, voom, voom; nee, nee, nee, nee, nee; zoom, zoom, zoom, zoom, zoom; etc. One or more of these sounds may be substituted for the words of a song. The effectiveness of different consonants varies from student to student, so it is advisable to experiment with a number of them. For some reason, the syllable "ding" is often successful.

One of the problems in correcting a breathy sound is that the student is unaware of it. It is so much a part of his natural sound that he does not hear it as breath. He must be made aware of it by means of tape recordings and the teacher's reminders until positive progress is being realized toward eliminating it; if not, he will keep slipping back into old habits.

Another problem which must be recognized is that most adolescent voices go through a stage when they are inherently breathy. There is a period when the interarytenoid muscles cannot or do not close the back one-third of the glottis; this results in a gap between the vocal processes of the arytenoid cartilages—the cartilaginous portion of the glottis. This opening is so prevalent in adolescent voices that it has become known as the *mutational chink*. Despite this chink, progress can be made toward reducing the amount of breathiness present. All of the methods that have just been presented may be employed with adolescents; however, a word of caution should be sounded. As Vennard states, "Young singers should not be driven to eliminate this breathiness impatiently."[11] Once the voice change is completed, there is no reason to allow breathy phonation to continue, however.

When all other methods have been tried and have failed, there is a last resort for correcting a breathy sound. This consists of going to the other extreme of phonation and asking the student to make a tight or tense sound. Since more indirect methods have not worked, something must be done to create enough tension to close the vocal cords more completely. There is some danger in this approach, for more voices are injured by excessive tension than by wasted breath. There is no point in substituting one bad habit for another. However, a person with a persistently breathy sound will seldom go too far the first few times he tries to sing a tight sound; usually he will come closer to a balanced sound than a tight one. Another suggestion which might work is asking him to imitate a hillbilly or a country-western singer, especially if the teacher asks for exaggeration or caricature. Any approach which encourages tightness, even as a means to an end, should be used with discretion and discontinued as soon as possible.

Summary of Corrective Procedures for Breathy (Hypofunctional) Phonation

1. Humming (vibration in roof of mouth);
2. using more energy by singing louder;
3. using more energy with gentle lifting exercises;
4. imitating an opera singer;
5. establishing good posture and breathing habits;
6. activating breath support mechanism by exercises;
7. singing to the last row of an auditorium;
8. becoming involved in the music;
9. adopting correct tonal goals by listening to good singers;
10. vocalizing on forward vowels; *nee*
11. vocalizing with nasal consonants; *ding*
12. imitating a tight sound as a means to an end.

Forced Breathiness.[12] There is one type of hypofunctional phonation which needs special mention because of complicating factors; this is the type known as forced breathiness. The complication arises because hypofunction in the laryngeal mechanism is accompanied by hyperfunction in the support mechanism. Correcting one problem can aggravate the other, or at least will do nothing to help it. Pulling in too hard on the abdominal muscles delivers too much air pressure to the larynx; since the vocal cords are not closing adequately, air is forced by them rapidly. The best approach is to correct the hyperfunctional breath support first, through the methods listed in the last chapter, and then correct the breathy phonation, by one or more of the methods just listed. Avoid any of those methods which might encourage a return to oversupport—such as numbers 2, 3, 4, 6, 7, 8.

Hyperfunctional phonation,[13] demanding too much from the laryngeal mechanism, results in a sound which is described in various sources as tight, tense, hard, edgy, or strained. The primary cause for this type of sound is excessive tension in the vocal cords themselves; however, they often are abetted in their action by too much tension in other muscles of the larynx and surrounding areas. When hyperfunctional phonation is accompanied by hyperfunctional breath support, the sound is further described as harsh, strident, rasping, grating, rough, constricted, or even strangulated.

Hyperfunctional phonation, if used persistently or if carried to the extreme, can result in severe vocal problems which may require the services of a medical specialist. It is beyond the scope of this book to discuss such problems at any length, but it should be mentioned that the offices of laryngologists are packed with people who have misused or abused their voices to the point that professional help is needed. Many other people do not recognize how badly they need help and go through life, for all practical purposes, as vocal cripples. It is very important that a teacher of singing be able to identify the symptoms of vocal abuse or misuse, and that the student who has such symptoms be urged to seek professional medical counsel. There may be nothing organically wrong or of serious consequence—the human vocal instrument is amazingly resilient and can withstand much punishment—but it is worth the doctor's fee and more just to find that out. If there is something of consequence, the earlier treatment is started, the better the chances of success. In any event, the teacher's help will be needed in teaching the student better vocal habits, so that the problem will not recur as soon as vocal use is resumed.

The most common symptom of vocal misuse or dysfunction is hoarseness. Morton Cooper states that hoarseness is the most prevalent clinical voice quality.[14] Just as headache is one of the most frequent complaints heard in a general practitioner's office, and does not identify any particular disease until other facts are accumulated and evaluated, so is hoarseness a widespread but nonspecific symptom. It may arise in conjunction with allergies, viral infections, laryngitis, growths on the vocal cords, medications, temperature changes, sinusitis, pollutants in the air, vocal misuse, and so on. Only a specialist is qualified to determine the correct cause of hoarseness, but a teacher can recognize that hoarseness is a danger signal and can alert the student to it. If it persists for any length of time (even after an illness),[15] if it occurs almost every time the student sings for more than a few minutes, or if there is chronic huskiness in the speaking voice, it is the better part of wisdom to consult a laryngologist. Greene reports on some interesting research which revealed abnormal patterns of vocal cord vibration in hoarse individuals.[16] Well-trained speakers and singers do not suffer from hoarseness as much as the average person; when they are hoarse, they seem to be able to cope with it better, for it is not such an apparent handicap.

Another common symptom of vocal misuse is the loss of range after singing only a few minutes. This usually occurs in the extremes of range—with loss of the highest notes, the lowest notes, or both of them—but may appear somewhere near the middle of the voice, especially with women. This is an indication that so much tension is present that the voice will begin to lose its normal function if it is used for any length of time. A voice which is properly produced has great powers of endurance. Cooper says that there is no such condition as overuse of the speaking voice if the speaking voice is properly used,[17] and quotes West, Ansberry, and Carr as stating, "No amount of vigorous vocalization can damage the edges of the vocal folds if the voice is properly used."[18] He identifies the causes of vocal misuse and abuse as lack of correct vocal knowledge, lack of proper vocal training, poor vocal models, emotional difficulties, and/or psychological problems. If a singer often experiences loss of range or eventual loss of voice after singing, it is a strong indicator that he is lacking in vocal knowledge and/or technique and that he should seek the help of a qualified teacher.

A common symptom which is found along with tight phonation is a limited or absent vibrato—the so-called "straight tone." Greene offers this conclusion:

> The easy rhythmic excursions of the vocal cords in normal, healthy voice production can be heard in the normal vibrato or pulses of sound. This is not heard in breathy, strained, or harsh voices and is therefore of diagnostic significance giving both physical and physiological clues.[19]

Vibrato will be considered in a later chapter. It is only mentioned here because of its importance as an indicator of vocal problems when it is absent. Laryngeal tension acts as an inhibitor of normal vibrato.

Some of the specific factors contributing to hyperfunctional phonation and its related vocal problems are:

(1) Singing in the wrong voice classification, especially in too high a tessitura;
(2) Speaking far above or below optimum pitch;
(3) Singing or speaking in a noisy environment;
(4) Habitually singing or speaking too loudly—with too much force;
(5) Screaming, shouting, or yelling;
(6) Wrong concept of breath support;
(7) Incorrect breathing techniques;
(8) Postural tension and rigidity;
(9) Wrong vocal models;
(10) Tension resulting from personality problems—feelings of fear, inferiority, insecurity, embarrassment, and so forth.

The corrective procedures for hyperfunctional phonation have one goal in common—the elimination of excessive laryngeal tension. Regardless of the cause, the net result is the same; the vocal cords are under too much tension to function effectively. Therefore, the corrective procedures employed must include relaxation techniques. It is also essential that the teacher establish a studio atmosphere in which the student can relax—a supportive environment based on sympathetic understanding and a genuine interest in the student's welfare.

A good starting place is the relaxation of general tension in the body as a whole. The techniques mentioned in the chapter on posture will apply here: bending and stretching exercises to tone the body; rolling the head around in circles; nodding the head; moving the shoulders in circles; shaking out the arms and legs; exercises to loosen the jaw, lips, and tongue; etc. A second step is to observe the student's posture, checking carefully for alignment and tensional faults.

Incorrect breathing and oversupport are frequent concomitants of laryngeal tension. Even if breathing and support seem to be correct, the teacher should check them while the student is singing. Check for expanding around the middle, setting up suspension, and starting the sound without pulling in strongly on the abdomen. Some students who do very well in nonsinging exercises abandon their technique in an actual song, particularly when there are "high" notes to be surmounted or consecutive long phrases, which tend to produce tension. There is the ever-present temptation to take in too much air, packing it into the chest in a vain effort to create more support.

Making a proper attack is very difficult for a person with tense vocal cords. The resulting phonation tends to start with an explosion of air because the glottis is firmly closed and breath pressure is increased until the vocal cords are almost violently blown apart. This type of attack has become known as a *hard attack* or a *tight attack,* and the explosion which accompanies it as a *glottal plosive* or *glottal shock.* Greene states that "hard attack is a symptom of laryngeal tension and if present in excess the sensitive membrane covering the folds may be damaged and the delicate laryngeal musculature strained."[20] In discussing the glottal plosive Vennard says, "Friction is thus created between the vocal processes as the cartilages are drawn together, and sometimes repeated glottal plosives actually produce contact ulcers between the cartilages."[21] Cooper cites an imposing list of authorities in support of the statement that vocal misuse and abuse are fundamental productive factors in the creation of vocal nodules, polyps, and polypoid degeneration, and bear a direct relationship to contact ulcers.[22] Obviously, it is highly important that the student master the skill of making the type of balanced or soft attack which is so widely recommended.

The secret of a balanced attack is the synchronization of breath pressure with the closure of the glottis. In a tight attack, the cords are closed first and then pressure is applied. In a breathy attack, the breath is flowing out before the cords start to close. In a balanced or soft attack, the breath and the cords arrive simultaneously, starting the sound cleanly, without any evidence of strain or wasted breath. The student should be urged to practice making soft attacks until it is a secure part of his singing technique. The following routine is designed for that purpose:

First do the relaxation exercises (rolling the head, moving the shoulders, etc.) to loosen and tone your muscles. Then stand in front of a mirror and watch yourself carefully for any signs of tension. Before you start any sound, always try to picture in your mind the pitch, dynamic level, and quality of the sound you want to make. Now breathe in easily as if beginning a yawn, expanding around the middle of your body as you do so, and suspending the breath just as you get comfortably full of air. When you get ready to phonate, leave the support mechanism alone and start the sound by merely thinking to do so. Be careful not to pull in consciously on your abdomen. Speak the sound "one" several times easily, prolonging the "n" sound and connecting each one to the next one without any break between them. Concentrate on the "buzzy" vibratory feeling of the "n," and the sensation that your voice is flowing easily from one "n" to the next. Next do the exercise again but substitute singing on a comfortable pitch for speaking. Do not pull in on the abdomen or accent the syllables; maintain a very smooth legato, and let each "n" carry your tone to the next one. Now repeat the entire routine using "no, no, no," then "nee, nee, nee," and finally "noo, noo, noo."

The teacher should monitor this procedure until it is apparent that the student is letting go of his laryngeal tension and that he is not supplying too much breath pressure to his larynx. Asking the student to imagine that the tone starts in his head instead of in his larynx may help to direct his attention away from the larynx. Stressing the idea of maintaining the beginning-of-a-yawn position while singing can be helpful because of the relaxation it creates and because it tends to put the larynx in its best position for singing.

Vowels and consonants may be used to combat a tight sound. It has been suggested that the frontal vowels are helpful in eliminating breathiness. The back vowels which require some lip rounding—such as [ɔ], [o], and [u]—are less tense than the frontal ones and therefore are more conducive to relaxing tension. Combining these vowels with the beginning of a yawn is one of the most effective means of reducing laryngeal tension. Preceding these vowels with "y" or "m" will help to reduce jaw tension and to encourage a free sound—for example, "you, you, you"; "maw, maw, maw"; and so forth.

The absence of vibrato has been listed as a prime indicator of laryngeal tension. When proper breath support has been established and some of the tension is released, the vibrato often will appear on its own accord as a side benefit. If it does not, special techniques must be employed to encourage it. These will be discussed in the chapter on coordination.

Going to the opposite extreme of a tight phonation by the deliberate introduction of breath into the sound is yet another possible approach. William Vennard was a strong advocate of this technique, asking his students to start a sound with an exaggerated [h] followed by a firm, clear vowel; once they had established this attack, they were instructed to use less and less breath until the [h] became an imaginary one. He also made frequent use of a "yawn-sign" exercise for this purpose.[23] Asking a student to sigh as if he is exhausted is an effective means of introducing breath into the sound. This approach is a means to an end—arriving at a balanced phonation by going from a tight sound to a breathy one and finally to the right sound.

Summary of Corrective Procedures for Tight (Hyperfunctional) Phonation

1. Exercises for relaxation of general body tension;
2. studio atmosphere conducive to relaxation and self-confidence;
3. establishing good posture and breathing habits, if needed;
4. reducing excess tension in support mechanism;
5. maintaining the beginning-of-a-yawn position;
6. exercises for balanced or soft attack;
7. making student aware of desired tonal goals;
8. vocalizing on vowels that require lip rounding—the back vowels;
9. vocalizing with consonants that help to free the jaw;
10. deliberately using a breathy sound as a means to an end.

The phonational problems caused by singing in a wrong voice classification and by speaking above or below optimum pitch have been omitted here. They will be included in later sections devoted to voice classification and the speaking voice. The same is true of registers, which definitely are related to the phonatory process. They will be discussed in the next chapter.

Notes

1. Sources recommended for their clarity and illustrative materials include Greene, *The Voice*, pp. 32-54; Vennard, *Singing*, pp. 50-78 and 97-108; and William H. Saunders, "The Larynx," reprinted from *Clinical Symposia*, Volume 16, Number 3 (1964). (Summit, N.J.: CIBA Pharmaceutical Company, © 1964.)

For a comprehensive study see Victor E. Negus, *The Mechanism of the Larynx* (London: Wm. Heinemann, Ltd., 1929) or *The Comparative Anatomy and Physiology of the Larynx* (New York: Hafner Publishing Company, 1962, © 1949).

2. The significance of knowing the skeletal framework of the larynx now becomes apparent. Both the names of the laryngeal muscles and some understanding of their function may be derived from the structural elements to which they are attached.

3. Greene, *The Voice*, p. 39.

4. Vennard, *Singing*, pp. 61-63.

5. For an explanation of the Bernouilli Effect and its relation to phonation, see Vennard, *Singing*, pp. 38-42.

6. Vennard, *Singing*, p. 260.

7. Greene, *The Voice*, pp. 50-51.

8. Christy, *Expressive Singing*, 2:35.

9. Listen to band 1 of the cassette tape for examples.

10. To test this statement, place a thumb on each side of your throat just below the lower jaw, pressing inward and upward with them. Say these syllables alternately: "bee, bah, bee, bah." Observe the difference in tension between the two vowels. Then try "bay, bah."

11. Vennard, *Singing*, p. 63.

12. Listen to band 2 of the cassette tape for an example.

13. Listen to band 3 of the cassette tape for examples.

14. Cooper, *Modern Techniques*, p. 23.

15. My own rule of thumb is about two weeks.

16. Greene, *The Voice*, p. 117.

17. Cooper, *Modern Techniques*, p. 16.

18. Cooper, p. 11.

19. Greene, p. 47.

20. Greene, *The Voice*, p. 46.

21. Vennard, *Singing*, p. 42.

22. Cooper, *Modern Techniques*, p. 12.

23. Vennard, *Singing*, p. 211.

6
Registration

What Is a Register?

No other area of vocal instruction is as shrouded with mystery, semantic confusion, and controversy as the subject of registers and registration.[1] The chief reason for the confusion is that the word *register* is used to describe so many different things. All of the following meanings are in current use: (1) a particular part of the vocal range, (2) a resonance area, (3) a phonatory process, (4) a certain timbre, and (5) a region of the voice which is defined or delimited by vocal breaks. While all of these meanings bear some relationship to registers, it is obvious that arriving at one basic usage of the term would eliminate much of the confusion.

Registers originate in laryngeal function. They occur because the vocal cords are capable of producing several different vibratory patterns. Each of these vibratory patterns appears within a particular range of pitches and produces certain characteristic sounds. From these statements it can be deduced that each register has three constituent elements: a certain vibratory pattern of the vocal cords, a certain series of pitches, and a certain type of sound. These three elements form the basis for a workable definition of the word *register*:

> A register in the human voice is a particular series of tones, produced in the same manner (by the same vibratory pattern of the vocal cords), and having the same basic quality.[2]

How Many Registers Are There?

Indiscriminate use of the word *register* has led to much confusion and controversy about the number of registers in the human voice. Various writers about the art of singing state that there are from one to seven registers present. (If you would like to perform an interesting but discouraging experiment, go to a major library and find the section devoted to books about teaching singing. Select about ten books at random and compare the discussions on registers. The diversity of opinion would confound a scholar, so think what it could do to a diligent student seeking some direct answers!)

One reason for this diversity of opinion is the use of such unfortunate terms as "chest register" and "head register." Since all registers originate in laryngeal function, it is meaningless to speak of registers being produced in the chest or the head. The vibratory sensations which are felt in these areas are resonance phenomena and should be described in terms related to resonance, not to registers. The terms "chest voice" and "head voice" are more legitimate as descriptions of resonance sensations, but even this usage is somewhat suspect from a scientific point of view. Their use is so widespread, however, that it will probably continue, whether it is accurate or not. Many of the problems which people identify as register problems are really problems of resonance adjustment. This helps to explain the multiplicity of registers which some authors claim. Relegating resonance problems to their own area will clear up some of this confusion.

Vocal registers arise from the different vibratory patterns produced by the vocal cords. Research has revealed that the vocal cords are capable of producing at least four distinct vibratory forms, although all persons cannot produce all of them. The first of these vibratory forms is known as natural or normal voice; another name for it—*modal voice*—is gaining currency and is the one recommended by this writer. In this usage, modal refers to the natural disposition or manner of action of the vocal cords. The other three vibratory forms are known as *vocal fry, falsetto,* and *whistle.* Each of these four registers has its own vibratory pattern, its own pitch area (although there is some overlapping), and its own characteristic sound. Arranged by the pitch areas covered, vocal fry is the lowest register, modal voice is next, then falsetto, and finally whistle.[3]

The Vocal Fry Register

Vocal fry has come into its own as an identifiable register only in recent years, although its characteristic sound was recognized much earlier. Glottal fry, glottal rattle, and glottal scrape are additional names for it, as is the German expression *Strohbass,* and are somewhat descriptive of its sound. The fry requires a loose glottal closure which will permit air to bubble through with a popping or rattling sound of very low frequency. Michel states that the vocal fry is extremely low in pitch with a mean fundamental frequency of 36.4 hertz.[4] According to Vennard, it is easier to perform on [a] (as in father) than it is on [i] or [u].[5] Discussion of vocal fry is much more frequent in books related to phonetics and speech therapy than it is in those dealing with singing. Some authorities consider the use of vocal fry in speech a dysphonia, while others consider it so only if it is used excessively. Hollien, Moore, Wendahl, and Michel make this statement:

> It is simply our intent to suggest that ordinarily vocal fry constitutes one of several physiologically available types of voice production on the frequency-pitch continuum and hence, of itself, is not logically classified among the laryngeal pathologies. Stated somewhat differently, while the excessive use of fry could result in a diagnosis of voice disorder, this quality is too often heard in normal voices (especially in descending inflections where the voice fundamental falls below frequencies in the modal register) to be exclusively a disorder.[6]

Cooper agrees that the vocal fry, used sparingly and intermittently, is a routine part of some speaking patterns, but says that the continued use of such a pattern does not make it utilitarian or nonpathological.[7] More will be said about the vocal fry in speech in a later discussion of the speaking voice in relation to singing.

The fry is more widely used in singing than many people seem to realize. Anyone who is familiar with the so-called gospel quartet or Stamps-Baxter idiom has heard the bass member of a group sing pitches which are below the range of the modal or normal register. The same thing occurs in the lowest voice part of some Russian choral pieces. According to Luchsinger and Arnold, these sounds, extending from F (87 Hz) to as low as E (41 Hz) and D (37 Hz), sound very much like the bass tones of an organ.[8] There are, of course, some basso profundos who can descend almost as low as these Russian anthems require in modal voice, but they are scarce, and many choral groups in the United States rely on singers who can "fry" these notes. The writer is a bass-baritone and has had the experience while singing a low E (82 Hz) of hearing a nearby singer drop that pitch an octave with sufficient volume to be heard in a choir of over sixty voices.

The chief use of the vocal fry in singing, then, is to obtain pitches of very low frequency which are not available in modal voice. It should not be used as the exclusive means of phonation and the attempt should not be made to carry the fry up into the range of the modal voice. Excessive use of vocal fry can limit the upward extension of the modal voice. Just as the assignment of girls in a high school choir to the exclusive singing of tenor parts can impair the upper notes of their range, so can excessive use of the vocal fry cause basses to lose the higher pitches of the modal voice. Moderate use of the fry in its proper range should not damage the normal voice.

Vocal fry may be used therapeutically with students who have trouble producing lower notes. Singers often lose their low notes or never learn to produce them because of excessive tension of the laryngeal muscles and of the support mechanism. Learning to imitate the sound of a vocal fry can help the student to release some of this tension. Once he has learned to make a fry with some ease, the student can usually produce some improved tones in his lower voice by starting the fry and then sliding up easily into the lower tones of his modal voice. Vennard says, "the 'rattle' is better for low notes, indeed it builds the low part of the range. It is especially beneficial for low voices."[9] Women are not usually required to sing in the vocal fry register (except in certain styles of folk singing), but are capable of doing so and may benefit therapeutically from its use. The writer knows of one interesting case where the wife of a bass could produce a fry on a lower frequency than her husband could.

In summary, vocal fry is the lowest phonational register, occupying the frequency range below the modal or normal register. It has a characteristic popping, frying, or rattling sound which is capable of very little variation of timbre. Its main use is to supply very low notes which are not available in modal voice; it may also be used therapeutically to improve the lower part of the modal register. Excessive use of the fry can result in vocal problems.

The Modal Voice Register

The modal voice is the normal register for speaking and singing. Some advocates of falsetto singing object to this statement because it seems to imply that the use of falsetto is abnormal. Their objection does not change the basic facts. It is rare to hear anyone speaking in falsetto, except for comic purposes; in fact, falsetto speech is classified as a functional dysphonia. Also, it is possible to attend the vast majority of concerts by major vocal artists without hearing more than the occasional use of falsetto for very high pitches or for soft high pitches. The fact that people can and do sing in falsetto does not qualify it as a normal register in actual usage. John Large states, "Current performance practice relegates falsetto to an auxiliary status along with Strohbass and whistle registers."[10] He cites some research by Rubin, LeCover, and Vennard which contains this statement: "It has been demonstrated by high-speed photography . . . that normal (chest) registration and the falsetto are two basically different mechanisms of voice production, the latter used only infrequently in conventional singing."[11]

The confusion which exists concerning what a register is, and how many registers there are, is due in part to what takes place in the modal register when a person sings from the lowest pitches of that register to the highest pitches. The frequency of vibration of the vocal cords is determined by their length, tension, and mass. As pitch rises, the vocal folds are lengthened, tension increases, and their edges become thinner. In other words, all three of these factors are in a state of flux in the transition from the lowest to the highest tones: length increases, tension increases, and thickness decreases. If a singer holds any of these factors constant and interferes with its progressive state of change, his laryngeal function tends to become static and eventually breaks occur, with obvious changes of quality. These breaks often are identified as register boundaries or as transition areas between registers. In actuality it is more likely that they are simply vocal problems which have been created by a static laryngeal adjustment that does not permit the necessary changes to take place.

On the lower pitches the vocal cords are thick and wedge-shaped. Because of this thickness, large portions of the opposing surfaces of the cords are brought into contact, and the glottis remains closed for a considerable time in each cycle. The glottis opens from the bottom first before it opens at the top; this imparts a fluid, wavelike motion to the cords. The modal voice has a broad harmonic spectrum, rich in overtones because of this rolling motion of the cords. It is comparatively loud because of the vibratory energy present, but is capable of dynamic variation. For the lowest tones, only the thyroarytenoid muscles are active; but as the pitch rises, the cricothyroids enter the action, thus beginning to lengthen the cords. As longitudinal tension increases, the glottis tends to develop a gap in the middle. To counteract this tendency, the lateral cricoarytenoids are brought into action, pulling forward on the muscular processes of the arytenoids. Vennard calls this process *medial compression*.[12]

In addition to the stretching of the vocal folds and the increasing tension on them as the pitch rises, the opposing surfaces of the folds which may be brought into contact become smaller and smaller as the edges of the folds become thinner. The basic vibratory (phonatory) pattern remains the same, with the whole vocal fold still involved in the action, but the vertical excursions are not as large and the rolling motion is not as apparent as it was on the lower pitches of the register. The physical limits of muscular strength of the internal thyroarytenoids (the vocalis muscle) are being approached. In order to sing above this pitch level it will be necessary to adopt a new phonatory pattern—to change registers.

A well-trained singer can sing two octaves or more in the modal register with consistent production, beauty of tone, dynamic variety, and vocal freedom. This is possible only if he avoids static laryngeal adjustments and allows the progression from the bottom to the top of the register to be a carefully graduated continuum of readjustments. Since every pitch in such a continuum requires its own adjustment, some purists say that each pitch, in essence, is a separate register. This is probably taking a good idea too far, but it does point up the need for readjustment throughout the modal register. When properly done, all evidence of "register" breaks or shifting of gears should disappear. There may be the need of some adjustments in the resonance system; these are not registration problems and will be discussed in a later chapter.

The semantic confusion about registers becomes most pronounced when one considers the upper part of the modal register and its relationship to the phonational register which lies above it and overlaps with it—the falsetto register. Some authorities call the upper modal voice "head voice"; others call the falsetto by that name. At one time Garcia further confused the issue by using both terms in relation to the female voice, with the head voice above the falsetto. Attempts have been made to clear up this confusion by substituting such terms as *thick register* and *thin register*, or *heavy mechanism* and *light mechanism*. These are better terms and are more accurate in regard to function, but some confusion still exists. For example, the falsetto is aptly described as the thin register, but the vocal folds can become thin in the upper modal register, also. The falsetto is produced by a light mechanism when contrasted with the heavy mechanism of the lower modal voice, but so is soft singing in the upper modal voice. As a further complication, some writers do not make it clear whether thick and thin or heavy and light refer to the lower and upper parts of the modal voice or to the modal voice and the falsetto.

After listening to singers in hundreds of public performances—in recital, opera, oratorio, and orchestral concerts—including many of the world's most acclaimed singers, this writer is convinced that the great majority of them sing almost exclusively in modal voice. When they use falsetto in public performance, it serves two main purposes: (1) to make available very high pitches which are above the range of the modal register, and (2) to make available some pianissimo tones that would be very difficult to sing in the modal register. Of course, there are obvious exceptions, such as Alfred Deller and the current vogue for countertenors and male altos in Great Britain, but these form a definite minority when compared to the whole vocal scene. Every singer should be able to sing in the falsetto register and should be aware when he is using it and when he is not. Unless he plans to make a career as a falsettist, he should view falsetto as a means to an end; that end is to assist his modal voice in the ways listed above, and to help in the development of the upper modal register. These and other uses of the falsetto will be discussed in the next section of this chapter.

The basic phonational faults of the modal register were presented in the last chapter; they were the two extremes of breathy and tight phonation— hypofunction and hyperfunction. The development of the modal voice will be considered in later chapters.

The Falsetto Register

The falsetto register lies above the modal voice register and overlaps it. The characteristic sound of falsetto is inherently breathy and flutelike, with few overtones present. This is due to the type of vibratory pattern set up by the vocal cords. As has been previously stated, the frequency of vibration is determined by the length, tension, and mass of the vocal cords. As pitch rises in the modal register, the cords are lengthened by the action of the cricothyroid muscles, tension is increased by the resistance which the vocalis muscles (the internal thyroarytenoids) offer to the pull of the cricothyroids, and mass is decreased as the edges of the vocal cords become thinner. The key factor is that the *whole* vocal cord is involved in the vibratory pattern of the modal register; this is not the case in falsetto. In falsetto only the ligamentous edges of the vocal folds enter into the vibratory pattern. When the transition from modal voice to falsetto takes place, the main body of each vocal cord (the vocalis muscle) relaxes its resistance to the pull of the cricothyroid muscles enough for the vocal ligaments to be stretched still further. Vennard describes this process as follows:

> With the vocalis muscle relaxed it is possible for the cricothyroids to place great longitudinal tension upon the vocal ligaments. The tension can be increased in order to raise the pitch even after the maximum length of the cords has been reached. This makes the folds thin so that there is negligible vertical phase difference, no such thing as the glottis opening at the bottom first and then at the top. The vocalis muscles fall to the sides of the larynx and the vibration takes place almost entirely in the ligaments.[13]

The essential difference between the modal and falsetto registers lies in the amount and type of vocal cord involvement: in falsetto, only the ligamentous edges of the folds enter into vibration—the main body of each fold is more or less relaxed; in modal voice, the wavelike motion involves the whole vocal cord, with the glottis opening at the bottom first and then at the top.

Research has revealed that all singers do not produce falsetto in exactly the same way. Some singers leave the cartilaginous portion of the glottis open (the so-called mutational chink), and only the front two-thirds of the vocal ligaments enter into vibration. The resulting sound, which is typical of many adolescents, may be pure and flutelike, but it usually is quite soft and somewhat anemic, as well. In other singers the full length of the glottis opens and closes in each cycle. In still others a phenomenon known as *damping* appears, with the amount of glottal opening becoming less and less as the pitch rises, until only a tiny slit appears on the highest pitches. The mutational chink type of falsetto is considered inefficient and weak, but there is little information available about the relative strengths and weaknesses of the other two types.

Falsetto is more limited in dynamic variation and tone quality than modal voice. Most trained singers have at least an octave of range which they can sing in either modal voice or falsetto. In this overlapping area a given pitch in modal voice will always be louder than the same pitch sung in falsetto. The type of vocal cord vibration which produces the falsetto precludes loud singing except in the highest tones of that register;[14] it also limits the available tone colors because of the simplicity of its wave form. Modal voice is capable of producing much more complex wave forms and infinite varieties of tone color.

In summary, falsetto is a phonational register occupying the frequency range just above the modal register and overlapping with it approximately one octave. It is produced by the vibration of the ligamentous edges of the vocal cords, in whole or in part. Its sound is inherently breathy and flutelike, with few overtones present, and is more limited in dynamic variation and tone quality than modal voice. Some of its typical uses will be discussed next.

Uses of the Falsetto Register. Falsetto has a number of highly specialized uses; the following list includes the more common ones:

1. In male choirs, to enable the first tenors to maintain the very demanding tessitura;
2. in yodeling;
3. for comic effects;
4. by some lyric (Irish) tenors, folk singers, and so forth;
5. by falsettists;
6. for pitches which are above the range of the modal register;
7. for pianissimo tones that would be difficult in the modal register;
8. for vocal development.

For choirs made up of adult men, composers often write cruelly high first tenor parts in an effort to spread the harmony and to avoid the excessive crossing of voices. Few tenors can maintain this tessitura for any length of time without resorting to falsetto for some of the quieter passages. Falsetto will be softer than modal voice on the same pitches and will involve less

modal - more waveforms / potential color

physical effort by the singer; when properly used, it can make possible some lovely tonal effects.

Yodeling is a technique which appears in the singing of Swiss and Tyrolean mountaineers and of certain Country-Western singers. It is achieved by switching back and forth between the modal and falsetto registers. There is no evidence that yodeling in itself is harmful to the voice; some cowboy yodelers are still singing at a ripe old age. Some teachers of singing, however, believe that a person should not engage in much yodeling if he plans to be involved in "serious" singing.

Falsetto is used for comic effect in opera and musical comedy, especially when men are mimicking women. This needs no further comment. It is also employed for special tonal effects by composers, who indicate in the score that falsetto should be used.

Some lyric tenors, especially the variety known as Irish tenors (or derisively as "whiskey" tenors), use the falsetto for all their higher tones, cultivating a light modal voice production which will permit an easy transition into falsetto without an obvious change of quality. Typical songs in their repertoire would include such favorites as "Danny Boy" and "Mother Machree." Also, folk singers of varying ethnic origins incorporate falsetto in their singing. It is common in Hawaii, the South Seas, Central and South America, etc., as well as in the United States. In addition, it appears rather frequently in "pop" singers and in rock groups, where it is used with so much force and strain at times that it can be permanently damaging to the voice.

Just as there is confusion about the number and nomenclature of the registers, so is there confusion about the proper name for persons who sing exclusively, or nearly so, in falsetto. Male falsettists have been called male altos or countertenors, but objections have been raised to both usages. The castrato singers of the sixteenth through the eighteenth centuries were male altos or male sopranos who sang in what was for them the modal voice; the normal masculine voice change was precluded by the surgical removal of the testicles. Thus, the castrati were not falsettists, but were modal voice singers with unique timbre and carrying power resulting from the combination of a female pitch range with the more powerful structure of a "male" body. In England there seems to be some justification for calling a male falsettist either a male alto or a countertenor:

> Originally the alto was a high male voice, which through the use of falsetto nearly reached the range of the female voice (contralto). This type of voice, also known as countertenor, was cultivated especially in England, where the church music of the 16th and 17th centuries definitely implies its use.[15]

The famous English singer Alfred Deller, who was a falsettist, at first listed himself as a male alto and then later as a countertenor. The present revival of interest in male falsetto singing apparently is due to Deller's artistry. Russell Oberlin, the noted American countertenor, does not believe that now or historically the name countertenor should be applied to falsettists. He states that the countertenor possesses an unusually high lyric voice and sings in the modal register.[16] Whether or not you accept his thesis, it will be informative to compare his recordings with those of Deller, both as to timbre and tessitura.

It is logical to assume that singers who have high modal voices will have higher falsettos than singers who have low modal voices. There is some evidence that basses and baritones are more effective falsettists in the upper reaches of the tenor range, and that tenors are more capable of negotiating the higher tones of the contralto range. A statement that Henry Purcell performed both as a bass and as a countertenor has been questioned by some authorities.

Up to this point the discussion has been limited to the male falsetto. Is the female voice capable of producing a falsetto? Many books about singing totally ignore this question or gloss over it. A few state categorically that women do not have a falsetto. This is difficult to understand; motion picture studies of laryngeal action reveal that women can and do produce falsetto, and electromyographic studies by Vennard, Hirano, and Ohala confirm this fact. There are women who sing exclusively, or nearly so, in falsetto.

One possible explanation for this failure to recognize the female falsetto is the fact that the difference in timbre and dynamic level between the modal and falsetto registers often is not as pronounced in female voices as it is in male. This is due in part to the difference in the length and mass of the vocal cords and to the difference in frequency ranges. Be that as it may, it is an established fact that women have a falsetto and that many young singers substitute falsetto for the upper portion of the modal voice. This type of singing is so prevalent that many choir directors accept it as the correct approach to the upper voice. It is so easy for contraltos and mezzos to sing in falsetto in the soprano range that they often are misclassified as sopranos. More about this later.

Women who sing exclusively in falsetto often are identified as coloratura sopranos; this is a questionable label, for there are coloraturas who use little or no falsetto. Technically, coloratura refers to a florid style of virtuoso vocal writing common in the eighteenth and nineteenth centuries; it should not be. applied only to those who sing in falsetto.

Perhaps a word should be said about the advisability of using the falsetto as your primary means of singing. First of all, the career opportunities for falsettists are somewhat limited; aside from certain styles and periods, there is little music written for the falsettist. The falsettist almost automatically must become a highly skilled specialist if he or she is to succeed. Second, many listeners soon weary of the tonal and dynamic limitations of falsetto singing; regardless of the artistry of the singer, the average listener will soon begin to long for the dynamic variety and broader tonal palette of the modal register singer. There is an appreciative audience for the falsettist, but it is a small one, especially outside of England. Third, and perhaps most important, there is a possibility that extensive singing in falsetto may be harmful to the vocal cords. It has been stated that the cricothyroid muscles can place great longitudinal tension upon the vocal ligaments. If this stretching action is too extreme, it is possible that the vocal cords will lose the ability to return to their unstretched condition; laryngologists call this problem "bowed vocal cords." The writer has observed that older singers who have sung extensively in falsetto tend to develop vibrato and intonation problems.

The remaining uses of the falsetto are functional ones for the assistance of the person who sings predominantly in the modal register. Their purpose is to supply pitches or dynamic levels that are difficult or impossible in modal voice, or to aid in the development of the upper modal range. Some pitches which lie above the upper limit of the modal register may be sung in falsetto if the singer can learn to make a smooth enough transition. This skill usually is attainable only by higher and more lyric voices. In lower voices, especially those with dramatic quality, the transition into falsetto is almost always obvious and sometimes quite humorous, as many basses can testify. (William Vennard once told the writer in a lesson that he had never taught a bass who could master the transition.) A number of sources recommend the technique of lightening the modal voice and lowering the dynamic level before attempting to make the transition into falsetto. This technique should be reserved for pitches which lie *above* the modal register, because if it is employed too frequently in the overlapping area, it will tend to rob the modal voice of some of its richness and brilliance.

Pianissimo tones which lie just below the upper limits of modal voice can be very difficult to produce. Here, too, the singer who can manage a smooth transition into falsetto may add some expressive possibilities to his singing. In addition to the technique already suggested, an actual vocal slide discreetly used may help to make a smooth connection with the falsetto. The slide can be discarded as soon as the technique is working.

Many teachers advocate the use of falsetto exercises to aid in the development of the upper portion of the modal voice. Here falsetto is not a substitute for the modal voice; rather, it is a means to an end. The ultimate goal is to free up the modal voice and strengthen it for use in public performance. Singing in falsetto can lessen the fear of "high" notes, particularly with male singers who adopt a static laryngeal adjustment and attempt to force the modal voice upward by sheer muscular effort. The sensation of singing freely in falsetto may encourage them to try an easier production in modal voice. It is also possible that the release of tension in the vocalis muscle which is prerequisite to the production of falsetto might encourage the release of some unnecessary tension in that same muscle while singing in the modal register. More will be said about this usage of falsetto in a later discussion of vocal development.

The Whistle Register

The whistle register is the highest phonational register, occupying the frequency range just above the female falsetto. According to Luchsinger and Arnold, it begins above the soprano "high C" (1047 Hz) and extends to C (2093 Hz) or D (2349 Hz); in young children it may extend as high as G (3136 Hz).[17] It is generally recognized that these highest tones of the female voice resemble the sound of a whistle, hence the name. Other names which have been used for the whistle register include flageolet, flute, small, and superfalsetto. There is not a great deal of available information about the nature of this register. Margaret Greene says that the whistle is difficult to film because the epiglottis closes down over the larynx and the resonating chamber assumes its smallest dimensions.[18] Earlier writers indicated that the vocal folds actually puckered like lips to form a whistle, but Van den Berg offers this description:

> When the laterals are active but the transversus inactive, a triangular opening is seen between the arytenoids, the vocal processes contact each other, but the posterior parts at the apex do not contact each other. This is true provided that the vocal folds are not stretched, as stretching of the vocal ligaments abducts the vocal processes. . . . This adjustment is used for the flute or whistle register, with very high (up to 2500 cps) and weak tones at small flows of air. . . .[19]

Although many babies and small children can produce sounds in the frequency range of the whistle register without any conscious effort, some adult women seem unable to do so. Like some of the lingual skills such as rolling an [r], if the whistle register has not been experienced by an adult woman, it can be a difficult skill to acquire. Some singers, such as Mado

Robin and Ima Sumac, who have incorporated the whistle register as a featured part of their singing technique, have achieved rather phenomenal ranges. However, the woman who cannot produce a whistle register should not feel that she has been slighted by nature. The vast majority of pieces written for the soprano voice can be sung without the use of the frequency range occupied by that register.

Small children of both sexes often can produce the whistle, but adult men seldom can do so. Even if they can produce a squeak or squeal at that pitch level, it is probably best that they not make a practice of doing so. There is some feeling that continued use of it could result in a vocal dysfunction, as can the abuse of such techniques as phonating on inhalation instead of exhalation or practicing diplophonia (forming two sounds at the same time by causing the vocal cords to vibrate simultaneously in two segments of unequal length or by using both the true and false cords).

In summary, the whistle register is the highest phonational register, occupying the frequency range just above the female falsetto. Its sound resembles that of a whistle, having a simple sinusoidal wave form with no prominent overtones. The sound is made by the passage of air through a triangular opening between the arytenoid cartilages. The available information about the whistle register is not extensive; more research into its use and abuse is needed.

Conclusion. This chapter has attempted to clear up some of the confused terminology relating to registers. The normal phonational register—the modal voice—and its three auxiliary registers—the vocal fry, falsetto, and whistle—have been described and their usage discussed. Those aspects of registration which seem to arise primarily from resonance phenomena have not been considered here but will be discussed in the chapter on resonation.

Notes

1. For an extensive discussion of this problem area, see Large, "Vocal Registers," pp. 18-25, 30-35.

2. Adapted from a definition in *The American College Dictionary.*

3. Listen to band 4 of the tape for examples of the four registers.

4. Quoted in Cooper, *Modern Techniques,* p. 19.

5. Vennard, *Singing,* p. 124.

6. Quoted in Cooper, p. 19.

7. Cooper, p. 19.

8. Quoted in Large, "Vocal Registers," p. 31.

9. Vennard, *Singing,* p. 48.

10. Large, "Vocal Registers," p. 34.

11. Large, p. 32.

12. Vennard, *Singing,* p. 63.

13. Vennard, *Singing,* p. 67.

14. The English practice of using male altos singing in falsetto in place of contraltos often results in unbalanced trio and quartet work because, except for his highest tones, the falsettist cannot produce as much volume as his modal voice colleagues.

15. *Harvard Dictionary of Music.*

16. Lecture by Russell Oberlin at the Guildhall School of Music and Drama, London, England, January 30, 1980.

17. Quoted in Large, "Vocal Registers," p. 31.

18. Greene, *The Voice,* p. 49.

19. Jw. Van den Berg, "Vocal Ligaments versus Registers," *The NATS Bulletin* 19 (December, 1963):18.

7
Voice Classification

A Rationale for Voice Classification

Voice classification presents an interesting paradox; it is one of the most important decisions teachers and students have to make, yet many teachers and students are too concerned about it.

If voice classification is so important, why shouldn't they be concerned? Perhaps the prior question should be, "Why is voice classification important?" It is important because misclassification can rob a voice of tonal beauty and freedom of production, can cause endless frustration and disappointment, can shorten a singing career, and can cause vocal damage of varying degrees of permanence. Greene says that singing outside the natural vocal range imposes a serious strain upon the voice,[1] and Cooper states that clinical experience indicates that singing at a pitch level that is either too high or too low creates vocal pathology.[2] Other speech scientists and singing teachers echo these opinions. Obviously it is very important that the proper voice classification be identified and established as early as possible in a singer's training.

If the proper classification is this important, how can it be said that many teachers and students are too concerned about it? The chief reason is that other priorities need to be established before classification is attempted. Premature concern with classification can result in misclassification, with all its attendant dangers. Many students want immediate decisions on classification and may push a teacher into a mistaken conclusion without realizing it. The first essential in singing is to establish good vocal habits within a limited, comfortable range. When correct techniques of posture, breathing, phonation, resonation, and articulation have become established in this comfortable area, the true quality of the voice will emerge and the upper and lower limits of the range can be explored safely. Only then can a tentative classification be arrived at, and it may need to be adjusted as the voice continues developing.

The first rule of voice classification is: *"Don't be in a hurry."* Vennard says:

> I never feel any urgency about classifying a beginning student. So many premature diagnoses have been proved wrong, and it can be harmful to the student and embarrassing to the teacher to keep striving for an ill-chosen goal. It is best to begin in the middle part of the voice and work upward and downward until the voice classifies itself.[3]

The second rule of voice classification is: *Assume that a voice is a medium classification until it proves otherwise.* There are two reasons for this rule: (1) the majority of the populace do possess medium voices; and (2) there is less chance of a harmful misclassification.

In a sufficiently large sample of the general populace, when people are grouped together by some measurable physical characteristic (such as shoe size, hat size, chest, waist, etc.), the distribution of the sizes will tend to fall into a standard configuration known as the Bell Curve, because of its shape. The majority of the people will fall under the dome of the bell, with a much smaller percentage at either extreme—the ones who are truly small or truly large. The same application may be made to voice classification. It is likely that in a large enough sample possibly 10-15 percent will be truly high voices, 10-15 percent will be truly low, and the rest—the great unwashed multitude—will fall in the middle. Most of the students who enter voice studios are mezzo-sopranos or baritones, by the law of averages. Of course, there are many variables which might alter these percentages for a particular studio— for example, a tenor teacher who attracts tenor students. This does not change the basic fact that most people have medium voices; it is safer to make this assumption until various factors prove otherwise.

In addition to recognizing the statistical majority of medium voices, the chances of making a harmful misclassification are reduced when a medium classification is assumed. The dangers of too much singing in the extremes of range has already been pointed out. Greene comments:

> The need for choosing the correct natural range of the voice is of great importance in singing since the outer ends of the singing range need very careful production and should not be overworked, even in trained voices.[4]

At the beginning of vocal study, establishing vocal freedom is more important than learning to sing high or low. Working in a comfortable medium range is much more conducive to good vocal habits than is an early attempt to increase the range of a singer. It is an easy matter to select song literature that will not push either end of the singer's range unduly before freedom is attained.

The typical choral situation affords many opportunities for misclassification to occur. The most common division of vocal parts is for high and low voices within each sex (SATB). Since most people have medium voices, they must be assigned to a part which is either too high or too low for them; the mezzo-soprano must sing soprano or alto and the baritone must sing tenor or bass. Either option can present problems for the singer, but for most singers there are fewer dangers in singing too low than there are in singing too high. This will be discussed further in the closing section of this chapter.

Some students are almost obsessed with the problem of voice classification. This may occur because they want to be something which they are not. The high voice in both sexes seems to be the most popular classification currently in "serious" music circles. An examination of the rosters of vocal concert artists put out by the major booking agencies will verify this, especially with female singers. Despite statistical evidence to the contrary, there usually are more sopranos listed than the combined total of contraltos and mezzos. In fact, one could surmise that the contralto voice is disappearing! A more likely explanation is that contraltos have discovered that they get more chances to sing if they call themselves mezzos, and the mezzos do so if they call themselves sopranos. Students get caught up in this popular trend and often try to force themselves to be something which they are not. The student is "whipping a dead horse" and will encounter much frustration. A teacher can help this situation by impressing upon the student the advantages of forgetting classification until his vocal technique has become secure in a comfortable range. This is sound advice for all singers.

Criteria for Establishing Voice Classification

There are several criteria which teachers of singing traditionally have applied in determining voice classification, but no one of them has gained widespread acceptance to the exclusion of the others. This would seem to indicate that the best approach is a composite one in which all available data are considered.[5] The most frequently applied criteria would seem to be (1) range, (2) tessitura, (3) timbre, and (4) transition points (breaks or lifts). Other considerations are physical characteristics, speech level, and scientific testing. An evaluation of each criterion follows.

Range. To avoid unnecessary hairsplitting and endless detail, only the six major voice categories will be considered here. Subclassifications such as buffo, cantante, and profundo have their place, but would only cloud the issue. There is little enough agreement among authorities about the precise ranges of the six basic categories without going further afield. According to Greene an exact definition of the ranges of singing voices is not possible since individuals vary greatly according to nature and the excellence or otherwise of their teaching.[6]

Classification by range has one practical application which is often overlooked or ignored. If a person is to call himself a tenor, this implies that he has the range needed to sing most of the literature written for that voice. Why call yourself a tenor if your upper range is so limited that most tenor literature is closed to you? This is parading under false colors, to say the least. One way to arrive at the range of the tenor voice is to examine a wealth of vocal literature written for that voice to see what sort of range is required to sing not all but most of it. The same approach is valid for all the voice categories.

There is fairly general agreement that a professional singer should have a usable two-octave range in order to sing most of the literature written for his or her classification. However, a great deal of literature can be negotiated with a range of a twelfth (an octave and a fifth) if that twelfth is located in the right place. The following chart of ranges shows three things: (1) the "practical" twelfth with which the singer can probably handle 75 percent of the literature for that classification; (2) the "ideal" two octaves which will cover 90-95 percent of it; and (3) the extreme ranges which are sometimes demanded.

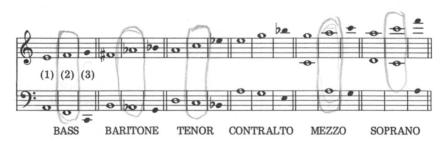

Figure 3

Range can be an effective criterion for use in determining voice classification, but it is most effective when used in conjunction with other factors. It is least effective with beginning students.

Tessitura. Range and tessitura are often confused with each other. Range is concerned with the total compass of a voice part or of a singer. Tessitura is concerned with that part of the range which is receiving the most use; it may refer to the voice part itself or to how the singer relates to it. Two songs may have the same general range but different tessituras, as shown in this example.

Figure 4

There are some singers who can sing both of these tunes comfortably; there are others who can handle the range without any problem, but who find the tessitura of the second tune very demanding because it lies so high within the octave. It is in this sense that tessitura can become a very valuable determinant of voice classification. Even though two voices may have identical ranges, one of them may actually be a higher voice than the other because it finds the tessitura comfortable while the other voice does not. Singers with very wide ranges often have to make a choice between tenor and baritone or between soprano and mezzo because they have the range to sing either part. The decision should be made, in part, on the basis of which tessitura proves to be more tiring. *Vocal longevity bears a direct relationship to vocal comfort.* If you can sing well in two different tessituras, it is the better part of wisdom to choose the one which is less fatiguing vocally. Normally this will be the lower one.

Tessitura should play an important part in any classification decision. It can be especially helpful when used in conjunction with range and timbre.

Timbre. Timbre (quality) is relied on heavily by experienced voice teachers in arriving at a voice classification. This is the most intangible criterion used, however, because the teacher must hear the voice as it sounds now and picture in his mental ear how it will sound when it is fully developed. To do this the teacher must recall other voices, other students, desired tonal images, and so forth. Obviously, it is an inexact science, as many phases of voice teaching are, but still vital to many classification decisions. Timbre is the most risky criterion for the inexperienced teacher, simply because he does not have all those tonal memories to call upon.

The inexperienced teacher should beware of certain pitfalls. Many persons assume that all light, lyric voices are high voices; this is not so, for there are lyric basses and baritones and lyric contraltos and mezzos. Another wrong assumption is that all heavy, dramatic voices are low voices; this, too, is not so, for there are dramatic tenors and dramatic sopranos. Any voice classifica-tion can have a heavy dramatic sound, although it is granted that it is probably more common in lower voices. Terms such as lyric and dramatic refer primarily to size of voice, kind of tone quality, or style of singing, rather than to range. A man with a light, lyric tenor voice should not be classified as a tenor unless he also has the range and tessitura of a tenor. Many young or undeveloped voices are misclassified as sopranos or tenors just because they sound light; this is especially true of young girls who replace the upper modal voice with falsetto. It should be remembered that the medium voice classification is the predominant one; all of those girls cannot possibly be sopranos.

Other pitfalls are the students who have misclassified themselves and those who have adopted a wrong tonal image. Some basses think they are tenors and do everything possible to lighten and brighten the voice, thereby offering misleading clues; or a mezzo decides that she is a deep contralto and makes the darkest sound possible. Morton Cooper finds a strong correlation between the vocal image an individual adopts and the creation and continuation of most functional and organic voice disorders.[7]

Timbre is an important, but somewhat illusory, criterion of voice classifica-tion. The new teacher may find it full of pitfalls, but it will grow more and more meaningful as he gains experience, particularly when he counter-balances it with range and tessitura.

Transition Points. Some teachers depend almost exclusively on the so-called register transition points (also called lifts or breaks) in determining voice classification. The confusion about terminology, number of registers, and so forth previously discussed in the chapter on registration enters the picture here, too. Nevertheless, it is generally accepted that most singers have more-or-less clearly defined areas in the voice where there is a "register" change, a change of quality, or the necessity for some change in technique. It is also generally agreed that the transition points of high, medium, and low voices follow that same sequence, with the higher voices having higher "lift" notes, etc. The actual pitches on which the transition should occur are not so widely agreed upon, however. It is interesting to observe that the most obvious transition occurs in the lower part of the female voice (usually spoken of as going from middle voice into chest voice) and in the upper part of the male voice (going from chest voice into head voice), but on the same pitches. The following chart of transition tones is an attempt to average the pitches given in various sources.

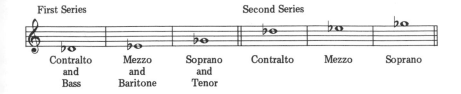

Figure 5

Female voices tend to exhibit a second series of transition tones approximately one octave higher (usually spoken of as going from middle voice to head voice). There is some agreement that these upper transition tones are more conclusive for categorizing voices.[8]

Classification by transition points is far from foolproof. Singers can learn to make a transition on any of several different pitches, or can learn to camouflage the change until it is almost imperceptible. This is particularly true of highly trained singers. It has also been clearly demonstrated by Appleman[9] and others that the different vowels have different transition points. In order for classification testing by transition points to have any kind of consistency the choice of vowel must be strictly controlled. A third type of problem arises with the student who will not accept his real classification; he may adopt the "lift" note of his desired classification just to prove his point.

Because of the problems just listed it has been this writer's experience that classification by transition points seems to work best with untrained voices who have not learned to manipulate or camouflage them. It may be especially helpful in a choral situation where large numbers must be tested. At any rate, the recognition of transition points can supply additional information for use in making a decision based on all available criteria.

Other Considerations. Other factors which may enter into voice classification include physical characteristics, speech level, and scientific tests. It has been observed by several writers that, as a general rule, persons with high voices tend to have round faces, short necks, large chests, and short stature, while those with low voices tend to have long faces, long necks, flat chests, and tall stature. Other writers would examine the appearance and dimensions of the hard and soft palates, or the bone structure and physiognomy as classification determinants. As general rules, these statements no doubt are valid, but they must be applied with caution. Only a moment of reflection will probably bring to mind several famous singers who have few, if any, of the indicated characteristics for their particular classification. The writer has directed a male chorus for a number of years; although the highest tenors and lowest basses generally resemble the accepted body types, there always are excellent singers who do not resemble the norms. Information on physical characteristics should be added to the data bank used in voice classification, but should not be considered as the definitive factor.

Speech level as a possible determinant of voice classification has received more attention in recent years. The relationship between good singing and good speaking has long been recognized, and teachers of singing have found it helpful to encourage their students to establish good speech habits, especially in regard to arriving at the optimum pitch level for speech. It is easier for some students to establish good habits in regard to timbre, volume, resonance, and phonation with the speaking voice than it is with the singing voice. Some efforts have been made to correlate the optimum pitch level of a person's speech with his or her voice classification, but the results are not, as yet, conclusive. This writer places so much importance on the advantages for the singer of speaking at the proper pitch level that a separate chapter has been devoted to the speaking voice.

In all probability the time will come when a singer's voice classification can be accurately determined by scientific tests. At the present the tests which are available are cumbersome, requiring specialized equipment, trained operators, and sometimes prohibitive costs. Definite correlations have been found between laryngeal dimensions and voice categories; although there are exceptions, it is accepted that vocal cord length is a primary determinant of voice type. Research has been done relating tonal spectra (vowel formants) of singers to voice types, and shows some promise. It is possible, eventually, that someone will develop portable equipment of modest cost which can be used in a voice studio to aid in classifying voices. For the foreseeable future, however, it is likely that teachers will continue to evaluate voice classification subjectively, using the same criteria they traditionally have—range, tessitura, timbre, and transition points, with a possible assist from physical characteristics, speech level, and scientific tests. The best classification decisions probably are reached by considering all the available data and not just one criterion. However, when all data have been considered and it is still difficult to decide, comfortable tessitura probably is the most important factor.

A Quick Classification System for Choral Auditions

The first rule of classification is: *Don't be in a hurry.* This is a very important rule, but what if you are giving choral auditions in which you must evaluate fifty singers in three or four hours? In order to protect the voices of your choir members and to obtain the best choral tone possible, it is essential that you be able to make an on-the-spot evaluation of considerable accuracy. As many as possible of the traditional criteria—range, tessitura, timbre, and transition points—will need assessment. Before beginning the auditions it is a good idea to prepare audition cards or sheets which have headings for all the information you hope to ascertain—items such as total range, tessitura (high, medium, or low), timbre, faults of tone quality (nasality, hoot, too dark, etc.), blend, vibrato, intonation, sight-reading ability, or whatever else you may want to know. Select a tune which has a range of at least an octave and a fourth. The familiar AUSTRIAN HYMN of Haydn and the one printed below are good examples.

Figure 6

Step 1: Ask the student to sing the melody and words in the key of E flat. Check the performance against the following statements:

If he sings the lowest note easily, but has some difficulty with the highest note or has to sing it loudly, he probably is a low voice.

If both the lowest and the highest notes seem comfortable, he probably is a medium voice.

If the lowest note is nonexistent or quite weak, he probably is a high voice. Omit Steps 2, 3, and 4 for high voices.

Step 2: Move the key down a minor third to C major. Ask the student to sing the tune again. Check against these statements:

> If the lowest note is strong and the highest note comfortable, he probably is a low voice.

> If the lowest note is weak or nonexistent, he probably is a medium voice. If you are uncertain, have him attempt Step 3.

> If not, omit Steps 3 and 4.

Step 3: Move the key down a whole step to B flat (starting note is F). Ask him to sing the first half of the tune. Check the following:

> If the lowest notes are easy, he probably is a low voice. Proceed to Step 4.

> If the lowest notes are weak or nonexistent, he probably is a medium voice. Omit Step 4.

Step 4: Move the key down a whole step to A flat (starting note is E flat). Ask him to sing the first half of the tune. If he can sing the lowest notes, keep moving down a whole or half-step until the lowest note disappears. This will isolate his lowest note for your records. Low voices may stop the procedure here, unless you like to see them suffer on high notes!

Step 5: Move the key up to G flat major (starting note is D flat). You have already identified the low voices and are now trying to separate the medium voices from the high ones. Ask the student to sing the whole tune. Check these statements:

> If he sings the lowest note easily, but has trouble with the highest note or has to sing it loudly, he probably is a medium voice.

> If he sings both extremes comfortably, he may be either a medium or high voice.

> If the lowest note is weak or nonexistent, he probably is a high voice.

Step 6: Move the key up to A flat (starting note is E flat). Student sings the whole tune.

> If the highest note is quite difficult, he probably is a medium voice and could stop here.

> If the highest note is easy, he probably is a high voice.

Step 7: Move the key up to B flat. Student sings *last* half of tune. If he can sing the highest note, keep moving the key up by whole or half-steps until he can go no higher.

The procedure may seem complicated, but it actually is not. Few auditions will require more than four of the steps and exactly the same procedures will work for female voices. If you want to observe transition points, the selected keys will facilitate this. The writer has used this approach successfully for a number of years. The key to it is using the appropriate keys for a song of wide enough range to expose in a hurry the customary problem areas in range, tessitura, timbre, and transition points. If the tune has a shorter range, it will have to be repeated too many times to accomplish the same purpose. Obviously, there will be some students with unusually wide ranges which will be harder to classify; in those cases comfortable tessitura probably should be the final determinant.

Dangers of Misclassification

The dangers which can result from misclassification have been listed already: loss of tonal beauty and freedom of production, a shortened singing career, continuing frustration and disappointment, and the possibility of serious vocal damage. Unfortunately, some of these dangers are not immediate ones; the human voice is quite resilient, especially in early adulthood, and the damage may not make its appearance for months or even years. Continual singing outside of your best range eventually will take its toll.

Singing at either extreme of the range may be damaging, but the possibility of damage seems to be much more prevalent in too high a classification. A number of medical authorities have indicated that singing at too high a pitch level may contribute to certain vocal disorders. Dr. F. S. Brodnitz relates singing at too high a pitch level to the development of vocal nodules,[10] and Margaret Greene states, "Sopranos singing above their natural range may develop vocal nodes since many are mezzo-sopranos but the fashion today is for soprano singers."[11] Extensive singing in the upper limits of your voice is somewhat like driving a car at top speed all the time. You may cover a lot of miles, but the motor will wear out much sooner than it would if you drove at normal speeds; and you probably will have to pay some speeding tickets. Increasing tension on the vocal cords is one of the means of raising pitch. Singing above your best tessitura keeps your vocal cords under a great deal of unnecessary tension for long periods of time, and the possibility of vocal abuse is greatly increased.

Singing at too low a pitch level is not as likely to be damaging unless you try to force your voice down. When a person sings his lower notes correctly, there is an element of relaxation of subglottic air pressure which permits the vocal cords to vibrate freely. If a pitch drops below a person's singing range, the sound will become almost inaudible or will turn to breath. This will not harm the voice unless the singer tries to force out a low pitch; and, paradoxically, forcing will usually cause the voice to cut off even higher because of the increased breath pressure. The secret of successful low notes is the relaxation of the support mechanism as the pitch descends. If this is done, there is little chance of vocal damage.

What about the dilemma of the people with medium voice classifications—the mezzo-sopranos and baritones—who outnumber the highs and lows? What should they do in a choral situation where the usual division of parts is only high and low? If the person sings correctly, there is less chance of harming the voice by singing on the low side. If he sings properly, his low notes just will not be heard; or, if he insists on being heard, he can sing the lowest notes up the octave. In either case, he will not hurt his voice just by singing low. But regardless of how well he sings, if he keeps singing above his best range, he will be keeping his voice under too much tension, and that can be harmful. If he is assigned to the upper part by the director, he should have the wisdom to protect his own voice by dropping the octave when the notes lie too high or by just faking it—pretending to sing. It is his voice he is hurting, not the director's! Of course, the ideal thing is to sing in a choir that has eight voice parts; then the baritone can choose between first bass and second tenor, and the mezzo between first also and second soprano, and be much closer to the best range. Most directors are sympathetic to this problem and will move a singer if he finds a high tessitura too demanding.

If the proper voice classification is found and if the proper singing technique is used, there is no reason why a person should not be singing in his sixties or seventies, provided that his general health is good. There are famous singers who have proved this statement, over and over again. There are four major reasons for shortened vocal careers, and three of them can be avoided: wrong classification, wrong technique, singing too much and too often without proper rest, and health problems. It should be added that if classification and technique are right, it is usually possible to sing longer and more frequently without damage. If you know the vocal truth, you will be free to sing for a long time!

Notes

1. Greene, *The Voice,* p. 79.
2. Cooper, *Modern Techniques,* p. 18.
3. Vennard, *Singing,* p. 78.
4. Greene, *The Voice,* p. 79.
5. For a similar conclusion, see Robert Shewan, "Voice Classification: An Examination of Methodology," *The NATS Bulletin* 35 (Jan./Feb. 1979):17-27.
6. Greene, *The Voice,* p. 79.
7. Cooper, *Modern Techniques,* p. 36.
8. Shewan, *"Voice Classification,"* p. 22.
9. Ralph Appleman, *The Science of Vocal Pedagogy* (Bloomington, Indiana: The Indiana University Press, 1967).
10. Brodnitz, *Vocal Rehabilitation,* p. 63
11. Greene, *The Voice,* p. 123.

resonators=
secondary vib.
set in motion
   by initial vib.
(create end prod.)

column of air

8

Resonation

The Nature of Resonators

Resonation is the process by which the basic product of phonation is enhanced in timbre and/or intensity by the air-filled cavities through which it passes on its way to the outside air. Various definitions related to the resonation process include such terms as amplification, enrichment, enlargement, improvement, intensification, and prolongation, although in a strictly scientific usage acoustic authorities would question some of them. The main point to be drawn from these terms by a singer or speaker is that the end result of resonation is, or should be, to make a better sound. In a technical sense resonance is a relationship that exists between two bodies vibrating at the same frequency or a multiple thereof. In other words, the vibrations emanating from one body causes the other body to start vibrating in tune with it. A resonator may be defined as a secondary vibrator which is set into motion by the main vibrator and which adds its own characteristics to the generated sound waves.

There are two basic kinds of resonance—*sympathetic* and *conductive*.[1] The essential difference between them lies in what causes the resonator to start vibrating. In sympathetic resonance (which is also called free resonance) there is no physical contact between the two bodies. The resonator starts functioning because it receives vibrations through the air and responds to them sympathetically. In conductive resonance the resonator starts vibrating because it is in physical contact with a vibrating body. This type of resonance is also called forced resonance, because the resonator is forced to vibrate.

Both types of resonance are at work in the human voice. When you are singing, much of the vibration that you feel is the result of conductive resonance. The vibrations created by the vocal cords travel along the bones, cartilages, and muscles of the neck, head, and upper chest, forcing them to vibrate. There is little evidence that these vibratory sensations make any significant contribution to the external sound, for reasons to be given later.

However, these same conductive vibrations are good sensation guides for the singer, regardless of their effect on the external sound. These sensations provide evidence to the singer that his vocal cords are forming strong primary vibrations which are being carried from them to the head and chest. Thus these vibratory sensations can supply feedback about the efficiency of the phonatory process.

What a person listening to you hears, however, is mainly the product of sympathetic resonance. Vibrations created by the vocal cords travel through air from the larynx into the cavities of the throat and head, setting them into vibration. This is sympathetic resonance, for there is no physical contact between these cavities and the vocal cords. Vennard makes the point that the vocal resonator is not a sounding board of some sort, as comparisons with stringed instruments would make it, but a column of air, whose shape is not only complex, but highly variable. He continues:

> Thus it may vibrate as a whole or in any of its parts. It should not be too hard to think of it as vibrating several ways at once. Indeed most vibrators do this, otherwise we would not have timbre, which consists of several frequencies of different intensities sounding together. Air is fully as capable of this as any other medium; indeed, the sounds of many diverse instruments are carried to the ear by the same air, are funnelled into the same tiny channel, and can still be heard as one sound or as sounds from the individual sources, depending upon the manner in which we give attention.[2]

Factors Affecting Resonators. There are a number of factors which determine the resonance characteristics of a resonator. Included among them are (1) size, (2) shape, (3) type of opening, (4) composition and thickness of the walls, (5) surface, and (6) combined resonators. The quality of a sound can be appreciably changed by rather small variations in these conditioning factors.

In general, the larger a resonator is, the lower the frequency it will respond to; the greater the volume of air, the lower its pitch. But the pitch also will be affected by the shape of the resonator—for example, whether it is conical, cylindrical, or spherical—and by the size of opening and amount of lip or neck the resonator has. A conical resonator, such as a megaphone, tends to amplify all pitches indiscriminately; this is why it fulfills its purpose so well. The pitch of a cylindrical resonator is affected primarily by the length of the tube. A spherical resonator will be affected by the amount of opening it has and by whether or not that opening has a lip. The following experiment should prove interesting:

> Find two bottles with the same shape but different sizes, such as a pint and a quart. Blow across their openings and see which sounds the

lower pitch. (The larger one should, because of its greater volume.)

Now find two jars or bottles which have the same volume, such as pints or quarts, but have different size openings. A pint soft-drink bottle and a pint fruit jar would be ideal. Blow across both openings and see which has the lower pitch. (It surprises most people to discover that the smaller opening will produce the lower pitch. A bottle which has a longer lip than another of the same volume also will tend to sound a lower pitch.)

This experiment has some interesting implications for vocal technique that will be presented later.

Three factors relating to the walls of a resonator will affect how it functions—the material it is made of, the thickness of its walls, and the type of surface it has. The resonance characteristics of a musical instrument obviously will vary with different materials—wood, brass, tin, silver, lead, etc.—and the amount of the material used (the thickness) will have some effect. Of special importance to singing is the relationship of the surface of a resonator to its tonal characteristics. Resonators can be highly selective— meaning that they will respond to only one frequency (or multiples of it)—or they can be universal—meaning that they can respond to a broad range of frequencies. In general, the harder the surface of the resonator, the more selective it will be, and the softer the surface, the more universal it will become. Hardness carried to the extreme will result in a penetrating tone with a few very strong, high partials. Softness carried to the extreme will result in a mushy, nondirectional tone of little character. Between these two extremes lies a whole gamut of tonal possibilities.

Scripture experimented with resonators of different materials, including a simulation of the fleshy texture of the walls of the human resonators. According to Vennard he showed that a hard resonator will respond only when the vibrator contains an overtone that is exactly in tune with the resonator, while a soft resonator permits a wide range of fundamentals to pass through undampened but adds its own frequency as an overtone, harmonic or inharmonic as the case may be.[3] This also has some implications which will be discussed later.

The final factor to be mentioned is the effect of joining two or more resonators together. This is a complicated area, but in general it may be said that the effect will be to lower the resonant frequency of each in different proportions according to their capacities, their orifices, and so forth. The rules governing combined resonators apply to the human voice, for the throat and mouth and sometimes the nose function in this manner.

Combined resonators

The next step will be to list the possible vocal resonators and to evaluate them as to their location, adjustability, and possible contribution as judged by their resonance characteristics.

The Vocal Resonators

There are seven areas that may be listed as possible vocal resonators. In sequence from the lowest within the body to the highest, these areas are the chest, the tracheal tree, the larynx itself, the pharynx, the oral cavity, the nasal cavity, and the sinuses.[4]

The Chest. Although strong vibratory sensations may be experienced in the upper chest, and although numerous voice books refer to chest resonance, the chest, by virtue of its design and location, can make no significant contribution to the resonance system of the voice. The chest is on the wrong side of the vocal cords and there is nothing in the design of the lungs that could serve to reflect sound waves back toward the larynx. If you were trying to construct a good resonator, one of your last choices would be the spongy matter composing the inside of the lungs, which would tend to absorb rather than reflect.

Place the palm of one hand firmly on your upper chest and say one of the following: "boom, boom, boom" or "mum, mum, mum, mum," prolonging the final [m] in each work. Repeating "ding" or "ninety-nine" will work well, also. The vibrations which you feel under your hand result from conductive resonance and reach a dead end (cul-de-sac) in the chest. Vennard refers to them as wasteful vibrations because they contribute so little to the external sound. However, they can be used to supply feedback to the singer. It must be concluded that the chest is not an effective resonator.

The Tracheal Tree. The trachea and the bronchial tubes combine to form an inverted Y-shaped structure known as the tracheal tree. It lies just below the larynx, and, unlike the interior of the lungs, has a definite tubular shape and comparatively hard surfaces. The internal diameter of the tube can be increased or decreased to a moderate extent (as in labored inhalation or coughing), but this is not under conscious control, so for all practical purposes the size and shape of the tracheal tree are not adjustable during the act of singing. This means that the response of the tracheal tree will be the same for all pitches except for its own resonant frequency. When this resonant frequency is reached, the response of the subglottic tube is to act as an acoustical impedance or interference which tends to upset the phonatory function of the larynx.

Research by Van den Berg has placed the resonant frequency of the subglottal system (the tracheal tree) around the E flat above middle C for both males and females, varying somewhat with the size of the individual.[5] This coincides with one of the transition areas discussed in chapter 7 (see Fig. 5.), where it was mentioned that both men and women may encounter problems between middle C and the G a fifth above it. It is this writer's opinion that this problem is caused by the resonant frequency of the tracheal tree, which creates acoustical impedance and interferes with the normal phonatory function of the larynx. This interference will continue until the singer learns to adjust the supraglottal resonators (the ones above the glottis) to compensate for it. If this is true, there is no need to consider this problem area as a change of registers; it is an area of resonance adjustment and modal voice can properly be used on both sides of it and during the adjustment. The tracheal tree makes no significant contribution to the resonance system except for a negative effect around its resonant frequency.

The Larynx. Since the larynx contains the vocal cords, which function as the primary vibrator, the fact that it may also serve as a resonator could pass unnoticed. However, it is a cavity, although a rather small one, and therefore should be evaluated. If it is a resonator, it would function only for high frequencies, due to its size. Research by Bartholomew[6] and others has indicated that one of the desirable attributes of good vocal tone is a prominent overtone lying between 2800-3200 Hertz, with male voices nearer the lower limit and female voices nearer the upper. This attribute is identified as brilliance, or more frequently as "ring." There are several areas in or adjacent to the larynx which might resonate such a high pitch. Among them are the collar of the larynx, the ventricles of Morgani (the pockets between the true and false cords), the vallecula (the space between the tongue and the epiglottis), and the pyriform sinuses (between the collar of the larynx and the thyroid cartilage). Another more distant area is that between the faucial pillars and the back wall of the pharynx.

Vennard seems to feel that "ring" is more likely to come from the vibrator itself than from a resonator—that the conditions under which it appears are more related to vocal cord action than to resonance. He makes these comments:

> In any case, it apears that what is commonly called "getting resonance in the voice," is really getting "2800," and this is fully as much a matter of proper vibration as it is proper resonance. Also, even if it is really resonance, it is in some small cavity below the level of consciousness, which is only controlled indirectly, largely by ear. We cannot relegate it to indifference, however, because it does appear in some tones and not in others, and any means that will build it, no matter how indirect, must be taught.[7]

There has been considerable research relative to these various cavities, with some of the most interesting work centering around the ventricles, but nothing definitive has emerged as yet. All that can be said at this point is that the larynx is not under conscious control, but whatever produces "ring" can be encouraged indirectly by awareness on the part of the student and the teacher of the sounds which contain it.

The Pharynx. By virtue of its position, size, and degree of adjustability, the pharynx (throat) has to qualify as the most important resonator. It is the first cavity of any size through which the product of the laryngeal vibrator passes; the other supraglottal cavities have to accept whatever the pharynx passes on to them. Greene states:

> The supraglottic resonators being in the main muscular and movable structures must be voluntarily controlled to produce conditions of optimal resonance either by varying degrees of tension in their walls, or by alterations in the size of their orifices and cavities during the articulatory movements.[8]

The pharynx is ideally suited to function in this capacity. Its vertical and horizontal dimensions can be increased or decreased, the tension in its walls is highly variable, and the size of the orifices leading to the mouth and nose can be varied, as can the entrance to the larynx itself. Because of its size, the pharynx is capable of bringing out the lower partials of the vocal tone when it is properly used. The resulting quality is described by terms such as fullness, roundness, warmth, richness, or mellowness. Various authorities place the frequency range of the pharynx somewhere between 330 and 750 Hz.

The pharynx extends all the way from the back of the nose down to the larynx and the mouth of the esophagus. Three large bands of constrictor muscles form its walls—the upper, middle, and lower constrictors. The upper portion of the pharynx is called the naso-pharynx; it can be shut off from the rest of the pharynx by the action of the upper constrictor and the elevation of the soft palate. The part directly behind the mouth is called the oro-pharynx; the lower part is called the laryngo-pharynx. The laryngo-pharynx can virtually be cut off from the rest of the pharynx by the juxtaposition of the back of the tongue and pharyngeal wall.

The Oral Cavity. The oral cavity or mouth is second in importance only to the pharynx. It, too, is well suited by location, size, and adjustability to serve as an effective vocal resonator. Its dimensions are altered by movements of the tongue, soft palate, jaw, and lips, and the shape and size of both its front and back orifices are capable of alteration. The main functions of the mouth are to form the vocal tone into understandable units by supplying consonants for communication, to get the sound out where it can be heard, and to join with the pharynx in the formation of vowel sounds. Vennard says that the function of the mouth is to shape the tone into words, and the skill one must acquire is that of articulating without spoiling the quality which has been generated in the larynx and resonated by the pharynx.[9] Greene sees it from another perspective:

> Possibly the most important function of the front resonator is the provision of a funnel for the projection of sound, like a speaking trumpet or megaphone. The more open this funnel can be kept by the relaxed position of the jaws and tongue and the lips the better projection the voice will have.[10]

The Nasal Cavity. The nasal cavity or nose is third in rank in the hierarchy of vocal resonators; it is much less important than the pharynx and mouth, being essential for the production of only three sounds in the English language, the nasal consonants [m], [n], and [ŋ], and the nasalized vowel sounds of languages such as French and Portuguese. Aside from a slight change in dimension effected by flaring the nostrils (which can make a singer look afflicted if done too assiduously), the cavity itself is not adjustable. However, it can be switched in or out of the resonance system to varying degrees by the action of the soft palate and the related musculature. The opening between the back of the mouth and the back of the nose is referred to as the nasal port.

The design of the nose is ideal for its main purpose: cleaning, adjusting the temperature of, and adding moisture to the incoming air. The factors which make it ideal are counterproductive for resonance. Like the inside of the lungs, the interior of the nose has little to recommend it as a resonator.

Research by Wooldridge, Vennard, and others has confirmed that it is necessary for the nose to function as a resonator only on the nasal consonants and vowels previously mentioned. Expert auditors were unable to distinguish between sounds made by singers with normal nostrils and the same singers with their nasal passages stuffed full of cotton gauze, and the vowel spectra revealed no significant differences. This means that the vibratory sensations experienced in the roof of the mouth, the nose, the cheekbones, or the sinuses by many singers may feel good and may provide evidence of a good sound, but contribute nothing to the external sound being produced. If they did contribute anything, blocking the nasal passages with gauze would alter the sound, which it did not. Like the chest vibrations, they may supply valuable feedback, but that is about all. Authorities are not in complete agreement as to the nature of their transmission. There is some feeling that the vibrations are carried to the bony structures of the head by conductive resonance, but others feel that the nasal cavity is made to vibrate sympathetically by the vibrations of the hard and soft palates, even when the nasal port is closed. These vibrations may testify to a good phonatory process or to the fact that the pharynx and mouth are functioning effectively as resonators; but, if so, it should be remembered that the vibrations are a *result*, not a *cause* of the sound you are producing.

Vocal authorities differ as to how much nasal resonance, if any, is acceptable on sounds other than the nasal consonants. More about this later.

The Sinuses. Because of their size, location, minuteness of orifice, and lack of adjustability, the sinuses cannot exert any significant influence on the vocal tone. In the past, various theories have attached great importance to the sinuses as resonators and even as the source of vocal tone (!), but research similar to that carried out on the nasal cavity has confirmed that their contribution to the external sound is negligible, despite all the wonderful vibratory sensations which may surround them. The singer should be aware of these sensations and even encourage them; but he should know, as stated earlier, that they are the result of the sound being produced, not the cause.

Summary. There are at least seven possible vocal resonators. Two of them—the chest and the sinuses—make no significant contribution to the external sound, despite the vibratory sensations which may be experienced in those areas and the considerable importance assigned to them in earlier days. Two others—the tracheal tree and the larynx itself—have some effect on the external sound, but are not under conscious control and are considered of secondary importance. The tracheal tree exhibits the same response for all pitches except its own resonant frequency, where it tends to create a negative effect through acoustical impedance. The larynx may be the source of "ring" in the voice (2800-3200 Hz), either through its vibratory pattern or a small cavity such as the collar of the larynx.

The most important resonators of the human voice are the pharynx and mouth, and, in a more limited sense, the nasal cavity. The nasal cavity is necessary for the production of the three nasal consonants in the English language and some nasalized vowels in other languages. It is not adjustable, but it can be switched (shunted) in or out of the resonance system to varying degrees by the action of the soft palate (velum) and related musculature. Vocal authorities differ as to how much nasal resonance, if any, is acceptable on sounds other than the nasal consonants. This will be considered more fully later in this chapter in a discussion of nasality.

The pharynx and mouth, because of their location, size, and degree of adjustability, must be considered the most important resonators, with the pharynx having a slight predominance because it gets the first shot at the

laryngeal product. The pharynx is capable of bringing out the
of the vocal tone, thus imparting a quality variously described a
round, rich, or mellow. The mouth helps to shape the vocal
understandable units for communication by supplying consonants   ..as a
function somewhat like a megaphone in transmitting the vocal sound outside
the body. The mouth and pharynx work cooperatively in the formation of
vowel sounds, functioning as combined resonators in a highly variable and
complex system, with constantly changing apertures, capacities, and degrees
of firmness in the walls in moving from one vowel to another. A third
resonator, the nasal cavity, is shunted in or out of the resonance system as the
necessity arises for nasal consonants or vowels.

Adjusting the Resonators

There are certain optimal conditions in the vocal resonators that must be
sought after and established if the resonators are to function effectively. These
conditions are related to such factors as laryngeal position, dimensions of the
resonators, relative firmness of the resonator walls, number of resonators in
use, and size and/or type of opening. There also are certain thought patterns
and physical actions that may be helpful in establishing these optimal
conditions for the singer.

The Position of the Larynx. The mechanism of the larynx was presented
in chapter 5. The extrinsic muscles of the larynx perform the important task
of positioning the larynx by raising, lowering, or stabilizing it. These muscles
may be divided into two groups: those that originate above the larynx (the
supralaryngeal muscles), and those that originate below the larynx (the
infralaryngeal muscles). As a general rule, those that originate above the
larynx pull up on it, and those that originate below pull down on it. Both sets
of muscles can play a part in stabilizing the larynx through the principle of
muscular antagonism. The downward-pulling muscles often are called the
yawning muscles, and the upward-pulling ones are rather loosely called the
swallowing muscles or the chewing and swallowing muscles. The opposing
action of the two sets can be illustrated by starting to yawn and then trying to
swallow. The swallow cannot take place until the yawning muscles have
stopped pulling down.

Most authorities now agree that the best position for the larynx is a
comparatively low one, and that the larynx does not need to make any
significant excursions up or down once phonation has started. These
conclusions were reached through a series of tests designed to establish a
relationship between desirable vocal tone and laryngeal position. It soon

)ecame apparent that the type of vocal tone favored by many teachers was associated with a comparatively low larynx, and that an undesirable type of tone often was associated with a high larynx. The scientifically controlled tests only confirmed what many teachers had arrived at empirically: that a high larynx and a tight, edgy sound often occur simultaneously.

Granted that a comparatively low larynx position is correct, how can you determine when it is low enough? The following experiment, which is repeated from chapter 5, should be helpful:

Place an index finger gently on the notch of your larynx. Observe what happens when you *begin* to yawn. You will feel the lower jaw drop freely open, the larynx descend slightly, and a gentle lifting in the area of your soft palate, as cool air goes deep within your throat and lungs. Now continue the action until it becomes a full yawn, noticing the tension which develops in the throat and lower jaw. Experiment with trying to speak or sing (1) in the beginning-of-a-yawn position, and (2) in the full-yawn position. You will discover that the first position is conducive to easy phonation, while the second is somewhat antagonistic to it.

The beginning-of-a-yawn position is ideal for singing and should be cultivated. The full-yawn position is exaggeratedly low and should be avoided; it is known as the depressed larynx.

Granted that the beginning-of-a-yawn position of the larynx is ideal for phonation, what does it have to do with resonance? Both the size of the pharynx and the tension in its walls are affected by the location of the larynx. When the larynx is high, the length of the pharynx is diminished, its walls are made harder, and its horizontal dimensions are decreased by the action of the constrictor muscles. All of these actions tend to restrict the resonation capabilities of the pharynx.

The "Open" Throat. Many writers concur on the value of an "open" throat; there is not as much agreement on what it is or how it should be achieved. Apparently some are referring to the vertical dimensions (a deep or long throat), others to horizontal expansion (a large throat). What are the desirable attributes of the "open" throat? There are several: (1) sufficient size to bring out the low partials, (2) sufficient flexibility to adjust (tune) to different pitches coming from the larynx, (3) sufficient softness to absorb undesirable high partials and respond to a broad range of pitches, and (4) sufficient muscle tonus to preserve the character of the tone.

If sufficient space is to be maintained in the pharynx, the swallowing muscles must not be allowed to take over. Their main functions are to raise the larynx and to make the throat as small as possible, so that food or drink may be squeezed into the esophagus. Start to swallow and try to phonate at the same time; you will quickly discover that the two processes are antithetical. One of the main causes of bad vocal sounds is tensing the constrictor muscles; it hardens the resonator walls, reduces needed space, and tends to create tension in the primary vibrator—the vocal cords. All of these results are contributory to a tight, hard sound.

The attempt to maintain space in the pharynx should not result in local effort, forcibly holding the throat expanded, or locking the jaw open. These actions are just about as harmful to the sound as singing with a high larynx. Singing in the full-yawn or depressed larynx position is an example of artificially maintaining pharyngeal space, which results in a great deal of tension.

The ideal way to arrive at a proper concept of the "open" throat is by learning to maintain the beginning-of-a-yawn position. The beginning of a yawn is not a panacea for all vocal ills, but it is a helpful stimulus to all four of the physical processes involved in the singing act, and should not be dismissed lightly. Sometimes a natural solution to a problem is overlooked because it seems too simple or inconsequential. Analyze the beginning of a yawn carefully and you will find that it can accomplish all of the following: it (1) opens the pathway for a noiseless and almost effortless taking in of air; (2) positions the larynx in a comfortably low position, without tensing to do so; (3) increases the size of the throat, especially in the vertical dimension, by lowering the larynx, gently lifting the soft palate, and relaxing the constrictor muscles of the pharynx wall; and (4) relaxes the muscles controlling the articulators, thus freeing them for action. There are few situations where a singer can get so many beneficial results with so little expenditure of effort.

The Position of the Soft Palate. Students are often confused about the position and functions of the soft palate. According to Greene:

> The velum is an entirely muscular structure forming a mobile flap which is attached to the posterior edge of the hard palate in front and hangs free behind terminating in the uvula. It is composed of several paired muscles.[11]

When at rest the soft palate hangs down almost vertically. This leaves the nasal port open, and the naso-pharynx forms a continuation upward of the oro-pharynx. In order to close the nasal port and cut off the nasal cavity the soft palate must be elevated until it makes contact with the back pharyngeal wall. This closure is more or less complete depending on the vowel to be sung and perhaps the tonal preference of the singer. The soft palate assumes its highest position (most complete closure) on the vowel [i], but also elevates considerably for the plosive consonants. On the nasal consonants the soft palate is down and the nasal port is open; this adds the nasal cavity to the resonance system. In swallowing, the nasal port is completely closed to prevent food or drink from being pushed into the naso-pharynx. It is easy to observe the raising and lowering action of the soft palate (especially of the uvula) in a hand mirror. Try singing an arpeggio to the upper octave and back down to the original tone while watching the uvula.

The External Orifice. The main discussion of the articulators will be reserved for the following chapter, but mention needs to be made here of their effect on the external orifice of the resonation system. For example, what effect will the lips have on the external sound if they are moved? Pull the lips back into a forced smile and sing the vowel [a]; is difficult to keep the sound from sounding hard and too bright. Pull your lips back hard again and notice the tension it creates in the region of the soft palate; you may feel a tightness around the larynx, too. Now pull your lips in over your teeth until your mouth is almost closed; notice how it muffles and darkens the sound, and also changes the vowel. Now protrude the lips forcibly until the front teeth are uncovered and you feel tension in the back of your throat and around the base of your tongue. Try to sing the [a] vowel; notice how tense it feels and how brilliant it sounds. Uncovering the teeth tends to encourage the high partials, and "trumpeting" the lips tends to lock the resonance system into a tight sound of considerable brilliance but little beauty or flexibility. While singing in this protruded lip position, relax your lips and open your jaw freely. Observe the almost startling contrast in tone quality and ease of production.

The purpose of these brief experiments has been to demonstrate the importance of the size and shape of the front orifice to the final vocal product, the sound that is leaving the body. Even if the rest of the resonance system is producing its best effort, the net result can be spoiled by the external orifice. The use of the mouth and lips will be discussed more fully in the next chapter, but for now it should be emphasized that the lips must avoid any rigid position; they should not be pulled back, pushed forward, or rendered almost immobile, but should be free to move at all times. The mouth should open freely, as in the beginning of a yawn, with the lower jaw dropping freely open, also.

Faults Related to Resonation

The faults related to resonation may be divided into two major categories: (1) those related to nasal resonance, and (2) those related to the basic harmonic spectrum of a voice—its tone color.

Faults Related to Nasal Resonance. The faults related to nasal resonance also may be divided into two categories: (1) excessive nasal resonance (nasality), and (2) insufficient nasal resonance. It has been pointed out that the only sounds in the English language which call for the addition of the nasal cavity to the resonance system are the nasal consonants [m], [n], and [ŋ]. Research has confirmed that all the other sounds can be formed acceptably with the nasal port closed or with the nasal passages blocked. Some authorities, such as Vennard, feel that the closure of the naso-pharynx should be complete for all sounds other than the nasal consonants. Others feel that a slight opening of the nasal port is not detrimental to the sound and may even add a desirable mellowness, while still others, such as Westerman, state that the soft palate should be lowered in singing. One of the difficulties in discussing nasal resonance is reaching a consensus on how much of it is good and desirable, and what limit must be passed before it becomes excessive. Another difficulty is that there are two distinct, but closely related, tone qualities that are identified as nasality. In some writings it is not easy to determine which type is being discussed. Perhaps the first step should be to attempt to clear away some of the confusion about these two types, before trying to decide how much nasal resonance is excessive.

True nasal resonance occurs when the nasal port is open enough for the nasal resonator to exert the *predominant* influence on the external sound produced. This occurs naturally in the nasal consonants, the French nasal vowels, and in a hum. If the nasal resonator is allowed to remain predominant in other sounds, however, it is classified as excessive nasal resonance or true nasality. It appears in an exaggerated form in cleft palate speech because the individual cannot close the nasal port completely enough with his soft palate to cut out the nasal cavity when it is not needed. One suggested name for this type of nasality is *postnasality* because the sound seems to be formed behind the nose; another is the descriptive expression apparently coined by William Vennard, *nasal honk.* In this true nasality the nasal cavity is coupled into the resonance system along with the mouth and pharynx, but dominates the tonal result.

There is a second type of nasality which may be identified as *forced nasality* or *nasal twang.* It is more widely recognized by the general populace as nasality than the true variety is, and is characterized by a tight, pinched sound which seems to be centered in the nasal cavity. Interestingly enough, true nasality may not be present with this sound, because nasal twang can be, and often is, produced when the nasal port is completely closed. Modern research has confirmed the earlier findings of Paget that nasal twang is caused by constriction somewhere in the pharynx. This constriction either forms a small resonator of high pitch (possibly in the area of the palatopharyngeal pillars) or emphasizes a high partial through muscle tension, for researchers have found that nasal twang is associated with a high overtone somewhere in the range of 2500-2800 Hz. (Vennard has pointed out the proximity of this frequency range to that of the "ring" in the voice.) If the nasal port is open, postnasality (nasal honk) may be present also; but if so, it will tend to be covered up by the characteristic penetrating quality of nasal twang, in which the nose is forced to vibrate.

Now back to the question of how much nasal resonance is excessive. The majority opinion seems to favor a vocal tone for sounds other than the nasal consonants in which the nasal port is closed or only slightly open. Experiments have demonstrated that in some singers the closure of the nasal port is seldom complete, yet there is no obvious nasality. The test of excessive nasal resonance must remain a subjective one for the individual listener, but there is a guideline for him to follow. If the sound indicates that the nose is the most obvious part of the resonance system on nonnasal sounds, nasality is present. If the ear cannot hear the predominance of the nose, nasal resonance may be present; but it is within acceptable limits.

When there is insufficient nasal resonance, the resulting sound is said to be *denasal.* It occurs when some physical condition or organic factor prevents the normal formation of the nasal consonants and limits nasal resonance in other sounds. The best illustration of this is the speaking voice of a person suffering from a bad head cold; a similar speech pattern can be caused by adenoids, a deviated septum, or polyps. Some persons without physical or organic problems adopt this mode of speech, but it is seldom a concern with singers. If it should appear, the best approach is humming exercises and vocalises centered around the nasal consonants.

Corrective Procedures for Postnasality (Nasal Honk). [12] Postnasality occurs when the nasal port is not sufficiently closed by the elevation of the soft palate and the nasal cavity predominates on nonnasal sounds. Aside from organic problems the chief causes of postnasality are wrong tonal models and/or inactive palatal muscles. If there is any indication of organic problems, the student should be sent to a medical specialist. If not, both of the other possible causes should be investigated. First of all, find out if the student is aware that he is making such a sound; if he is, see if there is a reason why— such as a former teacher, tonal preference, easy to sing that way, etc. Second, try to develop a new tonal model for him; demonstrate a postnasal sound and a balanced one, preferably by singing them or by recordings. Show him the

tonal and dynamic limitations of the nasal honk. Third, try to d~~irect the~~
tonal sensations to a new location. Explain that a balanced sound has a lot of
hard palate vibration and seems to be centered more in the mouth, whereas a
honk has more vibration around the soft palate and seems to be centered up
behind the nose. Demonstrate the action of pulling the sound forward and
down into the mouth from behind your own nose. Ask him to imitate what
you are doing and to describe his own sensations; he may say something that
will reveal what he is not doing.

If the postnasal sound persists, approach it from another direction while
continuing the old one. Assume that the palatal muscles are inactive and
start exercising them. It would seem logical to assume that you should avoid
the nasal consonants since the sound is too nasal. Strange to say, the nasal
consonants all are useful, for the reason that they require palatal movement,
especially if they are formed vigorously. This is particularly true of the [ŋ].
Experiment with words like ding, gone, zoom, hung, bum, and voom,
putting the initial consonant on quite firmly and sustaining the nasal
consonant while repeating the same word several times. Even though nasal
sounds are being used, palatal activity is being stressed. Sometimes the
vigorous juxtaposition of a syllable ending in [ŋ] and one starting in [g] is
effective, such as hung-gah or ding-gah. Plosive consonants, such as [p] and
[b], are good because they require closure of the nasal port. Speech therapists
incorporate various blowing exercises, such as blowing up balloons, for the
same reason.

As a last resort, since postnasality can be caused by muscular inactivity, it
may be assumed that the pharyngeal resonator is too flabby and needs more
tension, and the suggestion may be made for the student to produce a more
twangy or even tighter sound as an intermediate step on the way to a balanced
one; the final step in the process would be the instruction, "Now let your
lower jaw open wider and let the sound drop down into your mouth." Any
approach of this kind is a means to an end and should be used with caution.
There is little gain in substituting one fault for another.

Corrective Procedures for Forced Nasality (Nasal Twang).[13] Forced
nasality is caused by constriction somewhere in the pharynx. Possible areas of
the constriction include all three parts of the pharynx—the naso-pharynx,
the oro-pharynx, and the laryngo-pharynx. Margaret Greene states:

> . . . it should not be forgotten that nasality may also be imparted to the voice by
> muscular constriction in the laryngeal cavity and the relative positions assumed by the
> ventricular folds, aryepiglottic folds and epiglottis, also elevation of the larynx by the
> suprahyoid muscles.[14]

Tension in the pharyngeal resonator, with possible involvement of the larynx itself, is the cause of the forced vibrations in the nose and the sound which is descriptively identified as nasal twang. Another factor which may contribute to twang is the lack of oral space—the failure to provide enough mouth opening for the resonance system. Any corrective procedure for twang must provide for eliminating unnecessary tension (constriction) in the pharynx and larynx, must help develop a new tonal model, and must encourage the use of more oral space. Faults resulting from tension, such as tight phonation from laryngeal tension and nasal twang from a constricted pharynx, often may be traced to a prior cause such as faulty breath support or posture. When one part of the mechanism fails to function as it should, another often must compensate for it. As a prelude to the elimination of twang, it would be wise to check first on posture, breathing, and support. Then try the following approach:

1. Use loosening-up exercises for the entire body first, as suggested in chapter 3.
2. Use exercises designed to relax and loosen the neck, throat, and lower jaw—rolling the head around in circles, nodding the head, flopping the jaw loosely while saying "yah, yah, yah," or "mah, mah, mah," practice the beginning of a yawn while inhaling.
3. Try to develop a new tonal model for the student; demonstrate and contrast a twangy tone and a balanced one. Caricature the twang and explain its tonal limitations.
4. Try to direct his tonal sensations to a new location. While sustaining a sound ask him to open his mouth wider (drop his jaw open) while feeling the sound drop down from the front of his nose into his mouth. (Since the twang overtone is so close to that of "ring," you do not want to eliminate it, but to bring it into better balance with the rest of the resonance system. Providing more mouth space and more relaxation in the pharynx will help to do this.)

Perhaps the most important thing is establishing a new tonal model so that the student will be motivated to change the kind of sound he is making. Physiologically, the beginning of a yawn must be maintained to eliminate the constriction, the mouth must open freely to provide more oral space, and the sensation of a more mouth-centered tone must be cultivated.

Faults Related to Tone Color. Aside from nasality, most of the faults related to resonation may be divided into two categories: (1) sounds that are classified as too bright, too white, too open, or too forward, and (2) sounds that are classified as too dark, too muffled, too swallowed, too covered, or too far back. Both groups of faults result from a failure to bring the vocal resonators into proper balance. In the "too bright" group there tends to be too much emphasis on the mouth as a resonator and not enough on the pharynx. In the "too dark" group the situation is reversed; there is too much emphasis on the pharynx and not enough on the mouth. (In the faults related to nasality it was the nasal resonator which upset the desired balance.)

Although it is far from a unanimous choice, the tonal preference of most teachers seems to lie in a balanced sound—one which has both highs and lows present. If the lows are cut out of a sound, the result is a too white or too bright tone quality; if the highs are cut out, the sound becomes too dark or too dull (often referred to as a "tubby" sound). It is easy to demonstrate these tonal extremes on any high-quality sound reproduction equipment by means of the treble and bass controls. Most listeners like to have both ends of the harmonic spectrum present in a sound, but differ as to the desirable amount of each. The point of this discussion is to say that there is plenty of room in the broad middle ground of tonal preference for persons who like brighter or darker sounds. It is somewhat like flavors of ice cream; debate will never settle the question of which is better; it comes down to individual choice. Brightness and darkness are not in themselves vocal faults; they become faults when a majority would identify the sound as too bright or too dark.

A word needs to be said also about focusing, placing, or projecting vocal sound. The teacher who attempts to use these words in any literal sense may end up in a scientific quagmire. Sound moves out from its vibrating source in a series of compression and rarefaction waves, filling any vocal resonator to which it has access. There is nothing in the human mechanism by means of which a singer can place, focus, or throw the sound anywhere. And yet all these terms have meaning within the experience of both teachers and students. Vennard refers to "the illusion of placement." The student feels vibratory sensations at certain places and discovers that when his teacher suggests moving the tone forward or backward, he can feel the sensations move. It is legitimate to call this "voice placement" if you understand that your sound actually has not been put anywhere.

Likewise, a student tries to sing so that he can be heard in the back row of a large auditorium by thinking about projecting his voice. He may succeed in his effort, not because he has thrown his voice anywhere, but more likely because he begins to phonate more efficiently and to tune his resonators better. The resulting sound may be heard more easily on the back row, but, strange to say, may not register any increase of decibels on a meter. It is possible to speak of "projecting your voice" if you understand that you really have not thrown or impelled it anywhere.

Finally, suggesting to a student that his voice lacks focus may help him to tune his resonators in such a way that the high partial associated with "ring" may appear in his voice. He has not focused his voice anywhere, but the thought process has helped him make a more desirable sound. It is probably all right to use such terms as placement, projection, and focus in your teaching, but be careful not to confuse them with scientific fact.

Corrective Procedures for Sounds That Are "Too Bright."[15] The chief cause of sounds that are too bright is placing too much emphasis on the oral resonator. There are several factors which can cause this to occur: (1) lack of space in the pharynx due to the action of the constrictor muscles and/or elevation of the larynx; (2) tension in the walls of the pharyngeal resonator making it too selective; (3) wrong tonal models; (4) exaggerated mouth opening, pulling the lips back in a forced smile, or protruding the lips too much; (5) excessive tension in the muscles of the lips, tongue, jaw, or palatal arches.

The tight sounds of hyperfunctional phonation and their associated remedial procedures were discussed in chapter 5. It should be noted that tight phonation often occurs in conjunction with too bright sounds. The tension which causes one tends to contribute to the other; therefore, any corrective procedure should begin with the elimination or reduction of tension. Try this approach:

1. After checking on posture, breathing, and support, use general body-loosening exercises (chapter 3 or section on twang).
2. Use exercises designed to relax and loosen the neck, throat, and articulators.
3. Extensive practice on establishing and maintaining the beginning-of-a-yawn position—the tension and constriction in the pharynx must be lessened.
4. Try to develop a new tonal model for the student; contrast sounds that are too bright with balanced ones; explaining tonal limitations of such sounds.[16]
5. Since the vibratory sensations a singer feels can be moved around, suggest that he think the sound more inside himself, more internally, further back, or similar expressions which might call attention away from the mouth.
6. Most beginning singers need to imagine a deeper, richer, more

dramatic kind of sound than they usually sing—direct their thoughts along these lines.

7. The back vowels, which require lip rounding (such as [ɔ], [o], and [u]), are less tense than the frontal ones and more conducive to a darker sound; try combining them with the beginning-of-a-yawn feeling; precede them with [b], [m], or [j] to help reduce articulatory tension.

Sounds which are too bright often are associated with a high laryngeal posture. Some singers, particularly ones with lower voices, start with the larynx comparatively low and then raise it progressively as the pitch ascends, somewhat like an elevator (lift) moving from floor to floor in a department store. Other singers, chiefly ones with higher voices, tend to elevate the larynx as soon as phonation begins and force it even higher for the upper pitches. There is nothing in the laryngeal mechanism which requires that the larynx raise as pitch ascends or lower as it descends, with the possible exception of the extremes of range and of minor height adjustments associated with different vowels. Research has revealed that there is little laryngeal movement in many well-trained singers.

When a singer has made high laryngeal posture a habit, it can be a difficult one to break. If possible, it is best to do so by adopting a new tonal model and trusting it to bring about laryngeal stability. If it does not, some type of physical reminder may be needed. Ask the singer to place the tip of a finger gently on top of the thyroid notch and to observe when and how the larynx starts to rise. Ask him to counteract this tendency by mental controls, not by holding the larynx down with his finger, but by thinking that it does not need to move; the finger serves as a warning each time the larynx rises. Usually this awareness of movement will result in its elimination. If it does not, you must try to find at least one pitch in his voice on which there is no upward movement; alternate this pitch with the whole step above until the larynx stays down for both pitches, then alternate the lower pitch with a major third until it is established, then a perfect fourth, and so on until the whole range is secure. This problem requires a great deal of patience from both the singer and the teacher, but it can be solved eventually.

Corrective Procedures for Sounds That Are "Too Dark."[17] The chief cause of sounds that are too dark is placing too much emphasis on the pharyngeal resonator. There are several factors which can cause this to occur: (1) overuse of the "yawning" muscles, with resulting spread throat and/or depressed larynx; (2) lack of oral space due to lip, jaw, or tongue position; (3)

wrong tonal models; (4) flabby surfaces of pharyngeal walls (not enough muscle tonus to give any character to the sound); (5) tongue pulled back into the pharynx.

Darkness in a sound can come from too much or from too little tension, so it is important to try to identify the specific causes before starting corrective procedures. Look first for lack of activity in the articulators, such as failure to move the lips or make any significant mouth opening; this can darken and muffle the sound even when no other faults are present. Such lack of movement usually is easily corrected by calling the student's attention to it and requiring him to practice in front of a mirror.

If this is not the problem, listen to the student's sound to see if it is breathy in addition to being dark. If so, it is best to work on the breathy sound first, since it is a phonatory problem. (For suggested techniques, see chapter 5.) Often the darkness will disappear when the breathiness is eliminated.

Next, find out if the student is aware that he is making such a dark sound; if he is, see if there is a reason why—such as, he was taught to sing that way, he likes the sound, etc. Then try to develop a new tonal model for him; demonstrate various sounds that are too dark and contrast them with balanced ones. Explain the tonal limitations of dark sounds. Then try to direct his tonal sensations to a new location. Explain that a balanced sound has a lot of hard palate vibration just behind the front teeth and seems to have a lot of mouth resonance, whereas a dark sound has more vibration near the back of the palate, and seems to be more centered in the throat. Try such suggestions as: bring your tone forward, sing outside of yourself, sing a brighter sound, try to feel vibration in the front of your face.

If you think that his tongue is being pulled back, ask him to stick his tongue out over his bottom lip and sing "ah" in that position; this is hardly an ideal singing position, but it will give him some new vibratory sensations. Singing with the tongue over the lower lip is a good countermeasure for a depressed larynx, also, since the tongue, hyoid bone, and larynx are joined together in sequence. Exercises on the frontal vowels—such as, [i], [I], and [eI]—may help to brighten the sound, and rapid articulation exercises or patter songs may be beneficial, as well.

Closing Section

There are other matters which might be considered in a chapter on resonation. Chief among these are the vowels, which strictly speaking are phenomena of resonance; however, it is more convenient to consider them along with the consonants in the articulation chapter. Problem areas—such as the transition from chest voice into middle voice for women, and from chest voice into head voice for men—which likely arise from the resonant frequency of the tracheal tree could be discussed here, but will appear in the final chapter, where problems of coordination will be treated. The phenomenon known as "cover," which is closely linked with adjustment of the resonators, also will be reserved for that chapter. The next chapter will deal with articulation and its related faults.

Notes

1. For more detailed information on resonance see the list of books on acoustics at the beginning of chapter 2.

2. Vennard, *Singing*, p. 82.

3. Vennard, *Singing*, p. 85.

4. For a more detailed discussion see Vennard, *Singing*, pp. 85-96.

5. J. W. Van den Berg, "On the Myoelastic-Aerodynamic Theory of Voice Production," *The NATS Bulletin* (May 1958).

6. Bartholomew, *Acoustics*, pp. 145-147.

7. Vennard, *Singing*, p. 90.

8. Greene, *The Voice*, p. 70.

9. Vennard, *Singing*, p. 93.

10. Greene, *The Voice*, p. 73.

11. Greene, *The Voice*, p. 59.

12. Listen to band 5 of the cassette tape.

13. Listen to band 6 of the cassette tape.

14. Greene, *The Voice*, p. 240.

15. Listen to band 7 of the cassette tape.

16. Greene states, "Undue emphasis upon acquisition of resonance of imaginary origin in the air-filled spaces of the head may lead to an unpleasant thin and tinny quality to the voice and of course neglects the important principles of satisfactory voice production" (p. 76).

17. Listen to band 8 of the cassette tape.

9
Articulation

The Articulatory Process

Articulation is the process by which the joint product of the vibrator and the resonators is shaped into recognizable speech sounds through the muscular adjustment and movements of the speech organs. The primary articulators are the movable ones—the tongue, the lips, the lower jaw, the soft palate, and, in a more limited sense, the glottis, the epiglottis, and the larynx itself. They work in cooperation with the teeth, the alveolar ridge, the hard palate, and the pharyngeal wall to form an almost infinite variety of speech sounds by altering the size, shape, apertures, and other physical characteristics of various parts of the resonance system. Detailed discussion of the production and classification of speech sounds is beyond the scope of this book.[1] An introductory approach to the classification of vocal sounds was made in chapter 2; the discussion here will be limited to the identifying characteristics of consonants and vowels, and the problem of phonemic identity.

The Nature of Consonants. The most important identifying characteristics of consonants are contained in these statements:

1. They are more or less restricted speech sounds.
2. They contain more or less conspicuous noise elements due to the degree of restriction present.
3. They are subordinate to vowels in sonority.
4. They do not form the center (nucleus) of syllables, but define the borders of them.
5. They function as sound interrupters or sound stoppers and thus separate the vocal tone into recognizable units which can communicate meaning.

Consonants may be divided into two groups—those which require vocal cord vibration (*voiced consonants* or sonants) and those which do not (*unvoiced* or *voiceless consonants,* or surds). There are nine pairs of voiced and voiceless consonants, in each pair of which the articulators are essentially in the same position; the presence or absence of vocal cord vibration is the determining factor. These pairs are:

Voiced	Voiceless		Voiced	Voiceless
b	p		w	hw
d	t		ð	θ
dʒ	tʃ		z	s
g	k		ʒ	ʃ
v	f			

There are two easy tests that you can use to determine whether a consonant is voiced or not: (1) Stop your ears up with your fingers and pronounce any of the above pairs; notice how much louder the voiced one seems.[2] (2) Place one hand around your throat as if you are about to choke yourself; pronounce one of the pairs and notice the laryngeal vibration on the voiced consonant.

The rest of the consonants in the English language are voiced, except for [h]. There are no other pairs.

Speech sounds also may be identified as one of three movement categories: continuants, stops, and glides. *Continuants* are sounds which can be sustained as long as the breath lasts; all the vowels fall into this category, as do consonants such as [m], [l], [s], [v], and [θ]. *Stops* are consonants which bring the flow of the airstream to a complete halt; they are also called plosives or stop-plosives and include [b], [p], [d], [t], [g], and [k]. A *glide* actually is a vowel sound which functions as a consonant; it starts in the position of one vowel but immediately slides or glides toward whatever vowel follows it. The three common glides in the English language are represented by the first sound in each of the following words: you, will, and what. (Their IPA symbols are [j], [w], and [hw].) A fourth glide, the first sound in the word "hue," is rarely used.

There are two other systems that are frequently used for classifying consonants: (1) by the way the sound is produced, and (2) by the place or articulatory position in which it is formed. In the first system, a speech noise made by the friction of the breath stream passing through a narrow aperture is called a *fricative*—sounds such as [v], [f], [z], [s], [h], or [θ]. Sounds formed by the explosion of compressed air through the mouth are called *plosives* or *stop-plosives*—sounds such as [p], [t], and [k]. Consonants made by the passage of air through the nasal cavity are called *nasals*. An aspirate is any breathy consonant. An *affricate* is a consonant formed when compressed air is exploded through the narrow aperture of a fricative instead of the normal mouth opening used for a plosive—[tʃ] and [dʒ].

Identifying consonants by the place or articulatory position in which they are made is a convenient method of doing so. Sounds made by closing the lips are called *bilabials*—[b], [p], and [m]. Sounds made with the lower lip touching the upper teeth are *labiodentals*—[v] and [f]. Sounds made with the tip of the tongue touching the upper teeth are *dentals*—[ð] and [θ]. The *alveolars* are sounds made with the tongue touching the alveolar ridge just behind the upper teeth ([d], [t], [n], [l]) or approaching it ([z] and [s]). The *velars* are sounds made with the back of the tongue touching the soft palate—[g], [k], and [ŋ]. *Glottals* are sounds made with the glottis closed or nearly so; the sounds made with the glottis nearly closed include one consonant ([h]) and the whispered vowels; the sound made through a closed glottis is the glottal shock or glottal plosive ([ʔ]).

Actually, there is no standard method for identifying consonants. It is not unusual to see all four of the above systems used in texts on phonetics—for example, [v] is a voiced, fricative, labiodental continuant; [k] is a voiceless, aspirate, velar plosive; [h] is a voiceless, fricative, glottal continuant. There are a number of other terms used in connection with identifying consonants, but they are not requisite for this discussion; the previous listing of terms is by no means exhaustive, but merely presents some approaches to identifying consonants.

The Nature of Vowels. The most important identifying characteristics of vowels are contained in these statements:
1. They are unrestricted speech sounds.
2. They are capable of being sustained (they are continuants).
3. They normally are voiced (phonated) sounds, but they can be whispered.
4. They are the basic building material of vocal tone; the vowel carries the tone.
5. They have a definite shape or form—they are molded by the articulators.

Vowels are said to be phenomena of resonance because they result from a complex series of relationships between the oral and pharyngeal resonators, which undergo an infinite variety of changes in size, shape, aperture, and surface of walls during speech or song. "The characteristic quality of the vowel sounds is produced, it is thought, by the coupling of the predominant resonance pitches of the oral and pharyngeal cavities."[3] Vowels may be identified by the presence of certain formants, which may be defined as resonant frequency bands made up of prominent partials or overtones. Wise states:

It is likewise well known that for every vowel there are characteristic concentrations of energy, evidencing themselves in pitch patterns which identify the vowel. These patterns are found in limited regions of frequency, within which they must remain. This is another way of saying that the identifying pitch characteristics of a vowel are relatively constant. It is possible, to be sure, to speak or sing a given vowel at several different pitches without distorting it beyond recognition. But if the pitch is changed so much as to go above the regions wherein are found the components which identify the vowel, the resultant sound will actually be some other vowel.[4]

The identity of a vowel, then, depends on the presence of strong partials located in specified frequency bands. The total number of formants present in a sound may vary widely, with, as a general rule, more formants present in speaking than in singing; research reveals diagreement on the subject. However, the vowels usually may be identified by two characteristic formants, one high and one low, apparently provided by the coupled oral and pharyngeal resonators.

The tongue is the primary determinant of the relationship between the two cavities and, therefore, is the primary differentiator of the vowels. Although research has indicated that the vowels can be produced without significant tongue activity, the normal procedure is for the tongue to move on all vowel sounds. In order to test this statement, all you have to do is touch the tip of a finger to the front of your tongue and pronounce any two vowels. If allowed to function unhindered, the tongue will change positions for the second vowel. However, the tongue is not the only articulator used in forming different vowels; some of the vowels—[u], [ʊ], [o], [ɔ], and [ɒ]—are shaped by lip rounding in addition to tongue position.

Vowels are grouped together in various ways—such as front, back, and central vowels; tense and lax vowels; stressed and unstressed vowels; the cardinal vowels and the Latin (singer's) vowels. They are presented on various charts or diagrams—such as the vowel triangle, the vowel trapezium, etc. The front, back, and central vowels draw their names from the position of the highest point in the arch of the tongue. For the vowels [i], [ɪ], [e], [ɛ], [æ], and [a], the highest point is in the front of the tongue and moves progressively back in that section if the vowels are pronounced in the stated sequence; these are the *front vowels*. For the vowels [ɑ], [ɒ], [ɔ], [o], [ʊ], [u], the highest point is in the back portion of the tongue and moves progressively back in that section if the vowels are pronounced in the stated sequence; these are the *back vowels*. For the *central vowels* [ɝ], [ɜ], [ɚ], [ə], and [ʌ] the arch of the tongue is in the center of the mouth, midway between the front and back. (The system can be extended by indicating whether the tongue elevation is high, medium, or low in the front vowels, the back vowels, and the central vowels.)

According to Wise, a major difference between certain vowels is that resulting from the difference of cavity texture produced by tension of the muscles of the mouth and throat. The softer the texture of the cavity walls, the more the cavity emphasizes low overtones. There are four pairs of vowels in which the second member of each pair may be recognized as a lax version of the more tense first member; these pairs are [i]-[ɪ], [e]-[ɛ], [o]-[ɔ], and [u]-[ʊ].[5] You may test the relative tenseness and laxness of the first pair by saying "bee bit" while pressing in on both sides of the front of your throat just below the lower jaw.

The principle of making some syllables in words more important than others—the stressed-unstressed principle—is an old one which is a prominent feature of the English language. *Stress* is a word designating the relative loudness (force, intensity) with which a syllable is uttered.[6] Since a vowel is the nucleus of a syllable, it provides the best evidence of the degree of stressing or unstressing present. Four different levels of stress are possible: primary, secondary, tertiary, and weak. Under conditions of primary or secondary stress, a vowel tends to retain its full or typical quality, but under tertiary or weak stress (unstressing) a vowel tends to be reduced to a shorter form of itself, or, in the greatest number of cases, to [ə] or [ɪ]. The [ə] symbol, which is called a *schwa*, is used to represent the neutral, indeterminant vowel sound (or sounds) of most unstressed syllables of English: such as "a" in "alone" or "sofa," "e" in "pungent," and so forth. The [ɪ] symbol tends to be used more often in unstressed syllables where it replaces one of the forward vowels, especially [i], [e], and [ɛ]: for example, in prefixes such as "ex" and "de," and in suffixes such as "ed," "ate," and "es." Sometimes either [ə] or [ɪ] may be used, according to local custom or personal preference.

In addition to tense-lax pairs of vowels, there are *stressed-unstressed* pairs. The ones usually linked together in this way are all members of the central vowels group, as follows: [ʌ]-[ə], [ɜ]-[ə], and [ɝ]-[ɚ].[7] The [ə] sound found in the first syllable of "abut" is the unstressed form of the [ʌ] sound in the second syllable. The second stressed-unstressed pair [ɜ]-[ə] is more typical of British speech than American; both sounds appear in the word *burner*. Americans can approximate these sounds by omitting both "r's" in the word—[bɜ nə]. The third pair [ɝ]-[ɚ] can be illustrated by the same word, *burner*, but with the "r's" pronounced as in standard American usage—[bɝ nɚ].

There are different methods for determining the primary or most important vowels, with varying results. One system speaks of four *cardinal vowels*. Wise states:

> A cardinal vowel may be defined as a theoretic vowel made with a tongue-position that is invariable, easily described in writing or printing so as to be communicable at a distance. By referring to this tongue-position of the theoretic vowel as a point of reference, other vowels can be described as higher, lower, farther front, or farther back . . . [i] is made with the tongue as high and as far front as possible. [a] with the tongue as low and as far front as possible. [a] with the tongue as low and as far back as possible. [u] with the tongue as high and as far back as possible.[8]

Another system speaks of the five *Latin vowels*, *Italian vowels*, or *singer's vowels*—[i], [e], [a], [o], [u]. They are also called the *long vowels* because in speech they are sustained longer than the remaining vowels, which are referred to as *short vowels*. It may be conditioned reflex, but almost any singer will affirm that it is easier to sing on these five sounds than on the other shorter ones. There is acoustical evidence, also, which supports the primacy of these vowels.[9] For whatever reasons, teachers of singing are convinced of the value of these basic sounds in almost any program of vocal development. It should be pointed out that in standard American usage the [e] and [o] of the five "pure" vowels are placed by the diphthongs [eɪ] and [ou].

Another system which is widely used in teaching foreign languages classifies vowels as closed (close) or open; it bears a strong relationship to the tense-lax pairings. Because the terms *open* and *closed* (covered) generally have other meanings in the teaching of singing, that system will only be mentioned here.

The Problem of Phonemic Identity. As with the vowel and the consonant, arriving at a simple, accurate, all-inclusive definition of a *phoneme* is not without its problems. According to the Collins *English Dictionary,* a phoneme is:

> one of the set of speech sounds in any given language that serve to distinguish one word from another. A phoneme may consist of several phonetically distinct articulations, which are regarded as identical by native speakers, since one articulation may be substituted for another without any change of meaning. Thus /p/ and /b/ are separate phonemes in English because they distinguish such words as *pet* and *bet,* whereas the light and dark /l/ sounds in *little* are not separate phonemes since they may be transposed without changing meaning.

Phonetically distinct articulations which can be substituted for each other are called *allophones.* Wise lists ten allophones of the /t/ phoneme and indicates that the list is not exhaustive. He points out that the word *till* is made up of three phonemes, /t/, /ɪ/, and /l/, each of which may exist in a number of constituent allophones.[10] If any one of the three phonemes is changed, the meaning of the word must change, by definition. For example, if the initial /t/ phoneme is changed to /d/, the word becomes *dill*. You have left /t/-territory and entered /d/-territory. As long as the initial sound could be recognized as some kind of [t] or an acceptable substitute for it, the phoneme had not changed. As soon as the ear accepts it as [d], the phoneme has changed. You have entered the family of [d] sounds.

Several conclusions can be drawn from this discussion:

1. A phoneme is a family of sounds in a given language.
2. If two sounds cannot be interchanged without changing the meaning of a word, they are phonemes.
3. If sounds can be interchanged without changing the meaning of a word, they are allophones (family members) of a phoneme.
4. Native speakers may not realize that different allophones are being used. (The same is true of singers.)

One of the best assets a singer can have is an ear capable of making fine discriminations in the sounds of the language in which he is singing. He needs to be able to recognize and preserve the phonemic identity of the sounds he is making, so that he may communicate meaningfully through understandable diction. At the same time he must be able to make tonal adjustments within sound families (phonemes) to permit the most efficient use of his vocal mechanism, so that beautiful sounds can enhance the meaning of the text. A singer can become so obsessed with the phonemic purity of certain vowels that his voice is robbed of its beauty; conversely, he can be so concerned with tonal beauty that almost all verbal communication is lost. The singer with a discerning ear can reach the twin goals of achieving tonal beauty and preserving phonemic identity; this is the mark of artistic singing.

Establishing Good Articulatory Habits

A singer does not have a separate instrument that he can see or touch while he is making music; the singer *is* a musical instrument. Since he has no keys or valves or fingerboard to press, he must learn to depend on his own mind and body as singing guides. In addition to being a self-contained musical instrument, the singer has another property which makes him unique. He alone of all the instruments has the ability to communicate meaning through word *and* tone. All performers can convey musical ideas through their interpretation of a piece of music. Only the singer can convey musical ideas *and* specific verbal messages. Because of this, it is essential that the singer learn to communicate words well; the only way he can do this is by mastering the skill of articulation.

The words *to articulate* have several meanings: one is to express oneself fluently and coherently; another is to utter clearly in distinct syllables; still another is to make the separate parts or segments of something distinct. All these meanings have something in common: making something so distinct and clear that it may be easily perceived. For the singer or speaker the basic meaning is to make the movements and adjustments of the speech organs necessary to form speech sounds *distinctly.* If he cannot do this, he might be better off playing an instrument, where the lack of words is no handicap.

Use of the Articulators. The most important articulators are the ones which are under the direct control of the singer—the lips, the lower jaw, and the tongue. The other articulators—the soft palate, the glottis, the epiglottis, and the larynx itself—are essential to the formation of certain sounds, but are not under conscious control and can be trained only indirectly. There are two basic principles which contribute to effective use of the articulators: (1) All movements of the articulators should be quick, precise, and positive, ending in a position which is free of unnecessary tension; (2) in singing, articulatory movements must be exaggerated, especially with beginning students, if the words are to be consistently understood. In order for these principles to function, certain thought patterns and articulatory habits need to be established for each of the important articulators. As a first step, imagine that all your articulatory movements are taking place *just in front* of your mouth, with everything moving very crisply and precisely, but without tension. This will help to ensure clarity and distinctness. Another helpful thought pattern is to imagine you are singing to someone who has to read your lips or to someone who does not know your language very well.

The *lips* must be free from tension and ready to move as needed if they are to function well as articulators. Imagine that your lips are made of rubber and that they bounce freely apart when contacting each other. The position of the lips should be such that it helps your face to have a pleasant, vital expression, as if you are about to smile; it is very important that you communicate with your face, as well as with your voice.

Since the lips are a primary determinant of the type of external orifice on the resonator system, they will have a strong effect on the timbre of a voice in addition to its articulatory effectiveness. Although a slight smile is desirable, be careful not to pull your lips back off your teeth into a forced smile. Pulling back on the lips can tighten the pharynx in the vicinity of the soft palate and can cause the tone quality to become too bright. This brightness may add clarity to your diction (as many "pop" singers have recognized), but it does so at the expense of tonal beauty. Pulling your lips in against your teeth or your upper lip down also is not good; this tends to darken the tone quality and make the voice sound muffled because of the restricted space and type of opening.

Just as a slight smile is desirable when singing, the feeling that your lips are not touching your teeth may be beneficial. Do not do anything artificial to get this feeling, such as lifting your top lip as if you are smelling something unpleasant, or protruding your lips. Just try to feel that your lips are very slightly off your teeth and free to move. When the lips are protruded, they resemble a megaphone and may help produce a loud, ringing tone that will carry a long way. However, the sound often is tight, hard, and capable of little tonal or dynamic variation because thrusting the lips forward tends to tighten the back of the throat and create tension in certain lip and facial muscles. Singers who adopt this approach are referred to derisively as "fishmouth" or "trumpet lips," for obvious reasons.

The lips must be free from tension and ready to move as needed, slightly off the teeth as if you are about to smile. Their movements should be quick, precise, and positive. Imagine that they bounce apart after contacting each other.

The lower jaw must be free from tension and ready to move as needed if it is to function well as an articulator. This ideal condition can be achieved easily through the beginning-of-a-yawn position (Does this statement have a familiar ring?). When you begin a yawn, the throat seems to drop open and you can feel cool air going deep within it; the jaw drops down freely, and there is a gentle lifting at the top of the throat as the soft palate rises.

Many of the muscles used in chewing and swallowing are attached to the lower jaw. It is very important that these muscles not be kept in a state of tension while you are singing; if they are tight, the throat will be tight, and the resulting sound will be tight. Many people have a hard time learning to relax the muscles which pull the jaw up and close the mouth. It is necessary to use these muscles to keep the mouth from hanging open as you perform your daily tasks; this means that these muscles may be kept under tension during all the hours you are awake, for some people truly relax them only when they go to sleep. If the muscles which raise the jaw are relaxed, the jaw will drop freely down. This is why the mouth often drops open when a person falls asleep. You should cultivate the feeling that your jaw is dropping open freely of its own weight while you are articulating.

When the mouth must be opened wide, the jaw should drop down first and then swing back. It should not be pushed forward on any sound; protruding the jaw creates tension in the throat and the jaw joints; and may be associated with a high laryngeal position. Cultivating the down-and-back motion will help to eliminate any forward pushing of the jaw. To acquire a full and easy opening of the mouth, you should practice two things: (1) the beginning of a yawn to free the jaw from tension, letting it drop down of its own weight; and (2) saying or singing "yah, yah, yah," while opening the mouth freely with a down-and-back motion of the lower jaw. The lips, also, must be free from tension and ready to move as needed; if the lip muscles are tense, the jaw can hardly drop freely open. The same thing is true when the chewing and swallowing muscles are tense; the free travel of the jaw is restricted.

The lower jaw must not stay in the same place all the time while you are singing; it should not be forced wide open and held there or locked in an almost shut position. Avoid any kind of rigidity or locking in one position. The reason that the jaw must be free to move at all times is that the amount of mouth space must be adjusted as you sing higher or lower, form different vowels, and change dynamic levels. Increasing the size of the external opening of a resonator will cause it to resonate a higher pitch; therefore, the mouth should increase its opening as you sing higher and decrease as you sing lower. If the jaw is locked in one position, it is difficult to adjust your oral and pharyngeal resonance as you change pitch levels. Be careful to avoid "vocal lockjaw."

It is possible to create two kinds of resonance space in the mouth—external and internal. *External space* is created in the front of the mouth and is controlled by the amount of mouth opening. *Internal space* is created in the back of the mouth, and is controlled by the action of the jaw joints. Pretend that you are yawning in public and are keeping your lips closed to try to avoid being seen; notice how the jaw joints seem to drop open and there is a feeling of added space in the back of the mouth and in the throat. Now try the beginning of a normal yawn, letting the mouth open this time; notice that the same feeling of internal space is still present, even though it may not be as obvious when the mouth is open. Some teachers feel that this space should be maintained when you sing, and should not be allowed to close back up; others feel that internal space is essential to the best production of the upper voice. It does seem to be of major assistance in establishing and maintaining the proper laryngeal position for singing.

The lower jaw must be free from tension and ready to move as needed. The beginning of a yawn is conducive to these conditions. Cultivate the feeling that your jaw is dropping open of its own weight. For a wider opening the jaw should drop down first and then swing back. The mouth opening should increase as you sing higher and decrease as you sing lower, without rigidity or locking. The right kind of jaw action can help supply both internal and external space, and helps to maintain the proper laryngeal position.

The tongue must be free of unnecessary tension and ready to move as needed if it is to function well as an articulator. Its movements must be quick, precise, and positive. The tongue is the most important of the articulators. It is involved in the formation of all the vowel sounds and many of the consonants. Because the tongue has to move for so many different sounds, it is important for it to have a resting place to return to—*a point of reference*. Vennard makes an analogy between this aspect of tongue position and the best defensive position of a tennis player.[11] Players in a number of different sports employ reference points to enable them to repeat certain actions with a minimum of effort and a maximum of accuracy. This is the purpose of locating a resting place for the tongue.

For most singers the best point of reference seems to be the gum ridge just below the lower teeth. When you are singing any vowel, the tip of the tongue should rest lightly on the gum ridge, with the body of the tongue making the needed adjustments for a particular vowel. The tip will leave the point of reference to make various consonants, but should return to it quickly. It does not need to leave it for vowel sounds. It is very important for the singer to practice returning his tongue to this point of reference on the lower gum ridge consciously until it becomes an automatic reaction—a conditioned reflex.

The tongue must not be pulled back into the throat to form any consonant or vowel. If it is pulled back far enough, it may tighten the surrounding areas of the pharynx, depress the larynx, and almost block off the lower pharynx; all of these results will hurt the quality of the sound and the articulatory capabilities of the tongue will be limited. Neither should the tongue be pushed forward or tensed unduly in singing.

Some vowel and consonant sounds are formed with moderate tension in the tongue muscles—for example, [i] and the retroflex [r]. You must be careful not to tighten these sounds too much or to let the tongue become rigid and inflexible; excess tongue tension will always manifest itself in the tone quality being produced. The tongue must be free to move, even when some tension must be present. Nothing can upset good diction as much as a stiff, sluggish, or lazy tongue.

When the tip of the tongue is resting on the point of reference, the body of the tongue should lie fairly low in the mouth with its upper surface forming a gentle arch. This is the position the tongue assumes naturally to begin a yawn or an inhalation, and should be maintained during phonation, except for the changes in elevation needed for different vowel sounds. In a full yawn the tongue usually is pulled back into the throat; this is not the preferred position for singing. Observe the action of your tongue in both the beginning of a yawn and a full yawn; the tip of the tongue should not pull away from the lower gum ridge (the point of reference) during the beginning of a yawn.

The tongue must be free of unnecessary tension and ready to move as needed. Since it is involved in the formation of all vowels and many consonants, it is the most important articulator. To facilitate its work it should have a point of reference which it occupies for all vowels and to which it returns after forming consonants. The movements of the tongue must be quick, precise, and positive. When the tip of the tongue is resting on the lower gum ridge—the point of reference—the body of tongue lies behind it in a gentle arch. The location and height of the arch will change for different vowels, but the tip should remain in contact with the lower gum ridge.

The Articulation of Consonants. A consonant is a subordinate sound which is used with a vowel to form a syllable; it does not form the nucleus of a syllable, but can define its borders. Some are voiced; some are not. The only thing consonants have in common is that to a greater or lesser degree some restriction or obstruction is placed in the path of the sound, causing more or less conspicuous noise elements. The sounds cannot emerge as freely as vowels, although certain consonants do resemble vowels by nature.

In singing, the consonants often serve as sound-stoppers or tone-interrupters. They break up the almost continuous flow of vowels into recognizable units and help a listener organize the sounds into words. As an experiment, sing any familiar song and leave out all the consonants; sing only the vowel sounds. It is immediately obvious that without consonants the words are incomprehensible; verbal communication has been lost. This brings home the importance of consonant articulation and its difference in function from vowel articulation. This is the chief reason why many writers and teachers speak only of consonants under the heading of articulation and discuss vowels under such headings as timbre, resonance, or a separate section on vowels alone.

The two basic principles for the use of articulators are especially pertinent to the articulation of consonants: (1) all movements should be quick, precise, and positive, ending in a position that is free of unnecessary tension; (2) articulatory movements should be exaggerated. First of all, consonants must be quick and precise because to some degree they all are tone-interrupters and place some obstruction in the path of the tone. If you either anticipate or prolong the use of such an obstruction, it can harm the quality of the tone or even block it completely. The stop-plosives, in particular, must be executed quickly and cleanly. The nasal consonants do not require this kind of precision since they can be sustained, as in a hum, but except for special effects, it is still a good idea to put them on quickly to maintain the discipline needed for other more restricted sounds.

Consonants should be put on firmly for two reasons: (1) consonants are subordinate to vowels in sonority and do not carry as well, especially in a large auditorium; (2) firm consonants help the singer to establish and maintain good, solid tone production on the vowels. In other words, firm consonants help to supply the necessary energy for firm phonation. All articulatory movements need to be somewhat exaggerated when forming consonants in a large room so that the sonority level of the consonants will more closely conform to that of the vowels. This needs to be impressed on beginning singers, who often cannot comprehend how much articulatory energy it requires.

Consonants are identified by their location in a word. A consonant which is the first sound in a word is called an *initial,* one at the end of a word is a *final,* and one within a word is a *medial.* An initial consonant can make or break the vowel sound which follows it. If it is made too slowly, the tension in the articulators may carry over into the vowel. If it is weak, the vowel may be weak. If it is below pitch, there likely will be a scoop up to right pitch on the vowel. To avoid starting below pitch, think the initial consonant on the same pitch as the following consonant and give it sufficient energy to start firmly.

A medial consonant is not as crucial as an initial one, since the tone is already under way. However, it is important not to upset the flow of tone from the preceding vowel to the one which follows, so quickness, precision, and sufficient energy are still important. Finals must be made just as quickly as initials or medials, but with even more firmness, at least for the average singer. There is a widespread tendency among American singers to ignore or slight final consonants. Avoid this tendency by exaggerating all finals. Weak finals can keep an audience from understanding the words and can make a poor ending to an otherwise good sound, for they can let both the tone and the pitch sag.

One fact which is often overlooked in singing is that many consonants require two distinct movements of the articulators if they are to be heard at any distance. For example, consonants such as [d], [t], and [l] require that the tongue leave its point of reference on the lower gum ridge, touch the upper gum ridge, and then return to its resting place; this return movement must be vigorous, as if the tongue tip is rebounding from the upper ridge. Unfortunately, many singers become scriptural and "let the tongue cleave to the roof of the mouth," for the tongue remains high in the mouth or slowly makes its way back down. The tongue must return quickly to its point of reference on the lower gum ridge. If it returns slowly or is allowed to remain high in the mouth, it may interfere with the production of the following vowel.

[b], [p], and [m] are made by bringing the lips firmly together and then letting them bounce apart for the second movement. [f] and [v] are made by bringing the lower lip firmly against the upper teeth and then letting them bounce apart. It may be instructive to work your way through all the consonants trying to ascertain which ones require two movements, and then practicing them. The vigorous return movement is very important in initial and final consonants. In initials it clears the way for a good vowel sound; in finals it removes the habit of ignoring or slighting them, and helps a listener understand the words of the text.

The Articulation of Vowels. Vowels are voiced, unrestricted speech sounds which are capable of being sustained and thereby become the basic building material of vocal tone. Vocal tone is formed of a chain or stream of vowels; this stream is interrupted or deflected from time to time by consonants. The function of the vowel is to carry the tone; the function of the consonant is to break the tone up into distinct, comprehensible units.

The articulation of both vowels and consonants must be quick, precise, and positive, but there is an essential difference in the objective. The objective of quick, precise, and positive consonants is to break the tone up into distinct, comprehensible units *without* seriously interfering with the flow of vocal tone. The objective of quick, precise, and positive vowels is to establish and maintain a consistent channel through which the tone can flow without unnecessary variations of quality or quantity of sound. This legato connection of successive vowel sounds is at the heart of beautiful, artistic singing.

In speaking, vowels often appear to be in a constant state of flux because of the rate of speed at which speech moves. In singing, however, the vowels appear as successive "steady states" in which the posture of each vowel is established immediately and maintained as long as possible in the duration of the note value assigned to it.[12] One steadily produced vowel sound changes almost abruptly into the next one, using the intervening consonants, if any, as stepping-stones in the stream of tone. The inability to establish and maintain these steady states of vowel posture is an ever-present problem with inexperienced singers.

The stressed-unstressed principle of the English language is not applied to the same extent in singing that it is in speech. The use of shortened vowel forms and the *schwa* is more prevalent in speech because of the rate of speed at which it moves. In singing, the vowel sounds are more stretched out, and the use of unstressed sounds is not as acceptable to the ear as it is in more transitory speech patterns. The neutral *schwa* ([ə]) should be employed only when the tempo of the music causes the sung words to approach the speed of speech. When the tempo is slower, the vowel should not be neutralized, but should be raised or elevated closer to its original sound. A similar situation exists with unaccented syllables which are stressed by being placed on a long note or on a higher note; once again the vowel should be elevated from the neutral sound. Authorities differ as to just how much the neutral vowel should be raised in such cases, but a fairly safe rule is to select the vowel sound that is most frequently associated with the orthographic symbol used.

The word *Hallelujah* is a good illustration of the principle. In ordinary speech the second and fourth vowels tend to become neutral and are represented by the *schwa*. In the familiar "Hallelujah Chorus" of Handel, the first two appearances of the word are at too slow a tempo for the neutral sound to be acceptable. Most choral directors seem to prefer [ɛ] or [e] for the vowel in the second syllable (represented by the orthographic symbol "e" and [a] for the vowel in the last syllable (represented by "ah"). The tempo of the third and fourth appearances of the word is much more speechlike, and the normal stressed-unstressed pattern of speech tends to reassert itself. The point to be remembered is that in singing, anytime a vowel is stressed by virtue of duration or position, the neutral sound should not be used.

Expressions such as "pure vowels" or "vowel purity" are widely used in the teaching of singing. There is some question as to what vowel purity really is and how desirable it is. The expressions "phonemic integrity" and "phonemic identity" are more meaningful. It is common knowledge that the same singer will sing the same vowel different ways, depending on the pitch level at which it lies, the sounds which precede and follow it, the dynamic level desired, the emotion being expressed, the tempo, and so forth. The advocates of vowel purity seem to imply that there is only one true or pure form of the vowel and that it never varies. This is neither a practical nor an accurate assumption.

What is important is that the phonemic integrity of a vowel be maintained—that an [i] vowel, for example, will still retain its basic [i]-ness, its phonemic identity, despite all the variations it may undergo. Only when it crosses the border of a neighboring phoneme will it lose its identity and integrity. In fact, research seems to reveal that when a singer tries to reach the goal of a consistently produced voice which gives the illusion of uniform tone quality from top to bottom, he makes a lot of compromises with "vowel purity" and chooses versions of phonemes which make it easier to move smoothly from one vowel to another without any drastic changes in vocal technique. Conversely, the more one concentrates on singing each vowel only one way, the more likely it is that problem areas will develop because of this inflexibility.

To illustrate the point, perform the following experiment:

Sing the words "to me" on the same pitch making the first vowel as round and mellow as you can and the second as bright and ringing as you can; exaggerate the lip position of each. Notice the contrast. Now sing the two words making both vowels as round and mellow as the first one. Then sing them again making both as bright and ringing as the second vowel. Now try a fourth version in which each vowel seems to lend some of its character to the other and the transition is easy to accomplish. In this last version, if it is properly done, each vowel retains its phonemic identity, but the relation between them has been enhanced by a little compromise of purity.

As pitch rises and a singer reaches the upper portion of his modal voice, the matter of phonemic identity is pushed closer to its acceptable boundaries. By the time this portion of the range has been reached, the different vowels approach their phonemic borders that are closer to the [a] or [ʌ] vowels. In other words, they tend to become more central or neutral in character. The front vowels tend to migrate back toward the central ones, and the back vowels tend to move forward toward the central ones. One evidence of this is the fact that the two extremes of tongue position—[i] and [u]—can be sung with a much wider mouth opening in the upper voice, the type of mouth position which [a] requires. Singers who resist this tendency of the vowels to migrate and insist on singing "pure" vowels in the upper voice are likely to encounter vocal problems such as loss of quality, tight phonation, elevated larynx, and vocal strain.

Teachers and singers approach the matter of *vowel migration* or *vowel modification* in several ways. Some feel that you should recognize that vowels do modify in the upper voice and should encourage it by allowing more space, internally and externally, while still thinking of the basic vowel sound you are trying to produce. Others think you should encourage migration by thinking the vowel toward which you are modifying. In other words, since [i] modifies toward [ɪ], you should think toward [ɪ] when singing a word such as "me" in the upper voice. Still others feel that since the vowels migrate toward the center, all vowels should be colored with either "ah" or "uh" in the upper voice. These systems are not mutually exclusive, for all of them seem to work at different times with different students.

Ralph Appleman has done extensive research on vowel modification and has assigned a specific place of migration to each vowel in a very complex system.[13] Without in any way questioning the validity of the approach, it seems a little too involved to have a great deal of studio application for the average teacher. The important factor in all these systems is to retain enough phonemic identity for the word to be recognized.

Faults Related to Articulation

Articulation faults can be approached from two directions: (1) from the articulator involved and (2) from the speech sound involved. A speech sound might be faulty because an articulator is not doing its job, because the singer is not thinking the right sound, or from a combination of both factors. If the articulator is not doing its job because of an organic problem, the singer should be referred to a medical specialist for help; if it is a problem of function, the articulator will need to be trained to function properly. These functional faults of the articulators will be considered first.

Faults Related to the Articulators. Most of these faults have been mentioned in the section on the use of the articulators, but they will be listed again here and possible corrective procedures given. The customary division into hypofunction and hyperfunction will be used where it is applicable.

Hypofunctional use of the lips, failing to maintain enough tonus or mobility in them, occurs most frequently among beginning singers. Immobile or flaccid lips tend to muffle the sound and contribute to sloppy diction; the other articulators tend to be inactive, as well, for this kind of lethargy is seldom limited to just one area. A corrective procedure which is beneficial to one articulator probably will help the others. Try the following:

1. Ask him to sing in front of a mirror.
2. Request some kind of facial response—a slight smile, a feeling that the lips do not touch the teeth, think of something pleasant, etc.
3. Use exercises which require lip, jaw, or tongue action, asking for exaggerated movements. Say or sing "mah, mah, mah, mah, mah," then change to "bah" or "lah" or "yah," etc.
4. Alternate pulling the lips as far back as possible and pushing them

as far forward as possible, to increase their mobility.
5. Ask him to sing as if someone is reading his lips or a child is trying to understand him.

Hyperfunctional use of the lips, demanding too much tension or physical activity of them, takes two forms. In one the lips are locked into a rigid mold of some kind; in the other the lips are hyperactive. Locking the lips into a rigid mold also affects the resonance system and limits its capabilities. Some people pull the lips back into a forced smile (overbrightening the voice), some pull the lips against the teeth (darkening and muffling the voice), and others push the lips forward (tightening the back of the throat and hardening the sound). In each case the lips are robbed of their mobility because of tension, and the sound suffers, as well.

Corrective procedures might follow this sequence:
1. General exercises for relaxation of body tension.
2. Ask him to sing in front of a mirror; point out the rigid lip position; suggest relaxation of excess tension in lips.
3. Demonstrate adverse effect of that lip position on the sound.
4. Suggest the beginning of a yawn to relax throat, jaw, and lips.

Hyperactivity of the lips results from a misconception about good diction. The singer equates amount of motion with quickness and precision; he looks as if he is chewing or mouthing the words, with his lips and jaw moving on almost every speech sound, including those on which the tongue is the primary articulator.
1. Ask him to sing in front of a mirror; point out the excessive activity; suggest finer, more precise movements.
2. Demonstrate (caricature) adverse effects of hyperactivity.
3. Have him experiment with all vowels and consonants to see the minimum movement needed to form them.
4. Insist that he watch himself in the mirror until definite progress has been made.

Hyperfunctional use of the jaw occurs when it is forced down too far, pushed forward on certain sounds, or locked in one position. The jaw must be free from tension and free to move quickly at all times. If it is forced down too far or pulled back into the throat, it will press down on the larynx, inhibiting its action and creating tension. Some singers push the jaw forward for the forward vowels (especially [i]) and for higher pitches; this tends to elevate the larynx. Locking the jaw anywhere tends to lock the resonators, too.
1. General exercises for relaxation of body tension.
2. Specific exercises to relax head, neck, shoulders, and jaw.

3. Use mirror to point out the nature of the problem.
4. Demonstrate adverse effects.
5. Practice the beginning of a yawn and dropping jaw down and back for larger opening without tension.
6. Practice "yah, yah" for free jaw action, watching in mirror.

Hyperfunctional use of the tongue manifests itself (1) in movements which are too gross and too slow because excess tension is limiting its mobility, and (2) in the tongue being pulled back into the throat, pushed forward against the teeth, or held elevated in the mouth. The tongue is involved in all vowels and many of the consonants, so it is essential that it be free to move quickly, precisely, and positively. Too much tension or putting it in the wrong position robs it of that ability. If it is not functioning properly, it must be brought under conscious control and trained to do so.

1. Use mirror to point out specific tongue fault. If possible, demonstrate both fault and correct action.
2. Explain significance of the point of reference and assign exercises to help student acquire it.
3. Work for tongue agility with exercises incorporating dental and alveolar consonants—such as [l], [d], [n], and [t].
4. If tongue does not respond well, use specific tongue exercises:
    (1) protrude tongue as far as possible, then retract tongue as far as possible alternately, slowly at first but then faster and faster;
    (2) run the tip of the tongue smoothly around the inner surface of the lips several times clockwise and then counterclockwise;
    (3) try to touch your nose and your chin alternately with the tip of your tongue;
    (4) lay your tongue out over your lower lip and vocalize on "ah"; persist until you can do so without tongue trying to pull back into your mouth, quivering, or constantly trying to change its shape.
5. Select songs that require fast articulatory movements.

Faulty Speech Sounds. Faulty speech sounds can result from the articulators not functioning properly, or from the lack of a proper concept of the sounds. People who have normally functioning articulators, and make some sounds quite acceptably, often have problems with other sounds without even being aware of it. Children pick up their sounds by ear from their parents, playmates, and teachers. If the model is a poor one, or if the child simply does not hear some sounds correctly, he may produce faulty sounds all of his life if the faults are not pointed out to him. It is not the purpose of this discussion to make an exhaustive survey of all possible speech sounds and their aberrations. The purpose is to suggest some basic corrective procedures which may be applied to consonants and to vowels. The only prerequisite is that the teacher must be able to discriminate between correct and faulty speech sounds. Corrective procedure for faulty consonants:

1. Isolate and identify the faulty sound; demonstrate correct sound.
2. Point out its identifying characteristics: voiced or voiceless; continuant, stop, or glide; nasal, fricative, plosive, etc.; dental, velar, bilabial, etc.
3. Explain how correct sound differs from faulty sound and which specific articulators are involved in both.
4. Establish a practice routine which will implement and encourage the establishment of a new set of reflexes to replace the previous incorrect ones.
5. Assign word drills from speech texts featuring the problem sound in various locations within the word—initial, medial, and final.
6. Use audiovisuals for reinforcement—practice tapes, records, a mirror, etc.

With some minor alterations the same procedure can be used for faulty vowels:

1. Isolate and identify the faulty vowel; demonstrate correct one.
2. Point out its identifying characteristics: front, central, or back; tense or lax; primary or secondary; long or short, etc.
3. Explain how correct sound differs from the faulty one; is the tongue movement different? the lip movement?
4. Use a vowel chart or word list showing the sequence of vowels; select familiar words to illustrate correct vowel and faulty one. (See list following.)
5. Establish a practice routine which will implement and encourage the establishment of a new set of reflexes to replace the old ones.
6. Assign vocalises or songs which make prominent use of the desired new vowel sound.
7. Use audiovisuals for reinforcement.
8. Once the student has established the new phoneme, he may need to be guided to a more discriminating choice of sounds within that phoneme.

The vowel chart which follows can be used to help the student discriminate between vowel sounds. The sequence of sounds from right to left follows the tongue movements from the front of the mouth to the back, with the central vowels listed above. The key words, numbers, and phonetic symbols may be used to point out the correct and incorrect sounds: for example, "You are saying no. 9 in place of no. 10; you are saying the sound in *bawl* instead of the one on *boat*; you are saying [ɔ] when it should be [o]."

[ɝ] 17 bird
[ɜ] 16 bird (silent r)
[ɚ] 15 butter
[ə] 14 bonus
[ʌ] 13 but

[i]	[ɪ]	[eɪ]	[ɛ]	[æ]	[a]	[ɑ]	[ɒ]	[ɔ]	[o]	[ʊ]	[u]
1	2	3	4	5	6	7	8	9	10	11	12
beet	bit	bait	bet	bat	by*	balm	bottom	bawl	boat	book	boot

*This is the so-called "French ah" and is represented by only the first element of the diphthong without saying the offglide: [baɪ].

Disconnected Sounds. Although it is not customary to consider the lack of good legato in singing an articulatory fault, that is actually what it is. It results from the failure to maintain the "steady state" of each vowel sound until the almost abrupt transition into the next one. There is a simple technique which is quite effective in teaching students how to establish and maintain a good legato.

1. Have the student sing an entire song on one vowel sound, breathing at the usual phrases but otherwise keeping up an absolutely continuous tone within each phrase, moving or even sliding smoothly from tone to tone without any bumps or hitches.
2. When the student can manage Step 1 acceptably, have him sing the same song using all the correct vowels, but no consonants, and the same smooth or sliding legato.
3. When the student can manage Step 2 acceptably, let him sing the actual text of the song, making every effort to maintain the same effortless legato of the first two steps. This drill puts the vowel and consonant in their proper perspective by function—the vowel carrying the tone and the consonant making it intelligible.

Notes

1. Readers are referred to Wise, *Applied Phonetics*, and Virgil A. Anderson, *Training the Singing Voice*, 2nd ed. (New York: Oxford University Press, 1961).

2. Be certain that you are making the actual consonant sound and not a vowelized version, such as "bee" for b, or "kay" for k. To isolate the [k] sound, say the word "back" and delay the final sound.

3. Greene, *The Voice*, p. 71.

4. Wise, *Applied Phonetics*, p. 53.

5. Wise, *Applied Phonetics*, p. 61.

6. Wise, *Applied Phonetics*, p. 13.

7. Wise, p. 115.

8. Wise, *Applied Phonetics*, pp. 85-86.

9. For an extended coverage of acoustical findings as to vowel formants, see Vennard, *Singing*, pp. 127-141.

10. Wise, *Applied Phonetics*, pp. 75-77.

11. Vennard, *Singing*, p. 110.

12. William Vennard and James Irwin, "Speech and Song Compared in Sonograms," *The NATS Bulletin* 23 (December/1966):18-23.

13. Ralph Appleman, *The Science of Vocal Pedagogy* (Bloomington: Indiana University Press, 1967), pp. 220ff.

10
The Speaking Voice

COMPARISON OF SPEAKING AND SINGING

The basic mechanism for speaking and singing is the same, and the physical processes involved are essentially the same. Speaking and singing share the same breathing apparatus, the same larynx, the same resonators, and the same articulators. There are obvious differences, for speech and song do not sound alike, but these are differences in degree or extent of usage. Persons who are skilled at both speaking and singing can pass from one to the other with apparent ease; this is a necessary skill in opera and musical comedy, where the medium shifts back and forth between singing and spoken dialogue with little or no pause. Regardless of the skill of the singer-actor, it is an easy matter to ascertain which medium is being used, for there are significant differences.

As a general rule, speech moves at a faster rate. In singing, the vowel sounds are much more extended and even the consonants last longer than in speech.[1] In one sense, singing is stretched-out or prolonged speech. Time yourself and you will discover that it takes about twice as long to sing a stanza of "America" as it does to speak it. Of course, this will vary with the character and tempo of the song.

Normal speech lies in a much more restricted range of pitches than singing. It usually does not exceed a perfect fourth or fifth, whereas an untrained singer is asked to sing about a twelfth and the trained singer at least two octaves. Because of this wider range, the average pitch level of singing is higher than that of speech. Singing has been called raised or elevated speech.

Because of this faster rate and restricted range, speech tends to be in a continual state of flux, with constant readjustment of the articulators and resonators. Vennard and Irwin state:

> Speech sounds are constantly changing, forming diphthongs and triphthongs. Their sonagram appears mottled. Song is characterized by "steady states" of sound that look as

if they were stroked on smoothly with a wide brush, or perhaps a roller that contains the vibrato pattern.[2]

They also found that for a person speaking and singing the same text at what was considered to be a normal dynamic level for an auditorium, the sung version was ten decibels louder than the spoken one. Another significant difference was in the distribution of sound energy. In the sung vowels the formants were strongly marked, being relatively few in number with clear spaces between them, whereas the spoken vowels had more formants and they were considerably weaker. It was pointed out that such a spoken tone would be considered "diffused" or "spread" in a singing voice.[2]

One difference which has already been pointed out in the preceding chapter is that speech makes more use of neutral, unstressed vowel sounds than singing does; this is because the slower tempo and elevated pitch of song often place stress on syllables that are not stressed in ordinary speech. Another difference is that a speaker does not need the breath capacity and control required by a singer; the faster rate brings him to logical breathing places much more often, and the pitch level of speech does not make as many demands on the support mechanism. And Greene states:

> Articulation of the consonants in singing must be somewhat exaggerated, while vowel articulation and resonance must be adapted to the pitch of the laryngeal note and often has little resemblance to speech articulation. . . . Singing requires a more exacting performance in every department than does speech.[3]

Good speech can be considered as one foundation of good singing, despite this rather extensive list of differences. Some teachers believe that students should be taught how to speak well before they are taught how to sing. It is true that many of the basic principles of singing (especially those related to posture, breathing, and articulation) can be learned while speaking at a comfortable pitch level.

SPEECH LEVEL

In writings about the speaking voice, two terms appear rather frequently— *habitual pitch level* and *optimal pitch level.* Habitual pitch level is the limited pitch range within which a person customarily expresses himself for everyday speech. Optimal (or optimum) pitch level is the pitch range within which a person can achieve the best quality and quantity of sound for the least expenditure of effort. Normal speech tends to lie within a range of a perfect fourth or fifth, except for more excited utterances, which may exceed the range of an octave, particularly in female voices.

There is some evidence that the optimal pitch level is closely related to the fundamental frequency of an individual's resonance system. According to Margaret Greene:

> The range of vocal pitch . . . must be attuned to the resonance pitch of the individual's total resonator system; a voice pitched too high or too low cannot benefit to full advantage from its resonator. The supraglottic resonators being in the main muscular and moveable structures must be voluntarily controlled to produce conditions of optimal resonance either by varying degrees of tension in their walls, or by alterations in the size of their orifices and cavities during the articulatory movements.[4]

It is generally agreed among speech authorities that habitually speaking too far above or below your optimal pitch level can result in vocal problems. When the habitual and optimal pitch levels coincide, it is considered to be an ideal situation. Cooper says:

> If optimal and habitual pitch levels are identical, vocal misuse does not occur. If the habitual pitch differs from the optimal pitch, vocal misuse prevails. Most individuals do not utilize the optimal pitch range as their habitual pitch range.[5]

There is no such general agreement concerning whether speaking too high or too low is more prevalent or more damaging. Anderson says that habitual use of a pitch level that is too high may produce vocal nodules,[6] a sentiment that is expressed by a number of writers. Vocal fatigue, chronic hoarseness, and various other dysphonias are said to be caused by speaking at too high a pitch. Cooper takes the other point of view with the categorical statement, "The most frequent form of vocal misuse involving pitch is the use of too low a habitual pitch."[7] He cites other writers who support this position. At least there is agreement that speaking habitually at either extreme can be damaging.

Perhaps part of this difference of opinion can arise from the type of person surveying the field and from the time when the vocal problem is encountered. Most of the voices encountered by a speech teacher or a teacher of singing will be voices that are not receiving maximum good usage but are not classified as dysphonic voices; they are the voices of people who want to learn to use them better. The voices encountered by laryngologists and speech therapists, however, are mostly dysphonic ones, a good portion of which may have been badly abused. According to Emil Froeschels' hypofunction and hyperfunction categories, a hyperfunctional voice, if the hyperfunction is severe enough, will end up losing its ability to function—it will become hypofunctional. Among the symptoms of this are huskiness, hoarseness, thickening of the cords, bowing of the cords, and lowering of pitch. Perhaps this is why a specialist would see so many patients with obvious lowering of pitch. The fact that a patient is speaking on too low a pitch could be a result of vocal abuse, or perhaps it could be a cause.

Finding the Habitual Pitch Level

It is relatively easy for a teacher to determine what a student's habitual pitch level is by identifying one particular pitch while he is speaking. This pitch is not *the* habitual pitch; rather, it is one of a limited range of pitches on which he talks. Habitual pitch *area* might be a better term. If possible, it is best not to tell the student what you are about to do; he may have some preconceptions about where he *should* talk. Just ask him to follow this routine:

1. Ask him (or her) to pronounce these nonsense syllables several times in his normal conversational voice: bah, bay, bee, boh, boo. Let him repeat them until he is comfortable with the sequence of sounds and seems to be natural.
2. Ask him to repeat the sequence two more times, stopping on "bee" the second time through and holding it.
3. As he sustains "bee," locate the pitch on the piano. (This gets quite easy after you have done it a few times.)
4. This note is near the center of his habitual pitch level; he probably covers one or two whole steps on either side of this note in everyday conversation.[8]

Finding the Optimal Pitch Level

There is little agreement as to the best method for determining optimal pitch. Unfortunately, the results obtained by some of the approaches may vary as much as a fourth or fifth, which is far too great a margin of error. Ultimately, the choice is a subjective one on the part of the teacher, since there are few objective criteria, but there are some guidelines to that choice. First of all, it may be assumed that, by definition, when the optimal pitch level is located, it ought to sound better than other choices. Greene says, "When the optimal pitch is sounded the voice leaps into prominence, being so much more rich and resonant that there is no mistaking its rightness."[9] She indicates that this resonance change is far more striking in strained than normal voices; this means that the optimal pitch may not be as obvious in the teaching studio, but it still should sound better than other choices.

Second, the student must understand that optimal pitch level refers to an area of his voice, not to one specific pitch. Assuming that it is a fixed pitch can lead to artificiality and monotony. It is granted that the area does center on one pitch, but speech inflections should move freely above and below that center.

Third, the student who has not yet learned to sing freely in the middle of his range may give misleading clues concerning his optimal pitch level. In other words, vocal problems can camouflage optimal pitch. Avoid making a firm decision in such cases until more freedom of production has been achieved.

Several approaches to finding the optimal pitch suggest singing up and down the scale on a vowel which the student finds easy to vocalize on (usually [u], [ɔ], or [o]) while the teacher listens for clues from the resonance or dynamic level of the sound. Others suggest speaking a set expression or sentence on each tone of an ascending and descending scale while the teacher makes value judgments about the most effective pitch location.

Some approaches are related to the overall compass of the voice and attempt to place the optimal pitch level at a set point in it. One problem with these approaches is that they seldom make it clear whether falsetto is included in the total range or not, or whether all possible notes in modal voice are included or just those which a singer would consider usable notes. Cooper warns, "Any method which uses the total pitch range, or a certain number of notes from the bottom of the pitch range, may have the individual speaking at the top of his pitch range or at too high a level."[10] Also, there are large variations in the total ranges of trained and untrained singers.

Some systems are based on what is termed *basal pitch*. This is a widely used approach, but requires some caution in application. Basal pitch has been defined as the lowest pitch on which a person can sustain utterance. As the expression is used, it is not always clear whether this refers to the lowest pitch on which "good" sound can be sustained or the lowest on which any kind of sound can be made; the choice of meanings can mean the difference of a third or fourth in the pitch level. It also is true that basal pitch may vary from one to three half-steps at different times of the day.

The writer believes that there is a strong relation between the lowest *good* singing note and the lower limits of optimal pitch. Many singers can vocalize a third or fourth below the lowest tone that they would feel comfortable singing in public. These lower notes are usually weaker in dynamic level, poorer in quality, and less dependable than the lowest good singing note. Some singers, usually higher voices, can only vocalize one or two notes below their lowest good singing note; for this reason, it is not safe to make a blanket rule stating that the lowest good note is always a certain distance above the lowest possible note. It is safe to say, however, that a singer's lowest good singing note often coincides with the lower limits of his optimal pitch level, and his best speaking range starts around that note and extends upward for a perfect fourth or fifth. Here are some applications of this principle to different voice classifications:

1. A bass enjoys singing low F's (just below the bass staff) in public; on a clear day he can growl down to a low C but finds these notes weak and unreliable. His best speaking range is likely from this low F to c, with the *average* speaking pitch in this optimal range around A-flat or A.

2. A baritone feels comfortable singing as low as A-flat, but no lower; he usually can vocalize down to an F or occasionally an E, but has never been able to count on these notes. His best speaking range is likely from about A-flat up to d-flat or e-flat. The average level of his optimal pitch is about B or c.

3. A tenor sings down to bass clef c when he has to, but is not too happy about it. Sometimes he can find a breathy B or B-flat, but not very often. His best speaking range probably is from d-flat up to about g-flat, with the optimal pitch around e. When he answers the telephone, people sometimes say, "Mrs. Doakes, is your husband home?"

Similar applications can be made to the contralto, mezzo-soprano, and soprano voices at a pitch level approximately one octave higher. None of the suggested notes should be considered as fixed standards for any particular voice classification; singers exhibit too many individual differences. It will become obvious that the lower limits of the contralto voice may duplicate the upper limits of the tenor's speaking voice. If the tenor's voice is high enough, it is likely that he may be mistaken for a woman when talking on the telephone.

If the principle of finding a singer's lowest good note is used judiciously as an approach to finding the optimal pitch level, by placing the lower limit of the best speaking range on that note and placing the upper limit a fourth or fifth higher, the writer believes it to be safe, practical, and effective for use with "normal" voices. Persons with dysphonic voices should be referred to medical specialists for evaluation and treatment. The next three methods for finding the optimal pitch level are among those employed by specialists working with dysphonic voices, but may also prove effective with normal ones.

> The hands should be placed lightly over the face and nose while humming so that vibrations may be felt beneath the fingers. The vibrations become much stronger when the optimum pitch is reached. The patient should feel the therapist's face and then his own. [11]

> Humming with the hands pressed over the ears which amplifies the voice is also a useful device for determining the best vocal range, as the harmonics buzz in the ears and are felt in the jaw under the palms. [11]

> The patient is simply asked to say "um-hum" using a rising inflection with the lips closed, as though he were spontaneously and sincerely agreeing with what was just said. It is vital to underscore the fact that this "um-hum" be spontaneous and sincere. . . . A natural "um-hum" which is easy and gentle, will be felt around the sides and lower portion of the nose and around the lips. . . . The therapist must guide the patient in producing a natural and not a forced "um-hum." The optimal pitch level is clearly evident when the patient follows this procedure in most cases. [12]

COMMON SPEECH FAULTS[13]

Speech faults may be grouped together under six headings: articulation, breathing and support, pitch, quality, quantity, and rate. Three of these groups—faults of articulation, breathing and support, and quality—have been discussed in previous chapters and will not be repeated here, since there are no significant differences in the speech approach. The other three—faults of pitch, quantity, and rate—occur with such frequency in the general public and in beginning students of both singing and speech that they will be considered separately. Only the more common faults will be discussed.

Faults Related to Pitch

There are four common faults related to pitch: (1) speaking at too high a pitch level; (2) speaking at too low a pitch level; (3) speaking in too restricted a range; and (4) speaking in stereotyped pitch patterns.

Aside from persons who have been trained to do so, there are remarkably few people in this country who speak at the optimal pitch level. The tonal models presented to many children are such that they adopt wrong levels of pitch at an early age without being aware they have done so. With the obvious exception of those people who have severe functional, organic, or pathological vocal problems, this writer is convinced that the majority of the general public speak at too high a pitch level. He has examined the speaking level of several hundred young adults over a period of about twenty-five years (these were students planning to enter professions which require extensive use of the voice) and has reached the following conclusions: less than one in four of them was using the optimal pitch level; almost two out of three were using too high a pitch level; and less than one in ten was using too low a pitch level. It should be pointed out again that these were what might be considered "normal" voices, drawn from all sections of the country and typical of American speech patterns. The small number of truly dysphonic voices encountered were referred to a laryngologist. There is a distinction between the average voice that is not being used with maximum effectiveness and one that is so impaired that it cannot function properly.

When the speech level is too high, a person's voice tends to sound (1) breathy and immature, or (2) tight and penetrating, perhaps with accompanying nasal twang.[14] When the speech level is too low, a person's voice tends to sound (1) growly or gravelly, or (2) hollow and sepulchral, as if it is down in a well. In addition, the pitch and dynamic level may drop off so much at the end of phrases that the sound is almost inaudible.[15] For either fault it is essential to establish a new tonal model, explain the advantages of optimal pitch, try to determine the optimal level, and set up a practice routine to help establish its use.

Many people who use too high a speech level actually avoid their best level because they are afraid it will sound "put-on" or artificial. There are some people, of course, who do go too far and sound pompous or too "cultivated," but the great majority do not go far enough in trying to have a rich, resonant, ringing sound. The following comments might be helpful to a person seeking to adopt a new speech level.

It is important to find your optimal pitch level and make use of it. At its optimal level your voice will have its best tone quality, good carrying power, and its greatest endurance.

If your speech level is too high, work for a lower, richer, deeper-feeling sound with lots of vibration in your upper chest and head. Don't be afraid of sounding affected; we will tape-record your voice both before and after you try to lower it. Your new speech level will not feel natural to you at first and it may not sound natural until you become used to it, but the tape recording will let you know what it sounds like to other people. Concentrate on the kind of sound you are trying to make (deeper, richer, rounder, more resonant, etc.) instead of trying to zero in on one pitch. Don't *force* your voice down; *let* it down.

If your speech level is too low, work for the feeling that your sound is being made in your head, not in your throat, and that your articulatory movements are being made in the very front of your mouth. Try to feel more vibration in the hard palate and in the nasal cavity. Make a humming sound and feel where the vibration takes place; now try to feel your speech sound make vibrations in the same area, as if the sound is actually starting there. Imagine that your voice is higher and more forward than it used to be, but don't try to put it on any particular pitch.

The chief results of speaking in too limited a speech range are monotony and lack of expressiveness.[16] The speaker must be made aware that the voice should inflect up and down within the range of about a perfect fifth. He should be assigned poems or song texts to be recited from memory, interpretive readings or character parts from plays, and exercises where he has to portray different emotions by variations in his tone quality and pitch level. It is not enough for a voice to be in the optimal pitch area; it must also use the entire area expressively and with good tone quality.

The same type of application can be made to stereotyped pitch patterns, such as the "ministerial groan," or the habit of starting each phrase on a high pitch and then dropping, and various other singsong types. The speaker must be made aware of such mannerisms and encouraged to adopt a new tonal image.[17]

Faults Related to Quantity

There are three common faults related to quantity of sound: (1) speaking too softly, (2) speaking too loudly, and (3) speaking with too much variation of force. Speaking too softly is far more prevalent in the general populace than are the other two. There are many reasons for this—such as fear of embarrassment, inhibition, wrong tonal models, inability to hear your own voice (assuming your voice is louder than it really is), and the desire to appear genteel, modest, ladylike, unassuming, or nonpushy, etc. Speaking too loudly is much less common, but is much more offensive to the average listener. Among the usual causes are hearing loss, a noisy environment in your job, wrong tonal models, inability to hear yourself (assuming your voice is softer than it really is), extroversion, and the desire to be noticed, to command respect, or to dominate a situation.

It is easy to find out if you talk too softly. Do people frequently ask you to repeat something, lean toward you when you say something, or seem to be studying your face intently? If so, you speak too softly or mumble or both of the above. To break this habit, you must adopt a new tonal image. Try to speak *at all times* with a fuller, more resonant sound. Keep reminding yourself constantly to talk louder. If you do not, old reflexes will take over and you will drop back to the old dynamic level. Practice speaking in large rooms such as an auditorium; imagine you are speaking to someone on the last row. Ask your friends to let you know (kindly) when you are reverting to your old habits.

A similar approach can be worked out for the person who speaks too loudly. Help him to adopt a new tonal image by such comments as, "Pretend you are talking to a little baby," "Approach all conversations as if the words are highly confidential," or "Imagine you are saying sweet nothings to your true love." In addition to reminding himself not to talk so loudly, he must concentrate on using less physical energy and on general physical relaxation.

The habit of speaking with too much variation of force is usually a learned reflex by a person who has concentrated on making himself heard and understood by sheer physical effort.[18] He has made such an effort to bring out important words and syllables that he has formed the habit of jerking in strongly on his abdominal muscles for every important accent. This causes the vocal energy to come in spurts or surges, which is a distracting mannerism and can be vocally fatiguing. This speaker needs a new concept of the use of the support mechanism that will stabilize it and cut down on the hyperfunctional use. (See the chapter on breathing and support.) He needs to establish a legato flow of sound and to realize that force is not the only means of stressing words; they can also be stressed by pitch level (position) and duration.

Faults Related to Rate

There are three common faults related to rate: (1) speaking too fast, (2) speaking too slowly, and (3) speaking with too much variation of rate. As a general rule, people who talk at too high a pitch level tend to talk too fast as well, and those who talk at too low a pitch level often talk quite slowly. Neither extreme of rate is harmful to the voice unless there are other mitigating factors present, but all disturbances of rate can be distracting to the listener and therefore should be corrected. Typical examples of too much variation of rate include speakers who rush through opening phrases or groups of unimportant words or syllables to land triumphantly on the important ones (known as telescoping a phrase) and others who leave you hanging interminably by unexpected pauses, hesitations, and groping for words. The best approach to all rate problems is to record the speaker, call attention to the nature of the problem, and set up a practice routine designed to establish the new pattern. Persons who speak too fast or who telescope phrases need to spend more time on their vowel sounds, almost as if they are singing; they must keep reminding themselves to be "s l o w" and deliberate until the new speed has become established. Persons who talk too slowly must concentrate on quick, precise, and positive movements of the articulators, especially on the consonants, and must remind themselves to keep moving along. For all rate disturbances, but especially those associated with too much variation of rate, exercises with a metronome can be very helpful. Ask the speaker to put one syllable on each tick of the metronome until the desired rate can be maintained; then cut off the metronome and allow natural word rhythms to be reestablished.

Notes

1. Vennard and Irwin, "Speech and Song Compared . . . " p. 20.
2. Vennard and Irwin, p. 22.
3. Greene, p. 80.
4. Greene, p. 69-70.
5. Cooper, p. 16.
6. Anderson, p. 81.
7. Cooper, p. 16.
8. This method was adapted from Robert Lawrence Weer, *Your Voice* (Los Angeles: By the Author, 1948), p. 64.
9. Greene, p. 171.
10. Cooper, p. 68.
11. Green, p. 171.
12. Cooper, p. 74.
13. For detailed coverage see the excellent text by Virgil Anderson, *Training the Speaking Voice.*
14. Listen to band 9 of the cassette tape.
15. Listen to band 10 of the cassette tape.
16. Listen to band 11 of the cassette tape.
17. A very helpful book for persons who need to read or speak more expressively is Jessica S. Driver, *Speak for Yourself,* rev. ed. (New York: Harper, 1956).
18. Listen to band 12 of the cassette tape.

11
Coordination

Introduction

In chapter after chapter of this book you have encountered some version of the statement, "More about this later." There are two reasons for these frequent appearances. First of all, it is difficult to discuss one of the processes involved in the act of singing without making reference to another. Phonation comes into its true perspective only when it is connected with respiration; the articulators affect resonance; the resonators affect the vocal cords; the vocal cords affect breath control; and so it goes. In discussing one aspect of the vocal art, you mention its connection with other aspects and indicate that when time permits you will cover those related areas more fully. Hence, the ubiquitous conversation stopper, "More about this later."

In the second place, singing is an integrated, coordinated act. The various technical areas and processes must be broken down into their component parts, so that they may be studied and their individual functions understood. This is what happens in the teaching studio; some particular phase of the singer's technique needs attention or development, so it is singled out for intensive work. For a while this facet of the vocal art dominates discussion, practice, and evaluative listening in the studio, almost to the exclusion of everything else. Eventually this technical problem is solved, and both teacher and student turn their attention back to the whole process of singing (at least until the next crisis arises!). However, some areas of the art are so much the result of coordinated functions that it is hard to discuss them under one of the traditional headings—respiration, phonation, resonation, or articulation. Consistent tone quality, range extension, and vibrato all depend on coordinated functions. Hence, they were postponed to the last chapter, and the remark was made frequently, "More about this later."

DEVELOPING THE VOICE

Once the student has become aware of the physical processes that make up the singing act and of how they function, he begins the task of trying to coordinate them. Inevitably he will become more concerned with one area of technique than another. The various processes may progress at different rates, with a resulting imbalance or lack of coordination. The areas of vocal technique which seem to depend most strongly on the student's ability to coordinate various functions are (1) extending the vocal range to its maximum potential, (2) developing consistent vocal production (tone quality) throughout that range, (3) developing flexibility and agility, and (4) achieving a balanced vibrato. The first three areas will be considered under the general heading just given—Developing the Voice. The vibrato will be treated in a separate section.

Exercising the Voice

Despite all the material you may read about natural singing, singing is not a natural process; it is a highly skilled art and requires highly developed muscle reflexes. Singing does not demand much muscle strength, but it does call for a high degree of muscle coordination. Just like the muscles needed for any sport, the muscles needed for singing can be trained effectively through a planned program of exercise. Vocal development is the result of careful and systematic practice of both songs and vocal exercises. You must learn to exercise your voice in an intelligent manner, not by merely repeating rote vocalises but by thinking constantly about the kind of sound you should be making and the sensations you feel.

There are several purposes for vocal exercises: warming up the voice, extending the range, "lining up" the voice horizontally and vertically, acquiring vocal technique (such as legato, staccato, control of dynamics, rapid figurations, learning to sing wide intervals), and correcting vocal faults.

It is a good idea to warm up your voice gradually before you try to sing anything that is very demanding. A pitcher knows better than to throw a fast ball before a number of warm-up throws, and all athletes know what lack of warm-up can do to their efforts; yet many singers will start belting high notes with hardly any exercise. Warm-up exercises should start in the most comfortable part of your range. Avoid any high singing until your voice is thoroughly warmed up; it is better to start with exercises of limited range and then move to wider and wider ones as the voice becomes more responsive.

Plan a warm-up routine which will include (1) sounds that require activation of the jaw, lips, tongue and soft palate—such as yah, bah, mah, lah, ding, hung-gah, etc.; and (2) sounds that will stimulate vibration in the head and chest—such as ding, mum, boom, noh, voom, none, one, zoom, or a simple hum. (These sounds which can stimulate vibration are referred to as resonance-inducing speech sounds.) The following sequence of events is recommended:

1. General bending and stretching body exercises designed to loosen and tone the muscles.

2. Particular exercises designed to release tension in the shoulders, neck, and throat.

3. Descending five-note exercises (5-4-3-2-1 in the major scale) designed to activate the articulators and induce resonance, starting on the midnote of your range and moving progressively downward by half-steps. (If you are a higher voice and have a usable range from B-flat up to B-flat two octaves higher, start on your middle B-flat and do the five-note pattern down to E-flat; then do it from A down to D, etc.)

   Continue downward easily until you have reached the lowest note you can sing without forcing; then return to the middle B-flat and start descending five-note patterns again, but this time work your way progressively upward by half-steps. Whenever the highest note in the pattern begins to feel strained, do not go any higher.

4. Arpeggiated exercises which start fairly low in the total range and extend upward, starting with ones of fairly limited range and then moving to wider ones. (A good sequence might be (1) an exercise which does not exceed a fifth, (2) one that does not exceed an octave, (3) a tenth, and (4) a twelfth.)

It is important that the teacher and/or student be able to improvise vocal exercises on the spot. No one vocalise is a magical formula for vocal success, although some people may leave that impression. Every vocal exercise should have a specific purpose for a particular student.[1] In supervising students who are practice teaching, the writer has observed that student teachers tend to use the identical vocalises used by their own teachers, without giving any attention to the purpose for which the vocalises were originally used or to the specific problems of their second-generation students. A favorite stratagem is to stop the student teacher in mid-vocalise and inquire with an innocent air, "Why are you using that particular exercise?" The usual response is a blank stare. Some exercises are so traditional that they are passed on from generation to generation with no thought given to their original purpose. If an exercise is not helping a certain student, it should be discontinued or revised on the spot; perhaps a change of vowel or consonant, a different sequence of pitches or speech sounds, staccato instead of legato, fast instead of slow—experiment until some improvement can be detected. If nothing works, discard it; no vocalise is sacred, despite all the traditions.

There is no need for the writer to fill these pages with his favorite exercises for acquiring agility, flexibility, legato, staccato, high notes, or low notes. There are literally hundreds of vocalises in print.[2] The important thing is for the individual teacher to select from various sources or to design vocal exercises which have a specific purpose for a particular student. A long-distance runner is not trained the same way as a sprinter, and all long-distance people are not trained the same way. Any system of vocal exercise should allow for individual needs and differences.

Songs or sections of songs can be used effectively for the same purposes as vocalises—the so-called "song approach"—but it requires much more time and discrimination on the part of the teacher. The chief problem with its use is that some technical areas tend to be overlooked or slighted. It must be admitted that some students make more vocal progress through songs than they ever do with vocalises, which comes back to the matter of allowing for individual differences.

Extending the Range

An important goal of vocal development is to learn to sing to the natural limits of your vocal range without any obvious or distracting changes of quality and technique. This calls for the coordinated functioning of all the physical processes involved in singing, for it is not just a matter of laryngeal action, breath support, resonance adjustment, or articulatory movements, but a combination of all these factors working together. The first step in coordinating these processes is to establish good vocal habits in the most comfortable tessitura of the voice. The second step is to begin trying to extend the area in which you can sing well, opening up the range in both directions with freely produced and consistent tone quality.

There are three factors which significantly affect the ability to sing higher or lower: (1) energy, (2) space, and (3) depth. These three factors can be expressed in three basic rules:

1. As you sing higher, you must use more energy; as you sing lower, you use less.
2. As you sing higher, you must use more space; as you sing lower, you use less.
3. As you sing higher, you must use more depth; as you sing lower, you use less.

In other words, as you sing from the bottom of your voice to the top, there should be a continuum of carefully graduated changes in the amount of energy, space, and depth being used, with all of these factors being increased by small increments. When you sing from the top to the bottom, the process is reversed, with all the factors decreasing by small increments. It has already been recognized that there are progressive changes in the vocal cords as pitch rises; the length, thickness, and tension of the cords changes, with the cords growing longer, thinner, and tenser. Those factors are not under conscious control, but energy, space, and depth are.

The *first rule* is that as you sing higher, you must use more energy. In this usage, the word *energy* has several connotations. It refers to the total response of the body to the making of sound. It refers to a dynamic relationship between the breathing-in muscles and the breathing-out muscles—the support mechanism. It refers to the amount of breath pressure delivered to the vocal cords and their resistance to that pressure, and it refers to the dynamic level of the sound.

As you sing up a scale, each tone requires a little more energy than the one just below it. The total body response is increased; the support mechanism increases its output; more breath pressure is delivered to more resistive vocal cords; and the sound gets louder, for there is a built-in crescendo as you sing up a scale. All of this is a complex explanation of a simple fact—it takes more energy as you get higher.

Psychologically it is better to approach this increase of energy as being supplied by your whole body or else to think that you are gradually getting louder. If you think too much about the support mechanism or breath pressure, you may end up exerting too much local effort. The main source of more energy in singing actually is increased breath support, but you should not try to achieve it by pulling in on the upper abdomen. You should use energy from your whole body, not from just one place. It is best to avoid any kind of local effort in singing, so think of singing more energetically with your whole body.

For singing down a scale, the reverse is true. There gradually is less body involvement, less support, less breath pressure, and the sound gets softer. This is more difficult for many people, for it often is harder to let go of tension in small increments than it is to add it gradually, but it still should be mastered.

The *second rule* is that as you sing higher, you must use more space. This added space is needed for several reasons. Placing a larger aperture on a resonator will cause it to resonate a higher frequency. Adding space will help maintain the proper laryngeal position. Adding space will help to keep the upper voice from whitening. Adding space can help in vowel modification in the upper voice. As you sing up a scale, your mouth should gradually open wider. On the same vowel, each tone of the scale requires a little more space than the one just below it. In an actual song, singing up from a more open vowel, such as [a], to a more closed one, such as [i], the rule will not apply, for obvious reasons.

As has been previously stated, there are two sources of more space in singing: one is to increase the mouth opening; the other is to create internal space in the back of the mouth. Internal space is created by establishing the beginning-of-a-yawn feeling and maintaining it as you open your mouth to sing higher. This also helps to maintain the correct larynx position and to tune your resonators for a full, rich sound. Two words of caution should be sounded: (1) the mouth can be opened too wide, and (2) the throat can be held too open. The mouth needs to open progressively wider as the pitch rises, but it never needs to reach its maximum opening. Even on the highest tones of your voice, there should be the feeling that you still could open wider without forcing. The throat should be relaxed open by the *beginning* of a yawn; it should never be forced open as in a full yawn.

When singing down a scale, the reverse is true; the mouth opening should be reduced gradually. Each tone needs a little less space than the one just above it.

The *third rule* is that as you sing higher you must use more depth. The natural tendency of the human voice is to thin out and tighten or whiten as the pitch rises; it is also natural for the larynx to be pulled up by the supralaryngeal muscles. Adding progressive depth as the pitch rises will help to prevent this thinning of the sound and will be a factor in maintaining the proper laryngeal position and consistency of tone quality.

In this usage, the word *depth* has two connotations. It refers to actual sensations of depth in the body and vocal mechanism; it also refers to mental concepts of depth as related to tone quality. As you sing up a scale, you should imagine a deeper, richer sound on each successive tone; this is not a drastic change between two adjacent tones, but is an almost imperceptible filling out or deepening of the sound which, if properly done, will resist the natural tendency to thin out or whiten the tone. The desired result is the illusion of a consistently produced voice with good tonal balance from bottom to top.

As you sing up a scale, you should also feel sensations move deeper and deeper within your body and vocal mechanism. Each tone requires a little deeper sensation than the one just before it. These deeper sensations can be related to the throat and larynx, to the chest, and to the support mechanism. First, the natural tendency of the larynx is to rise for higher tones; the thought of feeling sensations deeper in the throat and larynx will help to counteract this tendency and to maintain good laryngeal posture. In singing up the scale, as you open the mouth wider, create internal space, and seek depth in the throat and larynx, you will feel the sound seem to change from a mouth-centered one to one that starts *low* in the throat but vibrates *high* in the head.

Second, the natural tendency of the voice to thin out or whiten as pitch rises can be counteracted in part by trying to feel deeper vibrations in the chest cavity. This may not be defensible in the sense that the chest is an effective resonance cavity, but it is in terms of what the singer feels.

Third, the higher the pitch rises, the more deeply the support mechanism needs to be anchored within the body. The center of support needs to move deeper and deeper as the pitch rises; stated another way, the higher the pitch level, the more the whole body needs to become involved and with a lower center of gravity. To illustrate this point, try the following experiment.

Obtain three objects—a coin, a book of normal size, and an unabridged dictionary (or a ping-pong ball, a basketball, and a bowling ball!)—and ask a friend to toss them to you in the given sequence. What is your reaction? The first object you probably caught in one hand with little other involvement apart from the arm and shoulder on that side of the body. For the second you probably used both hands, with some consequent firming of the chest and abdomen. For the third you should have felt a response much deeper in your body; possibly a shift of foot position to achieve better balance, a flexing of the knees, the galvanizing of the whole body; without doubt, the center of gravity shifted lower in your body. (An amusing variant can be achieved by pretending to throw someone a supposedly heavy object which actually is quite light; the recipient definitely will overreact!)

The point of this discussion is that singers tend to have the wrong reaction to supporting high pitches; they often resort to local action by pulling in and up on the upper abdomen and pushing up the chest. This is exactly backwards; the singer should feel his center of gravity move lower in the body when he needs more support for higher tones. The feeling should be that he is supporting with his whole body, not just with the upper abdomen.

When singing down a scale, the reverse is true; on each successive tone you should feel the depth gradually leaving the tone. Each tone needs less depth than the one just above it.

Things to Avoid. When learning to sing high notes you should avoid the following bad habits:

1. Reaching up mentally for high notes.
2. Reaching up physically—raising the chin, tilting the head back, lifting the shoulders, elevating the larynx, forcing the chest up.
3. Pulling in too strongly on the upper abdomen—supplying too much breath pressure to the larynx.
4. Pulling back the corners of the mouth into the "operatic smile"— this may seem to help high notes, but they are achieved at the expense of elevating the larynx and/or excessive tension in the soft palate and pharyngeal walls, with consequent whitening or shrill- ness of the tone quality.

When learning to sing low notes you should avoid the following bad habits:

1. Reaching down mentally for low notes.
2. Reaching down physically—pulling the chin down against the throat, tilting the head forward, depressing the larynx.
3. Using too much support—low notes require release of support.
4. Leaving the mouth too open—low notes need less space.
5. Letting the sound become breathy or dark—think of a bright, efficient, more mouth-centered, more compact kind of sound.

Summary. There are three factors which significantly affect the ability to sing higher or lower: energy, space, and depth. By constantly adjusting these three variables, a singer can learn to sing to the natural limits of the vocal range without any obvious or distracting changes of quality and technique. In general, singing higher requires the gradual increase of all three factors— energy, space, and depth—while singing lower requires the gradual decrease of all three. It is recommended that the student practice a series of ascending and descending scales in which he focuses his attention on increasing and decreasing energy for the first scale, space for the second, depth for the third, and all three simultaneously for the fourth. It is very important that each factor should be changed gradually and continually; they will have a tendency to stop at some point in the scale and remain static for the rest of the way up or down, as the case may be. Any factor which stops in this way should be practiced until smooth continuation can be maintained; the eventual goal of the exercise is coordination of energy, space, and depth.

Lining Up the Voice

There is another facet of vocal development which is strongly related to what has just been said about range extension. This is the ability to maintain consistent tone quality. The process by which this consistency is achieved is known as lining up the voice, unifying the voice, equalizing the vowels, blending the registers, and various other names. Obviously, one way to approach this goal is through the coordination of energy, space, and depth; other approaches would be (1) through vowels, (2) through registers, and (3) through resonance.

Before discussing these three areas it might be well to propose a philosophy of vocal tone. The ideal vocal tone is a balanced one containing a distribution of both high and low partials—enough low partials to impart richness, warmth, mellowness, roundness, etc., and enough high ones to impart ring and brilliance. This is the basic tone which the singer seeks to produce throughout the voice; however, this basic tone must be produced with enough freedom that the singer can vary it at will in order to communicate the meaning and emotions called forth by a particular song. Certain words may call for a darker or brighter sound than the norm; ugly words may even call for an ugly sound. A good singer needs to have a whole catalogue of expressive sounds available for use, but first he must establish this basic consistency from which he may then depart when he needs to do so for interpretive reasons.

Lining Up the Vowels. Being able to move from one vowel sound to another on the same pitch without a noticeable change of quality is an important skill for a singer. A second, but related, skill is being able to sing vowels throughout the vocal range without any obvious changes of quality. The first skill is called *horizontal vowel alignment* and the second *vertical vowel alignment.*

Each vowel has its own phonemic identity which must be preserved; however, its position within that phoneme may be adjusted so that the transition from one vowel to another may be made with a minimum of effort and the least movement of the articulators. This is good vocal economy; a maximum result from a minimum effort is good business. Since tongue position is the primary determinant of vowel sounds, a basic tongue position must be found which will permit a minimum of movement and effort when going from it to any other vowel. It is apparent that a central or neutral position would most nearly meet this requirement because the tongue could then move either to the front or back as needed.

If the articulators are not consciously shaped, the resultant vowel is some form of "uh" (perhaps a nasalized one). When a person grunts or is hit in the abdomen unexpectedly, the sound nearly always is a kind of "uh." Speakers fill the gaps in their delivery with "uh" while searching for the next word. Therefore, "uh" meets the requirement of a central or neutral position of the tongue. (Some teachers prefer "ah," which is slightly back of the center, but works quite well for many singers.)

In order for vowels to be lined up horizontally or equalized, they need to make some minor compromises. For example, the jaw opens widest for [a] and least wide for [i] and [u]. If [a] can give up a little of its opening and [i] and [u] can increase theirs a little, each sound will keep its phonemic identity but will more resemble the others in basic quality; at the same time, the jaw has less work to do. Likewise, the tongue is farthest forward for [i] and farthest back for [u]; if [i] can be made a little farther back and [u] a little farther forward, each sound will keep its phonemic identity but will be closer to the other in basic quality. On the sounds which require lip rounding, the lips should move no further from the neutral position than is necessary to give the vowel its distinctive character.

The basic principle behind *horizontal vowel alignment* is that the tongue operates from a neutral (central) position, moving to the positions for other vowels with ease and economy of motion, not in any sense restricting the action of the articulators, but making their work easier without hurting the phonemic identity of each vowel. The neutral position of the tongue is best located by using the beginning of a yawn.

Exercises for horizontal alignment should include alternating the neutral position with a sequence of the other vowels; the object in each alternation is to make the minimum readjustment needed to produce the new sound without upsetting the legato flow of sound or the basic tone quality. Christy suggests a continuous line of vowels on the same pitch, in the sequence "Uh-Ah—Uh-Ay—Uh-Ee—Uh-Oh—Uh-Oo—," and states:

> Do not use any more lip change from the neutral loose Uh position than is necessary to form each vowel easily. Too much change alters resonation space and vowel color radically, destroying vowel evenness. It is surprising how little change of position is necessary.[3]

Christy also lists several helpful exercises for establishing this type of alignment. Teachers who understand the basic principles can design their own exercises. It should be emphasized once again that this horizontal alignment or vowel equalization is a very important skill; surprisingly, it is often overlooked in studio procedures.

Vertical alignment of the voice has two aspects: (1) singing throughout the range on the same vowel (such as on "ah"); and (2) singing on a random sequence of vowels (such as that normally encountered in a song). Many of the vocal exercises used in the teaching studio limit themselves to one or two vowels, or to a predetermined regular sequence of vowels, often with no consonants present, or only those which seem to be most favorable to good vowel sounds. An actual song is seldom so considerate of the singer; it scrambles up all the available vowel and consonant sounds in a seemingly indiscriminate manner and expects him to produce them intelligibly and with beautiful quality. Perhaps this is why so many singers seem to sing better on vocalises than they do on songs.

Vocal exercises limited to one or two vowels are valuable, especially as an aid in developing range. By limiting the number of vowel and consonant possibilities, the singer has fewer variables to take care of and can concentrate on adjusting energy, space, and depth until the extremes of range are more secure; then he can mix in some other sounds. However, songs require a much more complicated series of adjustments because of the multiplicity of different sounds, and there are few vocal exercises designed to ease the singer's transition from simple one-vowel vocalises into actual songs. This gap should be filled by the teacher. Discriminatory listening can reveal which vowel and consonant combinations are most troublesome for a particular student, and vocalises which exploit those sounds can be devised on the spot.

Another aspect of vertical alignment is the ability to sing wide intervals without distracting changes of tone quality or dynamic level. Many singers have problems with large upward leaps; often they can be seen tensing the body, shifting their stance, or giving other visual clues that a "high" note is approaching, even several measures in advance. Then they often make two cardinal errors: they grab a large breath just before the note, thus effectively interrupting or disconnecting the flow of tone, and they pour on an excess of breath support just to make sure they have enough.

There are several secrets to the ability to sing "high" notes. First, unless the music insists on it, always make a legato connection to the high note from the lower note immediately preceding it; do not disconnect and then jump at the upper note. If necessary, as a stage in the learning process, actually slide from the lower to the upper note; then speed up the slide; then eliminate it, but be certain to stay connected. Second, if the lower note is long enough, crescendo on it *before* moving to the upper tone; do not wait until you get up there or the high note will be too loud. Third, try not to think of the upper note as a "high" note; think of it as a note that requires more energy, more space, and more depth, with a smooth connection from the previous note. Stated another way, do not reach up for a high note; think *down* for it; feel a deeper center of support within your body; supply energy smoothly with your whole body. Be especially careful not to raise your chin or stretch your neck upward for the upper note. In fact, the converse is often true; many singers have found that slightly lowering the chin (called "tucking in the chin") just before a high note is beneficial because it helps them to maintain a good laryngeal posture and resonance adjustment.

Singing down wide intervals can present problems, also. The singer must learn not to maintain so much support after the upper note that he cannot be heard on the lower note; too much support tends to cut off the lower notes of a voice to the extent that they are almost inaudible. The secret of being able to negotiate large leaps down into the lower voice lies in relaxation of effort. The lower notes takes less energy, less space, and less depth. You should connect the two notes smoothly and try to feel the lower tone more in the mouth—brighter and more compact in feeling than the upper tone. Do not reach down for the lower note or pull your chin down into your throat; it may restrict the freedom of the larynx.

Lining Up the Registers? One of the most controversial areas of vocal study is the use of registers to develop the voice or help line it up. Previous discussion in the chapters on phonation and registration has indicated that much of the problem is a semantic one. Apparently a lot of people use different names for the same thing, and a lot of other people use the same name for different things. The labels don't mean that much if the end results are the same, which frequently seems to be the case. Despite all the disagreement about how many registers there are, what they should be called, and how they should be used, there is rather surprising agreement that the end result should be a voice which appears to be uniformly and consistently produced, with no apparent register changes (either because there are none or because the transition has been so smoothly made) from the lowest note of the voice to the highest.

The evidence of the concert platform and opera stage today is that the modal voice is by far the predominant register used in public performance. John Large states (as previously quoted), "Current performance practice relegates *falsetto* to an auxiliary status along with Strohbass and whistle registers."[4] He cites some research by Rubin, LeCover, and Vennard which contains this statement, "It has been demonstrated by high-speed photography . . . that normal (chest) registration and the falsetto are two basically different mechanisms of voice production, the latter used only infrequently in conventional singing."[5] The uses of falsetto as an auxiliary register in performance have been listed earlier in the chapter on registration, so the discussion here will be limited to its use in developing the modal voice.

A number of teachers advocate the use of falsetto exercises as a means of developing or finding the upper part of the modal voice, especially with male voices. The reasoning behind this usage is set forth quite clearly in the following remarks by Clippinger:

> There is one place in voice training where the practice of falsetto has a distinct value. I have seen many tenors and baritones who used the heavy chest voice up until they developed an automatic clutch, and could sing the upper tones only with extreme effort. To allow them to continue in that way would never solve their problem. In such a condition half voice is impossible. It must be one thing or the other, either the thick chest voice or falsetto. The falsetto they can produce without effort, and herein lies its value. They become accustomed to hearing their high tones without the association of effort, and after a time the real voice appears. The thing which prevented the head voice from appearing in the beginning was extreme resistance, and as soon as the resistance disappeared the head voice made its appearance. This was accomplished by the practice of the very light register known as falsetto. When the head voice appears the use of the falsetto may be discontinued.[6]

William Vennard also advocated the use of falsetto in vocal development. He gives further illumination to the subject with these comments:

> It builds muscular strength somewhere in the vocal instrument, which I shall not venture to identify, but which I am sure is valuable to the singer. The laryngeal musculature is given a special kind of exercise in one extreme register which the opposite extreme will not provide, but which would be generally beneficial. Second, this practice gives the singer a "feel" of something that he should be doing but which he probably does not when he uses only the other mechanism. Specifically, when a man sings in falsetto he overcomes some of his fear of high tones, and he gets the feel of relaxation of the vibrator and activation of the breath that he does not achieve in chest voice.[7]

Clippinger and Vennard have stated their case with clarity. Falsetto is a means to an end in the development of the male voice; that end is to help the singer find and achieve freedom in his true upper voice (whatever you may choose to call it!). There are some who believe that the true upper voice is the falsetto, and others who think it is a matter of mixed or blended registers. Until more refined research techniques are available, the determination will rest with the sound which singers produce. The evidence produced by many professional singers is that they sing in modal voice throughout the range, for the upper part of the voice sounds like the rest of it, and in no way resembles falsetto. If this be heresy, make the most of it!

There is not much agreement as to the best exercises for use in developing the voice through falsetto, but there do seem to be three major types: (1) those that start softly in falsetto and then move down the scale until a transition into "chest voice" occurs, with the dynamic level gradually being raised and more muscular strength being used in the transitional area (2) those that are based on a loud falsetto sound (called a "supported" falsetto or "resonated" falsetto)[8] and either are "pushed over" into modal voice on the same pitch or carried downward until a transition occurs; and (3) those that start quite low in modal voice with a firm ringing sound and then jump two octaves or a twelfth into a fairly loud falsetto sound on [u] usually or sometimes [o]. William Vennard has a record set and manual entitled *Developing Voices* (New York: C. Fischer, c. 1973) which demonstrates the use of falsetto in some of the exercises.

With women's voices falsetto often presents a totally different picture. Unless men have been taught to use the falsetto, they tend to avoid it, on the ground that it does not sound masculine. Women, however, often use the falsetto in place of the normal upper voice. If a female voice has a light, breathy sound, especially in the upper range, the singer probably is using falsetto instead of normal voice. Although such a sound may be sweet and pleasant, it can never be rich in quality and exciting to listen to. A woman who sings in falsetto very much will likely be called a soprano whether she really is or not. Any woman can sing high notes in falsetto; this is why many teenage altos and mezzos are misclassified as high voices. The characteristic sound of pure falsetto is light, breathy, and thin, somewhat like the sound of a flute. A woman who sings this way must be encouraged to adopt a new tonal model which may be described by words such as more energetic, fuller, rounder, richer, louder, more exciting. Vennard says:

> With a woman's voice it is usually the opposite. She has been singing a breathy falsetto tone which is lacking in the necessary power to produce high partials. She may have been "whitening" the tone with her teeth, or if she is a mezzo, she may have considered it more refined to "bottle up the tone" in the pharynx. In either case she lacks the true "ring of the voice." Frequently she will discover the "ring" at the same moment that she discovers her chest voice. . . . if you can persuade her to experiment with it until she discovers a more dynamic adjustment of this voice, she will never be satisfied with pure falsetto again, except perhaps for extremely high notes.[9]

The woman who uses falsetto in place of her upper modal voice probably shifts into it between B-flat and F on the treble clef.[10] She should be made aware of this shift by means of demonstration and tape recordings, and should be urged toward the new tonal model at every opportunity. Further mention of problems related to the female voice will be made in the next section.

Lining Up the Resonators? A case has been presented in this chapter and in earlier ones for the point of view that there are four phonational registers—vocal fry (Strohbass), modal voice, falsetto, and whistle—and that by virtue of its function and name, modal voice is the normal register for speaking and singing, and the other three are auxiliary to it. The three auxiliary registers will be left out of the remainder of this discussion, and attention will be focused on the modal voice.

It is widely, if not universally recognized that the modal voice tends to have some rather clearly defined segments or divisions in its total range. The issue is confused by the fact that all voices do not have the same number of segments, and some do not show any at all. In men's voices the usual number is two; in women's voices the usual number is three, but it is not uncommon to find two. These segments of the modal voice have been called many things in the past and in the present. The segments of the male voice traditionally have been called chest voice and head voice; the tradition with the female voice has been more varied, but more recent usage seems to have settled on chest voice, middle (or mid) voice, and head voice.

The usage is further confused by the fact that these same segments have been called registers—chest register, middle register, and head register (which is perfectly legitimate under some definitions of register) and the distinction between head and falsetto has not always been made clear. But, by the definition of register used here, some of the confusion could be cleared up. Where these segments do exist, they could be identified as the lower, middle, and upper parts of the modal voice register. Another possibility would be lower voice, middle voice, and upper voice—or, for the traditionalists, chest voice, middle voice, and head voice. For the remainder of this discussion they will be referred to as the lower, middle, and upper parts of the modal voice.

It is the opinion of this writer that the appearance of these segments is due primarily to resonance phenomena which necessitate some alteration of both resonance adjustment and laryngeal function. This may be why the number of segments is not the same in all voices. When a person consciously or subconsciously has made the proper adjustment of the resonation system, the segments can disappear, either because they no longer exist or because they have been camouflaged to the point that they are no longer audible.

The resonance system is adjusted in some way for every different vowel and every different pitch. The laryngeal mechanism supplies the basic frequency through variations of length, thickness, and tension, but it is the work of the resonators to tune themselves to the product of the vibrator and enhance its timbre. If for any reason the resonators fail to readjust, if their position becomes static, if tension is allowed to accumulate, sooner or later the ability of the system to function breaks down and an obvious readjustment will have to be made. As has been pointed out several times, the adjustment needs to take place in continual increments from the lowest note to the highest in the modal voice—more energy, more space, more depth. If this is done properly, the segments will tend to disappear. There are numerous voices that can demonstrate this unification of the segments.

However, many voices, both male and female, encounter a problem area somewhere between middle C and the G above it. Men are said to be moving from chest into head, and women from chest into middle; the difference in terminology attempts to account for the usual number of segments in male and female voices. There are four possible explanations for this problem area in the male voice: (1) the resonant frequency of the tracheal tree creates acoustical impedance at this pitch level; (2) this area coincides with the first formant, which plays a key factor in vowel determination; (3) this is the area where vowel modification plays a prominent part in the male voice; and (4) this is the area where a transition into falsetto can occur.

In the female voice this area lies between the lower and middle parts of the modal voice. Two of the possible explanations listed above apply here also: (1) the resonant frequency of the tracheal tree, and (2) the area of the first formant. At any rate, it can be seen that three out of four explanations for the male and two out of two for the female point to a resonance-related problem. This implies that if the resonators can be properly adjusted, the problem can be solved. In the male voice the correct answer lies somewhere in vowel modification and cover.

Cover is related to the deepening process which has already been mentioned. The term *cover* is used here in the desirable sense expressed in two recent articles in the NATS Bulletin,[11] where it refers to a tone quality characterized as mellow, rich, round, and darkened, appearing in connection with a longer and wider pharyngeal cavity (the larynx is low and the soft palate is high); it is contrasted with *open*, which refers to an unpleasant spread or yell-like quality appearing in connection with a raised larynx and constricted pharynx. (Cover apparently is confused sometimes with the expression "too covered," which refers to a tone which is "too far back in the throat" or "swallowed" or "too dark.")

It is the writer's opinion that progressive deepening (cover) in coordination with vowel modification toward a central or neutral vowel is the best solution for this problem area in the upper modal voice of the male. (Parenthetically, recent research seems to indicate that in *cover* the trachea is often found to have been bent. Is this perhaps one means of adjusting the resonant frequency of the tracheal tree?)

In the female voice there often are two problem areas which divide the modal voice into three segments—lower, middle, and upper. The problem area between the lower and middle parts coincides with the same pitch area for the male—middle C up to G. The tracheal tree resonance and the location of the first formant seem to be the main factors, because both cover and vowel modification are related to the problem area an octave higher. Whatever the primary cause is (which probably is the acoustic impedance of the tracheal tree), it is observed that some women have no apparent problem here and the two lower segments seem to function as one, while other women experience an almost insurmountable break in this area.

Chest voice has two meanings; the predominant and probably more traditional one is merely the lower segment of the female voice; the other is used to denote a hard, pinched, brassy quality in that same area, typical of women of questionable repute. There are some who think that this brassy sound is the only one which can be made in this pitch area and therefore the lower voice should never be used. This is a bad mistake, for the bad sound results from a constricted throat and an elevated larynx. If the resonators are adjusted properly, it is possible for a woman to sing just as low and with a much more beautiful quality than the woman with the "chesty" sound.

The first step in eliminating this break area is to make certain that the brassy high-larynx sound is not being used, for it will never negotiate the problem area. Once this has been ascertained, there are two useful exercises which can help smooth out this problem.

Start on the A or B-flat above middle C. Do five-note descending patterns down through the area, being careful not to apply too much breath pressure to the vocal cords or to allow the sound to lose focus and become breathy. Think of the sound becoming brighter and more toward the front of the mouth as the pitch descends. Experiment with different vowels to see if one is easier than the others. [i] works well for some people. If you feel that you must change something going into the lower voice, let it be a legato connection and try to avoid a sudden increase in dynamics.

Start on the A below middle C. Use the [i] vowel (ee). Make a slide like a siren up the octave to A and then come down on the five-note scale pattern to D. Don't let your voice stop during the slide, but move continuously, trying to maintain a consistent vowel sound. If you can do this smoothly, move it around to other octaves (G, A-flat, B-flat, B, C, etc.). If [i] does not work, experiment with [u] and other vowels.

The other problem area lies approximately an octave above this one. It is not as pronounced a change as the one in the male voice, but it probably has some of the same causes. It is in the area where vowel modification occurs; it coincides with a possible transition into falsetto; it is in the harmonic series of the resonant frequency of the tracheal tree. One problem in this area already has been mentioned; it is so easy for immature or lightly produced voices to slip into falsetto here that many women substitute it for the upper modal voice. The other transitional problems can be approached in the same way that they are in the male voice. This would include the tripartite approach of more energy, more space, and more depth, starting in the lower part of the voice and culminating in the use of vowel modification and cover for the transition into the upper part. Because of the pitch level and its relation to the first formant, the effects of vowel modification and cover are not as apparent to the listener as they are in the male voice, but nonetheless they are vital to the correct production of the upper voice.

There are psychological advantages for the singer in thinking that the voice is all one piece; that properly produced, it is a matter of making almost imperceptible adjustments which facilitate the flow of sound from pitch to pitch and from vowel to vowel. To call attention to breaks, gearshifts, or problem areas is likely to aggravate them and create new problems. The ideal is a freely produced continuum of beautiful and expressive sound.

VIBRATO

The traditional definition of vibrato is the one by Seashore: "A good vibrato is a pulsation of pitch, usually accompanied by synchronous pulsations of loudness and timbre, of such extent and rate as to give a pleasing flexibility, tenderness, and richness to the tone."[12] The average pitch vibrato rate is between six and seven times per second; the average extent of pitch variation is one half-step. The rate of the intensity (loudness) vibrato is approximately the same as that of the pitch vibrato, and the average variation between two and three dB. The timbre vibrato is a periodic change in the strength of individual partials effected by the variation in pitch and intensity.

Vibrato is a natural concomitant of beautiful and expressive tone. According to research by the Seashore group, vibrato was present in 95 percent of all artistically sung tones. There have been various movements, especially within the choral field, that have decried the use of vibrato in any form and have advocated the straight tone. Fortunately, the almost universal presence of vibrato in all types of musical performance has been verified time after time by research and classified as not only necessary for beauty of tone but necessary for physiological reasons. The following information is cited by Large:

> The vibrato is a modulation of frequency and amplitude resulting from the pendulum-like movements of the intrinsic laryngeal musculature. These movements are said to prevent fatigue at the laryngeal level; in other words, the musculature is alternately working and resting in vibrato. In the production of straight tone the musculature is constantly working.[13]

Various theories have been advanced about the origin of the vocal vibrato, but the complexity of the mechanism involved has made it difficult for researchers to speak with absolute certainty. The latest research seems to indicate that the physiological control of vocal vibrato is a combined laryngeal and respiratory mechanism, with the laryngeal factor predominating. "The acoustic properties of vibrato are obviously interdependent with aerodynamic events and muscle activities related to phonation."[14]

Faults Related to Vibrato

The vocal faults related to the vibrato may be approached in three ways: (1) faults related to rate, (2) faults related to extent, and (3) faults related to respiratory energy. These types of faults are not mutually exclusive, but can occur simultaneously.

The faults related to rate indicate that a vibrato may be too fast or too slow. The average rate is between six and seven times per second. Some famous singers have vibrato rates higher than this, falling in the eight to ten bracket. It is generally agreed that rates faster than these are unacceptable, and some listeners even find eight to ten objectionable. Research by Zemlin and by Vennard revealed rates around five per second, but this rate has not been confirmed by others. As soon as the rate falls very much below six, the individual pulsations can be readily detected and tend to be judged as too slow.

The average extent of pitch variation is one semitone—a half-step.

Research on audience reaction to vibrato extent has been limited, but an extent approaching a whole step is likely to be perceived as too wide, and one approaching a quarter-tone may sound too narrow. The narrower it becomes, the more likely it is to be judged as a straight tone.

To this writer's knowledge there has been no scientific research directed at determining how much intensity variation is permitted before it is considered objectionable to a listener. But from personal experience and observation of other voice teachers, it is believed that the vibrato aberrations arising from unbalanced respiratory energy are the most objectionable to the teacher because they are so strongly related to poor vocal technique. Imbalance in the support mechanism coupled with tension in the laryngeal mechanism is the primary cause of vibrato problems.

If a muscle is held under tension too long, it will start quivering because it is not being allowed to relax; eventually it can develop in an uncontrolled tremor known as a tetanic flutter. These quivers can show up in the tongue, the jaw, the whole laryngeal structure, the abdominal muscles, and the rib and chest muscles. If it is a fast quiver, the vibrato will sound fast and nervous—shakily insecure. If the larger muscles and body structures get involved, it takes longer for them to shake and the vibrato will come in slow surges, like ocean waves. Both the extent of the pitch and the intensity will tend to be exaggerated. All of these tension-related vibrato problems arise because some muscle is being kept under too much tension.

Trying to sing too big a sound or failing to support a big voice enough can result in a slow vibrato of wide extent. Supporting too much—supplying too much respiratory energy to the vocal cords—can have one of two results. If the larynx resists this excessive breath pressure, it may cause the tone to become almost straight; or, if enough tension is present, it may induce a quiver involving parts or all of the laryngeal musculature. If the larynx alternately resists and releases this excessive breath pressure, a vibrato problem develops which is particularly difficult to correct. This type of vibrato is called the "bleat" or the "billy goat." To understand how this sound is made, try to bleat like a sheep or goat, or try to imitate the sound little boys make when pretending they are firing a machine gun. You will feel the alternate grabbing and releasing of the vocal cords easily; but if you analyze farther, you will feel the strong pull you are exerting on your abdominal muscles at the same time.

One final vibrato problem should be mentioned—the irregular vibrato. Sometimes the tension in and around the larynx is so great that the vibrato keeps changing rate and extent at irregular intervals, perhaps even straightening out at times. Forcing the chin down against the larynx or otherwise forcibly constricting the throat or larynx can have this effect.

Corrective Procedures for Vibrato Faults[15]

Fortunately, most of the vibrato faults will respond to the same kind of treatment. There are two main causes of vibrato problems: excessive tension and unbalanced breath support. Sometimes both are present; sometimes only one or the other; it is good procedure to check for both.

The techniques for establishing balanced support were discussed at length in chapter 4 and will not be repeated here. Techniques for releasing excess tension have appeared throughout the book and also will not be repeated. However, you should be on the lookout for the location of the various shakes or quivers as a clue to the cause of the tension. If the vibrato fault is audible, but not visible, the cause is probably in the larynx itself and/or the support mechanism. But whatever you do, check the support; some authorities think that all vibrato faults originate in that area, regardless of where they show up.

Three types of vibrato problems need special mention. The *bleat* is difficult to eliminate because it has two causes which must be corrected. First, the pulling in on the abdominal muscles must be reduced and the support mechanism brought into balance. Then the vocal cords must be trained to stay in continuous phonation instead of alternately grabbing and releasing. Try some easy humming exercises combined with relaxed support to stabilize the larynx. Impress on the singer that he must not squeeze the breath.

The *straight tone* can be difficult to eliminate. The main cause physiologically is laryngeal tension, but often the real cause is the tonal model of the singer. Many people hold the vibrato out deliberately; they may have sung in a straight-tone choir; someone may have told them that their voice shook too much; or they may just like the sound. Find out if they are aware that they have no vibrato and if so why. Sometimes in extreme cases it may be necessary to stimulate the vibrato artificially by asking the singer to make the voice shake, or to imitate someone who has a lot of vibrato. Some people believe that vibrato can be induced by learning to time voice shakes or impulses with a metronome; others use an alternation of two pitches a whole or half-step apart, starting slowly and gradually getting faster until a trill results.

The third type which needs mention is the typical slow and wide (*ocean wave*) vibrato demonstrated by many older singers. It is particularly prevalent among choir singers. There are usually two main causes: lack of physical exercise and lack of vocal exercise. Many choir singers hasten the natural deterioration that comes to all people in old age by cutting down on exercise; this causes loss of muscle tone, slumping posture, sagging support muscles, and flabby vocal muscles, for they tend to sing only at choir practice and on Sunday. They may resist the cure, but physical and vocal exercise is the main answer. For best results, practice should be a daily routine.

Finally, remember that balanced support and released tension will go a long way toward solving all vibrato problems.

CLOSING SECTION

The main purpose of this book has been to encourage the use of the diagnostic process in the correction of vocal faults—to suggest methods of identifying and evaluating auditory and visual clues to vocal problems. This is the cornerstone of effective voice teaching and choral work—discriminatory hearing assisted by acute observation. If this book has helped you in any small way to know what is wrong with the sounds you are hearing and what you can do to make them sound better, the writer has been amply rewarded.

Notes

1. In a NATS convention master class some years ago, Bruce Foote brought down the house by turning to the audience and commenting, "This vocalise may not do much for the student, but it sure can kill a lot of time in a lesson."

2. Van Christy, *Expressive Singing*, Vol. I, contains a number of well-designed vocalises.

3. Christy, *Expressive Singing*, 1:96.

4. Large, "Vocal Registers," p. 34.

5. Large, p. 32.

6. C.A. Clippinger, *The Head Voice and Other Problems* (Philadelphia: Oliver Ditson Company, 1917), p. 26.

7. Vennard, p. 76.

8. It should be pointed out that falsetto can be sung with a high larynx and a shallow pharyngeal resonator or with a low larynx and a deep pharyngeal resonator. The sounds, obviously, are quite different, but both are still falsetto.

9. Vennard, p. 121.

10. Listen to band 13 of the cassette tape.

11. Meribeth Bunch, "A Survey of the Research on Covered and Open Voice Qualities," *The NATS Bulletin* 33 (February 1977):11-18. Meribeth Bunch and Aatoo Sonninen, "Some Further Observations on Covered and Open Voice Qualities," *The NATS Bulletin* 34 (October 1977):26-30.

12. Carl Seashore, *Psychology of Music* (New York: McGraw-Hill, 1938), p. 33.

13. John Large and Shigenobu Iwata, "The Significance of Air Flow Modulations in Vocal Vibrato," *The NATS Bulletin* 32 (February/March 1976):44.

14. Large and Iwata, p. 46.

15. Listen to band 14 of the cassette tape.

Appendix 1

Audition Evaluation Checklist

Student's Name _____ Date _____

Checkpoints[1]	Remarks	Code[2]
Posture		
Breathing		
Facial Expression		
Phonation		
Support		
Quality		
Quantity (Volume)		
Vibrato		
Intonation		
Articulation		
Vowel Accuracy		
Basic Musicianship		
Range		
Voice Classification		

1. For more advanced students checkpoints such as communication, interpretation, phrasing, sensitivity to the text, platform technique, and various phases of vocal technique (agility, dynamic control, flexibility, tone color, etc.) may be added, as desired.

2. To save time and to protect your remarks from inquisitive eyes, you can develop a code made up of abbreviations of frequently used expressions: for example, G = good, VG = very good, NB = not bad, F = fair, Br = breathy, T = tight, N = nasal, W = weak, L = lacking, etc. Anything which needs any explanation can be covered under the Remarks column.

Appendix 2

Phonetic Symbols Used in This Book

Symbol	Key Words	Symbol	Key Words
[b]	be, ebb	[a]	lottery, I (first sound)
[d]	dead	[aɪ]	buy, night
[dʒ]	jade, badge	[aʊ]	proud, how
[f]	fee, if	[ɑ]	balm, father
[g]	go, gag	[ɒ]	pot, spot (British)
[h]	he	[æ]	cat, that
[j]	yes, you	[e]	gable, naval
[k]	keep, eke	[eɪ]	day, pay
[l]	low, ill	[ɛ]	bet, get
[m]	me, dim	[ɜ]	fir, girl (British)
[n]	no, on	[ɜ˞]	fir, girl (American)
[ŋ]	ring, hang	[ə]	sofa, about
[p]	pat, tap	[ɚ]	butter, mother
[r]	red, car	[i]	bee, deed
[s]	so, boss	[ɪ]	bit, it
[ʃ]	she, cash	[o]	notary, probate
[t]	too, cat	[oʊ]	go, sow
[tʃ]	church	[ɔ]	bawl, fall
[θ]	thin, thick	[ɔɪ]	boy, hoist
[ð]	then, that	[u]	boot, boom
[v]	vat, love	[ʊ]	book, took
[w]	we, will	[ʌ]	but, come
[hw]	what, when		
[z]	zoo, buzz		
[ʒ]	azure, casual		

Bibliography

The American College Dictionary. New York: Random House, 1961.

Anderson, Virgil A. *Training the Singing Voice,* 2nd ed. New York: Oxford University Press, 1961.

Appleman, Ralph. *The Science of Vocal Pedagogy.* Bloomington, Indiana: The Indiana University Press, 1967.

Backus, John. *The Acoustical Foundations of Music.* New York: Norton, 1977.

Barlow, Wilfred. *The Alexander Principle.* London: Arrow Books Limited, 1973.

Bartholomew, Wilmer T. *Acoustics of Music.* New York: Prentice-Hall Inc., 1942.

Brodnitz, Friedrich S. *Keep Your Voice Healthy.* New York: Harper & Bros., 1953.

————. *Vocal Rehabilitation.* Rochester, Minn.: Whiting Press, 1959.

Bunch, Meribeth. "A Survey of the Research on Covered and Open Voice Qualities," *The NATS Bulletin* 33 (February 1977):11-18.

Bunch, Meribeth, and Sonninen, Aatoo. "Some Further Observations oñ Covered and Open Voice Qualities," *The NATS Bulletin* 34 (October 1977):26-30.

Christy, Van A. *Expressive Singing,* 2 vols., 3rd ed. Dubuque, Iowa: Wm. C. Brown Company, 1975.

Clippinger, C. A. *The Head Voice and Other Problems.* Philadelphia: Oliver Ditson Company, 1917.

Collins Dictionary of the English Language. London: William Collins Sons, 1979.

Cooper, Morton. *Modern Techniques of Vocal Rehabilitation.* Springfield, Illinois: Charles C. Thomas, 1973.

Culver, Charles A. *Musical Acoustics.* Philadelphia: Blakiston, 1951.

Driver, Jessica S. *Speak for Yourself,* rev. ed. New York: Harper, 1956.

Duarte, Fernando. "The Principles of the Alexander Technique," *Journal of Research in Singing* 5 (December 1981):3-21.

Greene, Margaret C. L. *The Voice and its Disorders,* 3rd ed. Philadelphia: J.B. Lippincott Company, 1972.

Harvard Dictionary of Music, 2nd ed., s.v. "Instruments," "Wind Instruments," "Brass Instruments," and "Reed."

Large, John. "Towards an Integrated Physiologic-Acoustic Theory of Vocal Registers," *The NATS Bulletin* 28 (February/March 1972):33.

Large, John, and Iwata, Shigenobu. "The Significance of Air Flow Modulations in Vocal Vibrato," The NATS Bulletin 32 (February/March 1976):44.

Negus, Victor E. The Comparative Anatomy and Physiology of the Larynx. New York: Hafner Publishing Company, 1962, c 1949.

————. The Mechanism of the Larynx. London: Wm. Heinemann, Ltd., 1929.

Oberlin, Russell. Guildhall School of Music and Drama, London, England. Lecture, January 30, 1980.

Pike, Kenneth. Phonetics. Ann Arbor: University of Michigan Press, 1943.

Ross, William E. Secrets of Singing. Bloomington, Ind.: By the Author, 1959.

Saunders, William H. "The Larynx," Clinical Symposia, Volume 16, Number 3. Summit, N.J.: CIBA Pharmaceutical Company, 1964.

Seashore, Carl. Psychology of Music. New York: McGraw-Hill, 1938.

Shewan, Robert. "Voice Classification: An Examination of Methodology," The NATS Bulletin 35 (January/February 1979):17-27.

Taylor, Robert M. Acoustics for the Singer. Emporia: Kansas State Teachers College, 1958.

Travis, Lee E., ed. Handbook of Speech Pathology. New York: Appleton-Century-Crofts, 1957.

Van den Berg, J. W. "On the myoelastic-aerodynamic theory of voice production," The NATS Bulletin (May 1958).

————. "Vocal Ligaments versus Registers," The NATS Bulletin 19 (December, 1963):18.

Vennard, William. Singing—the Mechanism and the Technic. New York: Carl Fischer, Inc., 1967.

Vennard, William, and Irwin, James. "Speech and Song Compared in Sonograms," The NATS Bulletin 23 (December 1966):18-23.

Weer, Robert Lawrence. Your Voice. Los Angeles: By the Author, 1948.

West, Robert; Ansberry, Merle; and Carr, Anna. The Rehabilitation of Speech, 3rd ed. New York: Harper, 1957.

Wise, Claude Merton. Applied Phonetics. Englewood Cliffs, N.J.: Prentice-Hall, 1957.

Index

A

B

C

H

I

J

L

215

N

O

P

T

Tense-lax pairs, 151
Tension, 37, 155, 157, 158, 164, 200, 201
Tension, elimination of, 45
Tensional faults, 44, 89, 142
Tessitura, 104, 115, 121, 122, 184
Tetanic flutter, 44, 200
Thick register, 102
Thin register, 102
Thyroarytenoid muscle, 73
Thyroid cartilage, 69
Tight sounds, 89-94, 135, 155
Timbre, 16, 24, 25, 115, 198
Tonal ideal, 13, 189
Tonal image, 116, 138, 140, 141, 178, 189, 201
Tone color, 140-145
Tongue, 142, 144, 147, 150, 157, 189, 190
Tonus, 37
Trachea, 72, 128
Tracheal tree, 128, 132, 197
Transition points, 116, 129
Transmitter, 21
Triphthong, 30, 169

U

Unvoiced consonants, 147

V

Velum, 132, 135
Ventricle, 73, 129

W

Y